Nāgārjuna on Mindfulness of the Buddha

To refrain from doing any manner of evil,
to respectfully perform all varieties of good,
and to purify one's own mind—
This is the teaching of all buddhas.

The Ekottara Āgama Sūtra
(T02 n.125 p.551a 13–14)

A Note on the Proper Care of Dharma Materials

Traditional Buddhist cultures treat books on Dharma as sacred. Hence it is considered disrespectful to place them in a low position, to read them when lying down, or to place them where they might be damaged by food or drink.

Nāgārjuna
on
Mindfulness of the Buddha

The Easy Practice
Nāgārjuna's *Treatise on the Ten Grounds*, Chapter 9

The Pratuyutpanna Samādhi
Nāgārjuna's *Treatise on the Ten Grounds*, Chapters 20–25

Recollection of the Buddha
Nāgārjuna's *Exegesis on the Mahāprajnāpāramitā Sūtra*
Chapter 1, Part 36-1

As Translated into Chinese by Tripiṭaka Master Kumārajīva
Annotated English Translation by Bhikshu Dharmamitra

Kalavinka Press
Seattle, Washington
www.kalavinkapress.org

Kalavinka Press
8603 39th Ave SW
Seattle, WA 98136 USA
(www.kalavinkapress.org)

Kalavinka Press is associated with the Kalavinka Dharma Association, a non-profit organized exclusively for religious educational purposes as allowed within the meaning of section 501(c)3 of the Internal RevenueCode. Kalavinka Dharma Association was founded in 1990 and gained formal approval in 2004 by the United States Internal Revenue Service as a 501(c)3 non-profit organization to which all donations are tax deductible.

Donations to KDA are accepted by mail and on the Kalavinka website where numerous free Dharma translations and excerpts from Kalavinka publications are available in digital format.

Edition: NMOB-EO-1019-1.0
Kalavinka Buddhist Classics Book 14b

ISBN: 978-1-935413-14-1 / Library of Congress Control #: 2019029481

Library of Congress Cataloging-in-Publication Data

Names: Nāgārjuna, active 2nd century. | Dharmamitra, Bhikshu, translator. | Kumārajīva, -412? translator.

Title: Nāgārjuna on mindfulness of the Buddha / as translated into Chinese by Tripiṭaka Master Kumārajīva ; annotated English translation by Bhikshu Dharmamitra.

Other titles: Daśabhūmivibhāṣāśāstra. Selections. English & Chinese Description: Nmob-eo-1019-1.0 | Seattle, Washington : Kalavinka Press, 2019. | Series: Kalavinka Buddhist classics; book 14b | Includes bibliographical references. | In English and Chinese; translated from the Chinese translation of the Sanskrit original. | Summary: ""Nāgārjuna on Mindfulness of the Buddha" consists of three extended passages from Bhikshu Dharmamitra's original annotated translations from Sino-Buddhist Classical Chinese of works written by Ārya Nāgārjuna (circa 150 ce). All three of these passages have been selected from Tripitaka Master Kumārajīva's early Fifth Century Sanskrit-to-Chinese translations of works by Nagarjuna, as follows: 1) "The Easy Practice" -- Nāgārjuna's Treatise on the Ten Grounds, Chapter 9; 2) "The Pratyutpanna Samadhi" -- Nāgārjuna's Treatise on the Ten Grounds, Chapters 20-25; and 3) "Recollection of the Buddha" -- Nāgārjuna's Exegesis on the Mahāprajnāpāramitā Sūtra, Chapter 1, Part 36-1"-- Provided by publisher.

Identifiers: LCCN 2019029481 | ISBN 9781935413141 (paperback)

Subjects: LCSH: Nāgārjuna, active 2nd century. Daśabhūmivibhāṣāśāstra--Criticism, interpretation, etc. | Tripiṭaka. Sūtrapiṭaka. Daśabhūmīśvara--Commentaries--Early works to 1800. | Bodhisattva stages (Mahayana Buddhism)--Early works to 1800. | Pure Land Buddhism--Doctrines--Early works to 1800.

Classification: LCC BQ1632.A1 D425 2019 | DDC 294.3/85--dc23

LC record available at https://lccn.loc.gov/2019029481

Dedication

Dedicated to the memory of the selfless and marvelous life of the Venerable Dhyāna Master Hsuan Hua, the Guiyang Ch'an Patriarch and the very personification of the bodhisattva's six perfections.

Dhyāna Master Hsuan Hua

宣化禪師

1918–1995

Kalavinka Press books are printed on acid-free paper.
Cover and interior designed by Bhikshu Dharmamitra.
Printed in the United States of America

Acknowledgments

The accuracy and readability of this translation have been greatly improved by many corrections, preview comments, and editorial suggestions generously contributed by Bhikkhu Bodhi (Parts 1 and 2), Feng Ling, and Nicholas Weeks.

Expenses incurred in bringing forth this publication were underwritten by generous donations from Craig and Karen Neyman, Madalena Lew, Shuyu Yang, Jiajing Li, Kam Chung Wong, Loritta Chan, David Fox, Nicholas Weeks, Yuen-Lin Tan, and the BDK English Tripiṭaka Project. Assistance with aspects of Adobe Indesign book layout was provided by Anagarika Mahendra.

Were it not for the ongoing material support provided by my late guru's Dharma Realm Buddhist Association and the serene translation studio provided by Seattle's Bodhi Dhamma Center, creation of this translation would have been much more difficult.

Additionally, it would have been impossible for me to produce this translation without the Dharma teachings and personal inspiration provided to me by my late guru, the awesomely wise and compassionate Dhyāna Master Hsuan Hua, the Guiyang Ch'an Patriarch, Dharma teacher, and exegete.

Finally, I owe an immense debt of gratitude to the members of the liver care and transplant teams at Seattle's University of Washington Medical Center who cured me of liver cancer in 2010, gave me a liver transplant several months later, and finally cured me of hepatitis C in the winter of 2014–15. Without their wonderfully attentive and compassionate care along with the marvelous generosity of an anonymous liver donor, I would have died a half dozen years ago and thus never could have completed the scriptural translations I have produced in the last eight years.

List of Abbreviations

AN	Aṅguttara Nikāya
BCSD	Hirakawa's *Buddhist Chinese-Sanskrit Dictionary*
BHSD	Edgerton's *Buddhist Hybrid Sanskrit Dictionary*
CBETA	Chinese Buddhist Electronic Text Association's edition of the Taisho edition of the Chinese Buddhist canon.
CDB	*The Connected Discourses of the Buddha*
DN	*Dīgha Nikāya*
EA	*Ekottara Āgama*
KB	Kumārajīva and Buddhayaśas (T286)
KJ	Kumārajīva
MDPL	*Materials for a Dictionary of the Prajñāpāramitā Literature*
MLDB	*The Middle Length Discourses of the Buddha*
MN	*Majjhima nikāya*
Mppu	*Mahāprajñāpāramitā upadeśa*
MW	Monier Williams' *A Sanskrit-English Dictionary*
N	Ārya Nāgārjuna
NDB	*Numerical Discourses of the Buddha*
PDB	Princeton Dictionary of Buddhism
PTS	Pali Text Society
SN	Saṃyutta Nikāya
SYMG	The Song, Yuan, Ming, Gong editions of the Chinese Buddhist canon.
SZPPS	*Shizhu piposha lun*
T	Taisho Chinese Buddhist Canon via CBETA (Version 2004. ed.) Taibei)
VB	Venerable Bhikkhu Bodhi

Outlining in This Work

The chapter titles in this work are from the Taisho Chinese text. All other outline headings originate with the translator. Buddhist canonical texts are often so structurally dense that they are best navigated with the aid of at least a simple outline structure such as I have supplied here.

General Table of Contents

Directory to Chapter Subsections

Translator's Introduction

In this volume I present Ārya Nāgārjuna's explanations of three closely related but rather different "mindfulness-of-the-Buddha" practices that are sometimes mistaken for each other:

"Mindfulness of the Buddha" as Pure land practice;
"Mindfulness of the Buddhas" as cultivation of the "seeing-the-Buddhas" (*pratyutpanna*) samādhi;[1] and
"Recollection of the Buddha" as a protective practice.

In order to facilitate the clear understanding of the first two of these three topics, I present exemplary chapters from Nāgārjuna's *Treatise on the Ten Grounds,*[2] and, to distinguish and clarify the final topic, I present a long passage from Nāgārjuna's *Exegesis on the Great Perfection of Wisdom Sutra.*[3]

In his *Treatise on the Ten Grounds,* a third of the way through his discussion of the first bodhisattva ground, Nāgārjuna explains the "pure land" practice that involves reverential devotion to and invocation of the name of a particular buddha with the aim of achieving irreversibility on the bodhisattva path with the option of gaining rebirth in that buddha's purified buddha world. It is my translation of that single-chapter discussion, "The Easy Practice" (Chapter 9) that constitutes the first section of this book.

Later in that same text, in the final third of his discussion of the first bodhisattva ground, Nāgārjuna explains in great detail how to engage in "mindfulness of the Buddhas" practice in such a way that one may then enter the *pratyutpanna* samādhi,[4] the samādhi in which one is able to see the buddhas of the ten directions and listen to them teach the Dharma. It is my translation of that marvelously detailed six-chapter discussion of "mindfulness of the Buddhas" that forms the second section of this book.

Two thirds of the way through the immense (34-fascicle) "Introduction" to his 100-fascicle *Exegesis on the Great Perfection of Wisdom Sutra,* Nāgārjuna presents a very detailed description of "the eight recollections" of which the initial subsection is his discussion of "recollection of the Buddha." It is my translation of that discussion that forms the third section of this book.

The Rationale for Issuing This Volume

My primary reason for bringing forth this volume is to introduce to the English-speaking Buddhist audience selections from two classic Indian Mahāyāna texts that serve to distinguish and clarify the meaning and practice of these three important Mahāyāna practices that may otherwise be so closely associated with each other as to be thought of as somewhat synonymous.

The first of these three practices, "mindfulness of the Buddha" as "pure land" practice, is seldom recognized in Western Buddhism as a very early and important classic Indian Mahāyāna practice used as a means of progressing on the bodhisattva path to buddhahood. Rather it is most often associated with the later pure land schools of, first, China, and then, much later, Japan, where pure land practice has often been most focused on mere recitation of Amitābha Buddha's name with the aim of being reborn in his pure land. I feel it is very important for students of the Dharma to understand this practice in accordance with its early Mahāyāna character and meaning wherein it was regarded as a practice to be integrated into one's practice of the bodhisattva path.

The second of these three practices, "mindfulness of the Buddhas" aimed at acquisition of the *pratyutpanna* samādhi, is not much known in Western Buddhism. Where it is known, it may be easily confused with the "mindfulness of the Buddha samādhi" that one may enter through recitation of Amitābha Buddha's name. But these are two somewhat different samādhis and it is important to distinguish them and understand them as such. Nāgārjuna's extensive explanation of the practice leading to acquisition of this "seeing-the-Buddhas" samādhi eliminates any such confusion.

The third and last of these three practices, "recollection of the Buddha," is also easily confused with pure land practice. In fact, it is an entirely different practice with very different purposes that is found in both Southern Tradition Buddhism[5] and classic Indian Mahāyāna Buddhism. It has as its principal aims the allaying of fear and the provision of protection for practitioners attempting to pursue practice of the path in frightening, dangerous, or discouraging circumstances. The initial section of Nāgārjuna's discussion of the "eight recollections" focuses exclusively on "recollection of the Buddha" and serves quite well to distinguish this practice from others while also clarifying precisely how to employ this practice as an aid to cultivation.

Part One: The Easy Practice

In Nāgārjuna's discussion of the first bodhisattva ground, in response to a discouraged interlocutor fearful of the difficulty of achieving "irreversibility" on the seemingly interminably long bodhisattva path, he offers an alternative means for the bodhisattva practitioner to very quickly and easily achieve irreversibility on this path to buddhahood. This alternative means which he refers to as "the easy practice" involves earnest invocation of the name of particular buddhas who have vowed to come to the aid of anyone who sincerely calls upon them. The practitioner who takes up this "easy practice" is then said to be able to achieve irreversibility on the path to buddhahood by this means.

In this chapter entitled "The Easy Practice," Nāgārjuna first lists the names of ten buddhas, one from each of the ten directions, stating that, through the practice of invoking these buddhas' names, one can swiftly reach the ground of irreversibility. He then quotes a long passage in the *Questions of Precious Moon Sutra*[6] that describes the purified buddha world of Meritorious Qualities Buddha off in the East and describes how, through faith in this buddha, one may achieve irreversibility on the bodhisattva path.

After quoting this sutra, Nāgārjuna then notes the identical circumstances and practices associated with the nine other exemplary buddhas that dwell off in the other nine directions. Having done so, he then names and describes each of these other nine buddhas and their buddha lands.

Next, in response to a questioner wondering if there are other such buddhas, Nāgārjuna lists the names of Amitābha Buddha and 108 other such buddhas, after which he presents a 32-stanza verse praising and describing Amitābha Buddha, his vows, his pure land, his audience, and the advantages of achieving rebirth in his land. This praise verse concludes with Nāgārjuna's declaration of his own personal aspiration to always be borne in mind by this buddha and to succeed in achieving eternal purification of mind in Amitābha Buddha's presence.

Having so extensively described and praised Amitābha Buddha, Nāgārjuna then instructs us to praise and revere the seven historical buddhas of this era (including Śākyamuni Buddha) as well as Maitreya, the next buddha to appear in this world, after which he sets forth verses in praise of each of them. Then he lists ten[7] more buddhas followed by corresponding praise verses after which he lists "all buddhas of the past, the future, and the present" and also sets forth corresponding praise verses to them.

"The Easy Practice" chapter then concludes with Nāgārjuna's instruction to also bear in mind all of the great bodhisattvas, after which he lists 143 great bodhisattvas and states: "One should bear in mind all such bodhisattvas and bow down to them in reverence as one seeks to attain the *avaivartika*'s "ground of irreversibility."[8]

Part Two: The *Pratyutpanna* Samādhi

Toward the end of his discussion of the first bodhisattva ground, the Ground of Joyfulness, Nāgārjuna sets forth a verse indicating that, once the bodhisattva path practitioner has already come to dwell on the first ground, "he will naturally be able to see several hundred buddhas," whereupon he is immediately asked by an interlocutor who is clearly worried about the immense difficulty of even reaching the first bodhisattva ground: "Is it solely through the power of roots of goodness and merit [resulting from completely fulfilling the first-ground practices] that one becomes able to see buddhas, or is there instead some other method by which one can do so?"

In answer to this question, quoting from the *Pratyutpanna Samādhi Sūtra*,[9] Nāgārjuna sets forth a very detailed explanation of the means by which, without first reaching the first bodhisattva ground, acquiring the heavenly eye, or acquiring the heavenly ear, one may nonetheless be able to see the buddhas of the ten directions and listen to them speak the Dharma.

In the extremely detailed and precisely organized subsequent discussion, Nāgārjuna describes how to envision the Buddhas as seated on a lion throne in the midst of a great assembly and tells how to recollect the qualities of the Buddhas, including their vows, their four immeasurable minds, their four bases of meritorious qualities, their six perfections, and their thirty-two major marks and eighty minor characteristics along with the causes for acquiring each of those physical signs. After describing many more qualities and skills of the Buddhas, this "Mindfulness of the Buddhas" chapter ends with a long reiterative verse.

This initial chapter on "Mindfulness of the Buddhas" is then followed by three chapters devoted to close explanation of "forty dharmas exclusive to the Buddhas," a single chapter consisting entirely of praise verses, and a final very detailed chapter on exactly which practices to cultivate and how to cultivate them in order to acquire this *pratyutpanna* samādhi wherein one can see and hear the buddhas of the present. This final chapter is entitled "Teachings to Assist the Mindfulness of the Buddhas Samādhi."

Part Three: Recollection of the Buddha

In subchapter 36 of the 52-part introductory chapter to his *Exegesis on the Great Perfection of Wisdom Sutra,* Nāgārjuna discusses the "eight recollections" of which "recollection of the Buddha" is the first part. It is preceded by a short prefatory introduction to this practice wherein its fear-allaying, protective, and practice-inspiring functions are described.

After noting the role of the eight recollections in allaying fear, depression, discouragement, or disgust to which an isolated practitioner may have become subject, particularly in the wake of cultivating the nine reflections on the deterioration of a corpse, the introductory part of this "eight recollections" discussion then turns to an explanation of the first of these eight recollections, "recollection of the Buddha." This discussion involves a detailed topic-by-topic treatment of a series of bases for carrying out an orderly reflection on the Buddha as an object of contemplation that inspires fearlessness, determination, and happiness. The main subsections of that reflection are as follows:

a) The listing and explanation of the underlying meanings of the ten names of the Buddha;
b) A description of the illustrious lineage and marvelous birth of the Buddha;
c) A description of the physical characteristics, strength, and extraordinary physical marks of the Buddha's body;
d) A long and detailed description of the Buddha's perfection of the five "accumulations," namely moral precepts, meditative absorptions, wisdom, liberations, and the knowledge and vision associated with the liberations;
e) A summarizing list of other qualities of the Buddha upon which one should reflect which includes: the Buddha's omniscience; his manifold types of knowledge and vision; his great kindness and great compassion; his ten powers; his four fearlessnesses, his four types of unimpeded knowledge, and his eighteen special dharmas.

Nāgārjuna's discussion of "recollection of the Buddha" then concludes with a summary of various *abhidharma*-related factors regarding the stations of existence in which it can be practiced, the presence or absence of the contaminants in the practitioner, its association with bliss, joy, and equanimity, and the potential for achieving facility in "recollection of the Buddha" either through practice or as a result of prior karmic actions. In the case of those who acquire it through practice, this refers to those who practice the "mindfulness of the Buddha" samādhi. As for those who acquire it as a karmic result, this refers to such beings as those that inhabit the purified buddha world of Amitābha Buddha.

On the Authorship of the Texts

The author of both these texts, the *Treatise on the Ten Grounds* and the *Exegesis on the Great Perfection of Wisdom Sutra,* is considered by the Sino-Mahāyāna tradition to be Ārya Nāgārjuna, the same 2nd century CE Indian monk who produced such works as the *Mūlamadhyamaka-kārikā,* the *Bodhisaṃbhāra-śāstra,* the *Ratnāvalī,* and the *Suhṛllekha.* Although there have been a number of scholars who have doubted the Nāgārjunian authorship of this *Exegesis on the Great Perfection of Wisdom Sutra,* there arguments tend to boil down to an abundance of opinionation, for there is nothing but very thin circumstantial evidence for their doubts. I have found the internal evidence of doctrinal consistency with other Nāgārjunian texts to be quite strong and I think that the testimony of Kumārajīva (the translator who produced the Chinese edition) is far more trustworthy on the issue of this text's authorship, not least because he lived within 200 years of the life of Nāgārjuna and was the foremost authority on these matters at the time.

In Summation

I hope that this volume of Nāgārjunian texts focused on "mindfulness of the Buddha" practices will be both useful and inspiring to students of Dharma who wish to study, understand, and correctly cultivate these closely related modes of contemplation and practice common in classic Indian Mahāyāna Buddhism.

Bhikshu Dharmamitra

Seattle

May 14, 2019

Introduction Endnotes

1 *"Pratyutpanna samādhi"* is an abbreviation for *pratyutpanna-buddha-saṃmukha-avasthita-samādhi,* "the samādhi in which one encounters the buddhas of the present face-to-face."

2 *Daśabhūmika-vibhāṣā* (十住毘婆沙論 / T26, no. 1521). This is Nāgārjuna's 17-fascicle, 35-chapter discussion on the meaning of the *Ten Grounds Sutra* (*Daśabhūmika-sūtra* [十住經 / T10, no. 286]).

3 *Mahāprājnāpāramitopedeśa* (大智度論 / T25, no. 1509).

4 The complete name of this samādhi is "the *pratyutpanna-buddha-saṃmukha-avasthita samādhi,*" lit., "the samādhi in which the Buddhas of the present stand directly before one."

5 "Recollection of the Buddha" constitutes the first of the "four protective meditations" in Southern Tradition Buddhism. (The other three protective meditations are loving-kindness, the unloveliness of the body, and death.)

6 See *The Sutra on the Youth Precious Moon's Questions on Dharma* (大乘寶月童子問法經 – T14n0437_p108c01-110a07).

7 Actually, the text lists eleven buddha names, but it is probable that one of those names is included only as a scribal error involving unintentional redundancy. This conclusion is corroborated by the absence of any mention of this "eleventh" buddha in the ensuing verses that individually praise each of these buddhas.

8 An *"avaivartika"* is one who has achieved irreversibility on the bodhisattva path to buddhahood.

9 "The Pratyutpanna Samādhi Sūtra" (*Pratyutpanna-buddha-saṃmukha-avasthita-samādhi-sūtra*) is preserved in the *Taisho* Canon as the *Banzhou Sanmei Jing* (般舟三昧經 / T13.no. 0418.902c23-919c05) of which Paul Harrison has produced a translation for the BDK English Tripitaka.

Nāgārjuna
on
Mindfulness of the Buddha

Part 1: The Easy Practice

Nāgārjuna's *Treatise on the Ten Grounds,* Chapter 9

As Translated into Chinese by Tripiṭaka Master Kumārajīva
Annotated English Translation by Bhikshu Dharmamitra

An Introductory Note on "The Easy Practice

This chapter on "The Easy Practice" is preceded by Nāgārjuna's very detailed description in earlier chapters of his "Treatise on the Ten Grounds" of the difficulties, hazardousness, and lengthiness of the bodhisattva path to buddhahood in contrast to the relative ease of the much swifter paths of śrāvaka disciples and *pratyekabuddhas*.[1] In the immediately preceding chapter on the *avaivartika*,[2] he describes the qualities of the bodhisattva who, while cultivating the ten grounds, finally achieves "irreversibility" on the bodhisattva path, qualities that are very rare, very hard won, and only acquired after a very long time on the bodhisattva path.[3]

In Chapter One, with regard to the length of time required to perfect the cultivation of the ten bodhisattva grounds and become a fully enlightened buddha, Nāgārjuna says:

> In the case of those who cultivate the Great Vehicle, some may require a number of great kalpas as numerous as the sands of a single Ganges River, and some may require a number of great kalpas as numerous as the sands in two, three, or four Ganges Rivers, and so forth until we come to kalpas as numerous as the sands contained in ten, one hundred, one thousand, ten thousand, or a *koṭi* of Ganges Rivers. They may require an even longer period of time than that.

With this background in mind, it should become much easier then for us to understand the rationale of the interlocutor in this chapter when, at the bottom of the first page, he asks Nāgārjuna for an easier alternative path, "an easily-practiced path by which one might rapidly succeed in arriving at the ground of the *avaivartika*."

Then again, given how much effort Nāgārjuna has just devoted in the first seven chapters of his treatise to describing the incredible heroism of the bodhisattva who so fearlessly conquers all obstacles on the ten grounds, it is perhaps understandable, too, why, at the top of the second page, he responds so harshly to a question that searches instead for an "easy" way to reach the "irreversibility" by which one avoids the possibility of falling down onto the śrāvaka or *pratyekabuddha* grounds.

Endnotes

1 In Chapter one, Nāgārjuna notes that it may require only as few as one or two lifetimes for someone to become an arhat and only as few as seven lifetimes for someone to become a *pratyekabuddha.*

2 An *avaivartika* is someone who has become irreversible on either the individual liberation path of the arhats or on the universal-liberation path of the bodhisattvas and buddhas.

3 In the immediately preceding chapter on the *avaivartika* (irreversible) bodhisattva, we have a verse describing such a bodhisattva's qualities:

> The bodhisattva does not apprehend the existence of any self,
> and also does not apprehend the existence of any being.
> He does not engage in discriminations as he discourses on Dharma,
> nor does he apprehend the existence of bodhi.
>
> He does not perceive a buddha by his [physical] signs.
> It is on account of these five meritorious qualities
> that he is referred to as a great bodhisattva
> and becomes an *avaivartika.*

Part One
The Easy Practice

Ch. 9: On the Easy Practice

I. Chapter Nine: On the Easy Practice

A. Q: How Difficult! Is There an Easier Path to the Avaivartika Ground?

Question: Given that this *avaivartika* bodhisattva's initial endeavors are such as previously discussed, one aspiring to reach the ground of the *avaivartika* would have to practice all manner of difficult practices for a long time and only then be able to reach it. [This being the case], he might become prone then to fall down onto the grounds of the *śrāvaka* disciples or *pratyekabuddhas*. If that were the case, this would be for him an immensely ruinous calamity. As stated in the Dharma of *The Provisions Essential for Bodhi* (*Bodhisambhāra Śāstra*):[1]

> If one were to fall onto the ground of the *śrāvaka* disciples
> or onto the ground of the *pratyekabuddha*s,
> this amounts to "death" for a bodhisattva,
> for he then loses all beneficial effects [of his bodhisattva practice].
>
> If one faced the prospect of falling into the hells,
> he would not become filled with such fear as this.
> If one were to [contemplate] falling onto the Two Vehicles' ground,
> then this would bring about great terror.
>
> If one were to fall into the hells,
> he could still ultimately succeed in reaching buddhahood.
> If one were to fall onto the grounds of the Two Vehicles, however,
> this would ultimately block the realization of buddhahood.
>
> In the scriptures, the Buddha himself
> explained matters such as these, stating that
> this is just as with a person who covets a long lifespan:
> If he is faced with decapitation, he is then filled with great fear.
>
> The bodhisattva is also just like this.
> If [confronted with the prospect of] the *śrāvaka* disciples' ground
> or the *pratyekabuddha*s' ground,
> he should react with great terror.

Therefore, if, as a skillful means, the Buddhas have mentioned the existence of an easily-practiced path by which one might rapidly succeed in arriving at the ground of the *avaivartika*, then please explain it for me.

B. A: How Weak & Inferior! But, If You Want That, I Will Explain

Response: Statements such as you have just made are symptomatic of a weak, pusillanimous, and inferior mind devoid of the great resolve. These are not the words of a heroic man possessed of determination and ability.

How is this so? If a person has brought forth the vow to strive for the realization of *anuttarasamyaksaṃbodhi,* during that interim period in which he has not yet gained the *avaivartika* stage, he must not be sparing of even his own body or life. Rather he should strive with vigor both day and night, acting with the same urgency to save himself as someone whose turban has just caught fire. This is as stated in the *Bodhisambhara Śāstra*:

> So long as the bodhisattva has not yet succeeded in reaching
> the ground of the *avaivartika,*
> he should always diligently practice vigor,
> acting with the urgency of one whose turban has caught fire.
>
> Taking up the heavy burden
> for the sake of striving to attain bodhi,
> he should always act with diligent vigor,
> refraining from developing an indolent mind.[2]
>
> Even were one to seek the *śrāvaka* disciples' vehicle
> or the *pratyekabuddha*'s vehicle,
> thus seeking only to perfect one's own benefit,
> even then, one should always diligently practice vigor.
>
> How much the more should this be so in the case of the bodhisattva,
> one who strives to liberate both himself and others.
> Compared to these men of the Two Vehicles,
> he should be a *koṭi's* number of times more vigorous than they are.[3]

In speaking of the practice of the Great Vehicle, the Buddha described it thus: "As for generating the vow to attain buddhahood, it is a challenge heavier than lifting all of the worlds in a great trichiliocosm."

As for your saying, "This dharma of the *avaivartika* ground is so extremely difficult to accomplish that one can only reach it after a long time" and "If there were only some easily-traveled path by which one could swiftly reach the *avaivartika* ground," these are the words of those who are weak and inferior. These are not statements of a great man possessed of determination and ability. Still, if you definitely do wish to hear of this skillful means, then I shall now explain it for you.

1. The Practice of Calling on Ten Buddhas, One in Each Direction

The Dharma of the Buddha has measurelessly many gateways. This is just as with the world's various routes among which there are those that are difficult and those that are easy. When taking overland routes, the traveling may involve suffering, whereas in the case of water routes where one boards a boat, it may instead be pleasurable.

So too it is in the case of the bodhisattva path. In some instances, one is diligently devoted to the practice of vigor, whereas in others that involve faith and skillful means, one adopts an easy practice by which one swiftly arrives at the station of the *avaivartika*. This is as described in the following verse:

In the East, there is Meritorious Qualities Buddha.
In the South, there is Candana Qualities Buddha.
In the West, there is Measureless Light Buddha.
In the North, there is Emblematic Qualities Buddha.

In the Southeast, there is Sorrowless Qualities Buddha.
In the Southwest, there is Giver of Jewels Buddha.
In the Northwest, there is Floral Qualities Buddha.
In the Northeast, there is Three Vehicles' Practices Buddha.[4]

Toward the Nadir, there is Brilliant Qualities Buddha.
Toward the Zenith, there is Vast Multitude of Qualities Buddha.
Bhagavats such as these
now abide throughout the ten directions.

If a person wishes to swiftly reach
the ground of irreversibility,
he should, with a reverential mind,
take up and maintain the practice of invoking these buddhas' names.

If a bodhisattva wishes in this very body to succeed in reaching the ground of the *avaivartika* and then attain *anuttarasamyaksaṃbodhi,* then he should bear in mind these buddhas of the ten directions and invoke their names. This is just as explained in the "Avaivartika Chapter" of the *Sutra Spoken in Response to the Questions of the Youth Precious Moon,*[5] in which the Buddha told Precious Moon:

Off in the East, going beyond a number of buddha lands equal to the sands in a measureless, boundless, and inconceivable number of Ganges Rivers, there is a world system named Sorrowless. Its ground is level and composed of the seven precious things. Strands of purple powdered gold are woven throughout that realm and rows of jeweled trees serve as adornments there.

There are no destinies of the hells, animals, hungry ghosts, or *asuras,* nor are there any places beset by difficulties. It is pure, free of any filth, and also free of gravel, ceramic shards, stones, mountains, hillocks, deep pits, and dark ravines. The devas' always rain down flowers that cover its ground.

That world now has a buddha named Meritorious Qualities Tathāgata, Worthy of Offerings, of Right and Universal Enlightenment, Perfect in Knowledge and Conduct, Well-Gone One, Knower of the Worlds, Unsurpassable One, Tamer of Those to Be Tamed, Teacher of Devas and Humans, Buddha, Bhagavat. He is respectfully surrounded by an assembly of great bodhisattvas. His body's characteristic radiance and appearance are like a great flaming gold mountain and like a great aggregation of precious jewels.

For the sake of everyone in that great assembly, he extensively proclaims the right Dharma that is good in the beginning, middle, and end, that is eloquently presented and meaningful. Whatever he proclaims is free of admixture, perfect in its purity, accordant with reality, and free of error.

What is meant by "free of error"? It is free of any error with respect to the [four great elements of] earth, water, fire, and wind, is free of any error with respect to the desire realm, the form realm, and the formless realm and is free of error with respect to [the five aggregates of] form, feelings, perceptions, formative factors, and consciousness.

Precious Moon, from the time this buddha achieved buddhahood until the present, sixty *koṭis* of kalpas have passed. Moreover, in that buddha's country, there is no difference between the day and the night. It is only by reference to the enumeration of days, months and years of Jambudvīpa that one describes his lifetime in terms of a particular number of kalpas.

The light from that buddha always illuminates that world. In the course of a single discourse on Dharma, he causes a measureless and boundless number of thousands of myriads of *koṭis* of *asaṃkhyeyas* of beings to abide in the unproduced-dharmas patience. Twice this number of people are thereby caused to abide in the first, second, and third type of patience.

Precious Moon, the power of that buddha's original vows is such that, if there are any beings in other regions who have planted roots of goodness under a previous buddha, he need only be touched by this buddha's light in order to immediately attain the unproduced-dharmas patience.

Precious Moon, if there is a son or daughter of good family who but hears this buddha's name and is then able to have faith and accept him, such a person will immediately achieve irreversibility with respect to the attainment of *anuttarasamyaksaṃbodhi.*

The circumstances related to the other nine buddhas are just like this. Now we shall explain the names of those Buddhas as well as the names of their lands.

As for "Meritorious Qualities Buddha," his qualities are associated with pure goodness and the possession of peace and happiness. They are unlike the meritorious qualities of devas, dragons, and spirits which delude and trouble beings.

As for "Candana Qualities Buddha," in the South, off at a distance from here of buddha lands as numerous as the sands in incalculably and boundlessly many Ganges Rivers, there is a world named Delightful. The name of the buddha there is Candana Qualities. He is right now proclaiming the Dharma that is as fragrant and cooling as *candana*.[6] The fame of that buddha's name is heard afar, circulating and spreading about like the fragrance of incense. It extinguishes the heat from the fire of beings' three poisons and thereby causes them to experience refreshing coolness.

As for "Measureless Light Buddha," off in the West, at a distance from here of buddha lands as numerous as the sands in incalculably and boundlessly many Ganges Rivers, there is a world named "Excellence." That buddha is named Measureless Light. He is at this very time proclaiming the Dharma. The light from that buddha's body and the brilliant illumination from his wisdom reach an incalculable and boundless distance.

As for "Emblematic Qualities Buddha," off in the North, at a distance from here of buddha lands as numerous as the sands in incalculably and boundlessly many Ganges Rivers, there is a world known as "Immovable." Its buddha is known as Emblematic Qualities. He is right now proclaiming the Dharma. That buddha's meritorious qualities are lofty and prominently displayed, appearing like a banner.

As for "Sorrowless Qualities Buddha," in the Southeast, off at a distance from here of buddha lands as numerous as the sands in incalculably and boundlessly many Ganges Rivers, there is a world named "Lunar Brilliance." The buddha who abides there is named Sorrowless Qualities. He is even now proclaiming the Dharma. That buddha's spiritual qualities are such that they cause all of the devas and men there to be free of any sort of sorrow.

As for "Giver of Jewels Buddha," in the Southwest, off at a distance from here of buddha lands as numerous as the sands in incalculably and boundlessly many Ganges Rivers, there is a world named "Multitude of Signs." The buddha who abides there is known as Giver of Jewels. Even now he is proclaiming the Dharma. That buddha always bestows on beings the jewels of the uncontaminated root-faculties, powers, limbs of enlightenment, the path, and so forth.

As for "Floral Qualities Buddha," in the Northwest, off at a distance from here of buddha lands as numerous as the sands in incalculably and boundlessly many Ganges Rivers, there is a world known as "Multitude of Sounds." The Buddha who abides there is known as Floral Qualities. Even now, he is proclaiming the Dharma. That buddha's physical body is like a marvelous flower and his meritorious qualities are incalculably numerous.

As for "Three Vehicles' Practices Buddha," in the Northeast, off at a distance from here of buddha lands as numerous as the sands in incalculably and boundlessly many Ganges Rivers, there is a world known as "Peaceful and Secure." The buddha who abides there is known as Three Vehicles' Practices Buddha. Even now, he is proclaiming the Dharma. That buddha always explains the practices of the *śrāvaka* disciples, the practices of the *pratyekabuddhas,* and the practices of the bodhisattvas. There are those who state that it is because he explains the superior, the middling, and the lesser levels of vigor that he is named Three Vehicles' Practices.

As for "Brilliant Qualities Buddha," in the Nadir, off at a distance from here of buddha lands as numerous as the sands in incalculably and boundlessly many Ganges Rivers, there is a world known as "Expansive." The buddha who abides there is known as Brilliant Qualities. Even now he is proclaiming the Dharma. "Brilliant" refers to the light that shines from his body, the light of his wisdom, and the light that shines from his jeweled tree. These three kinds of brilliance always illuminate that world.

As for "Vast Multitude of Qualities Buddha," in the Zenith, off at a distance from here of buddha lands as numerous as the sands in incalculably and boundlessly many Ganges Rivers, there is a world known as "Many Moons." The buddha who abides there is known as Vast Multitude of Qualities. Even now he is proclaiming the Dharma. It is because the meritorious qualities of that buddha's disciples are vast that he is known as Vast Multitude of Qualities.

Now, as for these buddhas of the ten directions, beginning with Meritorious Qualities Buddha and concluding with Vast Multitude of Qualities Buddha, if a person single-mindedly invokes their names, he will thereby immediately succeed in gaining irreversibility with respect to the attainment of *anuttarasamyaksaṃbodhi.* This is as described in a verse:

> If there is a person who is able to hear
> the utterance of all these buddhas' names,
> he will immediately acquire countless meritorious qualities,
> just as was explained for Precious Moon.

I bow in reverence to these buddhas
presently abiding throughout the ten directions.
Whosoever invokes their names
immediately attains irreversibility.

Off in the East, in the realm known as Sorrowless,
that buddha named Meritorious Qualities
has a form resembling a mountain of gold.
The reach of his fame is boundless.

If a person so much as hears his name,
he immediately attains irreversibility.
With palms pressed together, I now bow in reverence to him
and pray that worries and afflictions may be entirely dispelled.

Off in the South, in the realm known as Delightful,
there is a buddha named Candana Qualities.
His countenance is as pristine as the full moon
and the radiance of his light is measureless.

He is able to bring about the extinguishing of beings'
fiery afflictions produced by the three poisons.
If one but hears his name, he then attains irreversibility.
I therefore bow down in reverence to him.

Off in the West, in a realm known as Excellence,
there is a buddha known as Limitless Light.
The light from his body and the brilliance of his wisdom
are boundless in the range of their illumination.

If there be anyone who but hears his name
he will immediately attain irreversibility.
I now bow down in reverence to him,
praying that I may put an end to the limits imposed by *saṃsāra*.

Off in the North, in a realm known as Immovable,
there is a buddha named Emblematic Qualities.
His body is replete with the many signs and minor characteristics
with which he is personally adorned.

He utterly defeats the hordes of Māra, the enemy,
and skillfully teaches both humans and devas.
Those who hear his name attain irreversibility.
I therefore bow down in reverence to him.

Off in the Southeast, in a world known as Lunar Brilliance,
there is a buddha named Sorrowless.
His illumination surpasses that of the sun and moon.
Those who encounter it are thus able to extinguish their afflictions.

He always explains the Dharma for the sake of the multitude,
thus ridding them of all inward and outward sufferings.
The buddhas of the ten directions praise him.
I therefore bow down in reverence to him.

Off in the Southwest, in a realm known as Multitude of Signs,
there is a buddha named Giver of Jewels.
He always uses all manner of Dharma jewels
to engage in extensive universal giving.

All the devas bow down in reverence to him
so that their jeweled crowns are brought low at his feet.
I now, bowing in reverence with all five extremities,
take refuge in the Bhagavat, Giver of Jewels.

Off in the Northwest, in a realm known as Multitude of Sounds,
there is a buddha named Floral Qualities.
That world is graced with an abundance of jeweled trees
that send forth sounds expounding the sublime Dharma.

He always uses the flowers of the seven limbs of enlightenment
to bestow adornments on those beings.
His mid-brow white hair tuft mark is like the moon.
I now bow down in reverence to him.

Off in the Northeast, in a world known as Peaceful and Secure,
one that is composed of all manner of jewels,
there is a buddha named Three Vehicles Practices
whose body is adorned with the measureless marks.

The light from his wisdom is measureless.
It is able to dispel the darkness of ignorance
and cause beings to become free of worry and afflictions.
I therefore bow down in reverence to him.

Off toward the Zenith, in a world known as Many Moons,
adorned with the many types of jewels,
attended by a congregation of greatly virtuous *śrāvaka* disciples
and bodhisattvas who are incalculable in number,

there is a lion among the Āryas
named Vast Multitude of Qualities.
He is feared by all the *māras*.
I therefore bow down in reverence to him.

Off toward the Nadir, there is world known as Expansive
in which there is a buddha named Brilliant Qualities.
His physical marks are far more marvelous
even than a mountain of *jambūnada* gold.

He always uses the sun of his wisdom
to open the blossoms of beings' roots of goodness.
His land of jewels is extremely vast.
From afar, I bow down in reverence to him.

In the past, countless kalpas ago,
there was a buddha named Oceanic Meritorious Qualities.
These buddhas of the present era
all made their vows under him.

His lifespan was incalculably long
and the reach of his light's illumination was endless.
His country was extremely pure.
Those hearing his name became definitely bound for buddhahood.

These [buddhas] who now abide in the ten directions
are completely equipped with the ten powers.
I therefore bow down in reverence to them,
these most venerable ones among all humans and devas.

2. Q: Can One Instead Call on Other Buddhas and Bodhisattvas?

Question: Is it the case that one may only be able to reach irreversibility with respect to *anuttarasamyaksaṃbodhi* through hearing these ten buddhas' names and bearing them in mind? Or is it the case that there are yet other buddhas' and other bodhisattvas' names through which one may succeed in reaching the station of the *avaivartika*?

3. A: Yes, There is Amitābha as Well as Other Such Buddhas

Response:

There is Amitābha and also other such buddhas
as well as the great bodhisattvas.
If one invokes their names and single-mindedly bears them in mind,
one will also thereby attain irreversibility.

In addition, there is Amitābha as well as other buddhas to whom one should also respectfully bow down in reverence and utter their names. I shall now set forth their names in full:

Limitless Life Buddha, King of Sovereign Mastery in the World Buddha, Lion Mind Buddha, Dharma Mind Buddha, Brahman Signs Buddha, World Signs Buddha, Sublimity of the World Buddha, Kindness and Compassion Buddha, World King Buddha, King Among Men Buddha, Moon-like Virtues Buddha, Precious Virtues Buddha, Qualities of the Marks Buddha, Great Marks Buddha, Jeweled Canopy Buddha, Lion Mane Buddha, Destroyer of Ignorance Buddha, Flower of Wisdom Buddha, Tamālapattra Candana Fragrance Buddha, and Upholder of Great Meritorious Qualities Buddha.

There are also: Rain of the Seven Precious Things Buddha, Excellent Bravery Buddha, Enmity Transcendence Buddha, Great Adornment Buddha, Signlessness Buddha, Jewel Treasury Buddha, Summit of Virtue Buddha, Tagara Fragrance Buddha, Candana Incense Buddha, Lotus Fragrance Buddha, Adorned Path Buddha, Dragon Canopy Buddha, Rain of Flowers Buddha, Scatterer of Flowers Buddha, Floral Radiance Buddha, Solar Voice Buddha, Eclipsing the Sun and Moon Buddha, Lapis Lazuli Treasury Buddha, Brahman Sound Buddha, and Pure Radiance Buddha.

There are also: Treasury of Gold Buddha, Sumeru Summit Buddha, King of the Mountains Buddha, Masterful Voice Buddha, Pure Eyes Buddha, Lunar Radiance Buddha, Mount Sumeru Likeness Buddha, Sun and Moon Buddha, Acquirer of Multitudes Buddha, Flower-born Buddha, Proclaimer of the Brahman Sounds Buddha, Lord of the Worlds Buddha, Lion-like Practice Buddha, Sublime Dharma Mind Lion's Roar Buddha, Pearl Canopy Coral Appearance Buddha, Dispeller of the Darkness of Delusion and Desire Buddha, Water Moon Buddha, Multitude of Flowers Buddha, Opener of Wisdom Buddha, and Retainer of Various Jewels Buddha.

There are also: Bodhi Buddha, Flower Transcendence Buddha, Radiance of True Lapis Lazuli Buddha, Outshining Sunlight Buddha, Retainer of Great Qualities Buddha, Realizer of Right Wisdom Buddha, Heroic Strength Buddha, Beyond Flattery and Deception Buddha, Dispensing with Planting Roots of Evil Buddha, Great Fragrance Buddha, Path Splendor Buddha, Water Light Buddha, Roamer in Oceanic Clouds of Wisdom Buddha, Virtue Summit Flower Buddha, Floral Adornment Buddha, Solar Voice Buddha, Lunar Supremacy Buddha, Lapis Lazuli Buddha, Brahmā-like Voice Buddha, and Light Buddha.[7]

There are also: Treasury of Gold Buddha, Mountain Summit Buddha, Mountain King Buddha, Sound King Buddha, Dragon Vigor Buddha, Stainless Buddha, Pure Countenance Buddha, Lunar Countenance Buddha, Sumeru Semblance Buddha, Candana Fragrance Buddha, Awesome Strength Buddha, Blazing Lamp Buddha, Difficult to Overcome Buddha, Precious Virtue Buddha, Joyous Sound Buddha, Radiance Buddha,[8] Dragon Supremacy Buddha, Defilement Transcendence Light Buddha, Lion Buddha, and King Among Kings Buddha.

And there are also Supremacy of Powers Buddha, Floral Garden Buddha,[9] Fearless Brilliance Buddha, Fragrant Summit Buddha, Universally Worthy Buddha, Universal Flower Buddha, and Precious Signs Buddha.

These buddhas, *bhagavats*, abide now in pure worlds throughout the ten directions. One should invoke the names of all of them and bear them in mind.

a. Amitābha's Original Vows and a Praise Verse

The original vows of Amitābha are of this sort: "If any person bears me in mind, invokes my name, and takes refuge in me, he will immediately enter the stage of certainty with respect to attaining *anuttarasamyaksaṃbodhi*."

One should therefore always remain mindful of him. I set forth his praises here with a verse:

He possesses boundless illumination and wisdom
and his body is like a mountain of gold.
Paying homage to him with body, speech, and mind, I now
place my palms together and bow down in reverence to him.

His marvelous golden-colored light
everywhere streams into all worlds,
increasing in its brilliance in response to each being.
I therefore bow down in reverence to him.

If, when life's end comes, a person
succeeds in being reborn in that land,
he immediately acquires countless meritorious qualities.
I do therefore take refuge in him.

Whoever is able to bear in mind this buddha
possessed of measureless powers and awe-inspiring qualities
will immediately enter the stage of certainty.
I do therefore always bear him in mind.

That land is such that if, at the end of one's life,
one should otherwise undergo all manner of suffering,
even so, one will not then fall into those terrible hells.
Therefore, taking refuge in him, I now bow down in reverence.

If a person gains rebirth in his land,
he will never again fall into the three wretched destinies
or into the realms of the *asuras*.
Taking refuge in him, I now bow down in reverence.

Though his body is similar to that of humans and devas,
it resembles the summit of a mountain of gold.
This is the place to which all supreme [qualities] return.
I therefore bow down in reverence to him.

Those who have been reborn in his land,
gain the powers of the heavenly eye and ear
that reach unimpededly throughout the ten directions.
I bow down in reverence to the one honored among the Āryas.

All the beings in his land
perform supernatural transformations, know others' thoughts,
and are endowed with the knowledge of past lives as well.
Therefore, taking refuge in him, I bow down in reverence.

Those who are reborn in his land
have no conception of either "I" or "mine."
They do not have thoughts conceiving of "others" or "self."
I therefore bow down in reverence to him.

He has stepped beyond the prison of the three realms.
His eyes are like the petals of a lotus.
The assembly of *śrāvaka* disciples there is measurelessly vast.
I therefore bow down in reverence to him.

All the beings in his land
are in nature gentle and harmonious
and they naturally practice the ten good deeds.
I bow down in reverence to this king of the many *āryas*.

It is from such goodness that his pure light is produced
that, in the number of its rays, is measureless and boundless.
He is foremost among those who stand on two feet.
I do therefore take refuge in him.

If a person vows to become a buddha
and then bears in mind Amitābha,
when the time is right, he will appear for his sake.
I do therefore take refuge in him.

Through the power of that buddha's vows
the bodhisattvas of the ten directions
come to make offerings and listen to the Dharma.
I therefore bow down in reverence to him.

All the bodhisattvas in his land
are endowed with all the major marks and secondary characteristics
by which they thereby adorn their own bodies.
Taking refuge in him, I now bow down in reverence.

Three times every day,
all those great bodhisattvas
make offerings to the buddhas of the ten directions.
I therefore bow down in reverence.

If a person who has planted roots of goodness
retains doubts, then the flower will not open.
If one's mind of faith is pure,
the flower will open and one will then see the Buddha.

For many different reasons,
the buddhas of the present throughout the ten directions
praise the qualities of that buddha.
Taking refuge in him, I now bow down in reverence.

His land is especially majestic in its adornment,
surpassing in its excellence the palaces of all the devas.
Its qualities are especially profound and abundant.
I therefore bow down in reverence at the feet of the Buddha.

The Buddha's feet carry the sign of the thousand-spoked wheel.
They are soft and, in appearance, resemble the blossoms of a lotus.
Those who see them are all filled with delight
and bow down their heads in reverence at the feet of the Buddha.

The light from the white hair tuft between his brows
appears like a pristinely shining moon,
enhancing the radiance displayed by his countenance.
I bow down in reverence at the feet of the Buddha.

When he originally sought out the path to buddhahood,
he performed all manner of distinctive and marvelous works.
These are just as described in the sutras.
I bow down in reverence to him.

That which is proclaimed by that buddha
eliminates the roots of karmic offenses.
His eloquent discourse brings benefit to many.
I now bow down in reverence to him.

By resorting to such eloquent discourse,
he rescues beings from all maladies arising by clinging to pleasures.
He has already liberated such beings and now liberates yet more.
I therefore bow down in reverence to him.

The devas bow down in reverence
to he who is the most honored of all humans and devas.
Their seven-jeweled crowns are brought low and touch his feet.
I do therefore take refuge in him.

The Sangha of all the Worthies and the Āryas
as well as the multitudes of humans and devas
all join in taking refuge in him.
Therefore I too bow down in reverence to him.

One who boards his ship of the eight-fold path,
will be able to cross beyond that sea so difficult to cross,
delivering himself to liberation while liberating others as well.
I bow in reverence to he who has achieved sovereign mastery in this.

If, for countless kalpas, the Buddhas
proclaimed their praises of his meritorious qualities,
they would still be unable to come to the end of them.
I take refuge in he who has become such a purified person.

In this same manner, I now proclaim
the praises of his boundless qualities.
I pray that, due to the causes and conditions of this merit,
the Buddha may therefore always bear me in mind.

By whatever merit I have created in the present or previous lives,
whether it be but little or much,
I pray that my mind will become forever purified
in the very presence of the Buddha.

As for the supremely marvelous qualities that may be acquired
through the causes and conditions of such merit as this,
I pray that all of the many varieties of beings
shall all become able to acquire them as well.

4. Also, the Seven Buddhas of the Past as Well as Maitreya

One should also bear in mind Vipaśyin Buddha, Śikhin Buddha, Viśvabhū Buddha, Krakucchanda Buddha, Kanakamuni Buddha, Kāśyapa Buddha, and Śākyamuni Buddha, as well as Maitreya, the future Buddha. One should bear them all in mind and bow down in reverence to them. I set forth their praises here in verse:

The Bhagavat Vipaśyin
abides beneath an *aśoka* bodhi tree,[10]
having perfected all-knowledge
and all of the subtle and marvelous meritorious qualities.

Having rightly contemplated the world,
his mind has succeeded in gaining liberation.
I now, with all five extremities, bow down in reverence,
taking refuge in that unsurpassable Honored One.

The Bhagavat, Śikhin Buddha,
sat in the *bodhimaṇḍa*
beneath a *puṇḍarīka* bodhi tree
where he then achieved the complete realization of bodhi.[11]

His physical appearance is incomparable.
It resembles a mountain of flaming purple gold.
I now take refuge in the Honored One
who is unsurpassed by anyone in the three realms of existence.

Viśvabhū Bhagavat
sits beneath the *śāla* tree
where he naturally acquired the penetrating comprehension
of all forms of sublime wisdom.

Among all humans and devas,
he is the foremost and without peer.
I do therefore take refuge in the Honored One
who is the most supreme among them all.

Krakucchanda Buddha
succeeded in attaining
anuttarasamyaksaṃbodhi
beneath the *śirīṣa* tree.[12]

He perfected the great wisdom,
and became forever liberated from *saṃsāra*.
I now take refuge and bow in reverence
to that supreme and incomparable Honored One.

Kanakamuni,
the great Ārya and unsurpassable Honored One,
attained the perfect realization of buddhahood
beneath the *udumbara* tree

and reached the penetrating comprehension
of all the measurelessly and boundlessly many dharmas.
I do therefore take refuge in him,
that foremost and unsurpassable Honored One.

Kāśyapa Buddha, the Bhagavat,
with eyes like a pair of lotus blossoms,
achieved the perfect realization of buddhahood
beneath the *nyagrodha* tree.

Throughout the three realms, there is nothing he fears.
His gait is like that of the king of the elephants.
I now take refuge in him, bowing down in reverence
to that insuperable Honored One.

Śākyamuni Buddha,
beneath the *aśvattha* tree,[13]
conquered Māra, the enemy,
and perfected the unsurpassed enlightenment.

His countenance is like the full moon,
pure and free of any blemish.
I now bow down in reverence
To that heroically brave and supreme Honored One.

Maitreya, the buddha of the future,
sitting beneath the *nāga* tree,
shall attain the perfect realization of the vast resolve
and then naturally realize buddhahood.

His meritorious qualities are so extremely solid and durable
that no one is able to surpass them.
I do therefore take refuge in him,
that incomparable king of the sublime Dharma.

5. Also, by Calling on Ten Other Buddhas

Additionally, there are: Supreme in Meritorious Qualities Buddha, Universal Illumination Buddha, Victorious over Adversaries Buddha, Marks of the Sovereign[14] Buddha, King of the Marks Buddha,[15] King of Measureless Qualities' Brilliance and Sovereign Mastery Buddha, Unimpeded Medicine King Buddha, Jeweled Traveler Buddha, Precious Flower Buddha, Peacefully Abiding Buddha,[16] and Mountain King Buddha. One should remain mindful of them as well, respectfully bowing in reverence to them. I set forth their praises here in verse:

In the world known as Invincible,
there is a buddha named Supreme in Meritorious Qualities.
I now bow down in reverence to him
as well as to his Dharma Jewel and his Sangha Jewel.

In a world known as Joy in Whatever One Wishes,
there is a buddha named Universal Illumination.
I now take refuge in him
as well as in his Dharma Jewel and his Sangha Jewel.

In the world known as Universal Excellence,
there is a buddha named Victorious over Adversaries.
I now take refuge in him and bow down in reverence to him
as well as to his Dharma Jewel and his Sangha Jewel.

In the world known as Accumulation of Goodness and Purity,
there is a buddha named Marks of the Sovereign's Banner.
I now bow down in reverence to him
as well as to his Dharma Jewel and his Sangha Jewel.

In the world known as Accumulation of Stainlessness,
there is a buddha named Measureless Qualities' Brilliance
whose sovereign mastery extends throughout the ten directions.
I therefore bow down in reverence to him.

In the world known as Undeceptive,
there is a buddha named Unimpeded Medicine King.
I now bow down in reverence to him
as well as to his Dharma Jewel and his Sangha Jewel.

In the world known as Present Accumulation,
there is a buddha named Jeweled Traveler.
I now bow down in reverence to him
as well as to his Dharma Jewel and his Sangha Jewel.

In the Beautiful Sound World, there is Precious Flower Buddha.
[So too,] Peacefully Established and Mountain King Buddhas.
I now bow down in reverence to them
as well as to their Dharma jewels and sangha jewels.

All of these *tathāgatas* now abide
off in the regions to the East.
With a respectful mind, I spread their praises and,
taking refuge in them, bow down in reverence to them.

I only pray that the Tathāgatas
will bestow their deep kindness and sympathy
and thus manifest their bodies before me
so that I might be allowed to personally[17] see them all.

6. Also, by Calling on All Buddhas of the Three Times

Additionally, one should exhaustively and comprehensively bear in mind and respectfully bow in reverence to all buddhas of the past, the future, and the present. I set forth their praises here in verse:

All buddhas of the past
conquered the many *māras*, their adversaries
and, using the power of great wisdom,
provided vast benefit to beings.

The beings who existed in those eras
were entirely devoted to making offerings to them all,
showed them reverence, and proclaimed their praises.
I therefore bow down in reverence to them.

The incalculably many buddhas of the present
throughout the worlds of the ten directions
are so measurelessly and boundlessly many
as to surpass the number of sands in the Ganges River.

Out of kindness and pity for beings,
they always turn the wheel of the sublime Dharma.
I do therefore accord them respect,
take refuge in them, and bow down my head to them in reverence.

The buddhas of the future
shall appear with bodies resembling mountains of gold
that emanate measureless illumination
and display the self-adornment of their many characteristic signs.

They shall appear in the world and liberate beings,
after which they shall then enter nirvāṇa.
To all such *bhagavats* as these,
I do now bow down in reverence.

7. Also, by Calling on the Great Bodhisattvas

Additionally, one should bear in mind the great bodhisattvas, namely: Good Intentions Bodhisattva, Good Eyes Bodhisattva, Moon Hearer Bodhisattva, King Śibi Bodhisattva, Universally Supreme Bodhisattva, Knower of the Great Earth Bodhisattva, Great Medicine Bodhisattva, Kapotagṛha Bodhisattva, Arenemin Bodhisattva, Summit Born King Bodhisattva, Delightful View Bodhisattva, Uttara Bodhisattva, Sarvadāna Bodhisattva, Long Life King Bodhisattva, Kṣānti Bodhisattva, Velāma Bodhisattva, Flashing Light Bodhisattva, Moon Covering Bodhisattva, Brilliant Leader Bodhisattva, Dharma Leader Bodhisattva, Perfecting Benefit Bodhisattva, and Maitreya Bodhisattva.

In addition, there are: Vajragarbha Bodhisattva, Vajra Leader Bodhisattva, Treasury of Non-defilement Bodhisattva, Vimalakīrti Bodhisattva, Dispeller of Doubts Bodhisattva, Undefiled Virtue Bodhisattva, Net-like Brilliance Bodhisattva, Immeasurable Brilliance Bodhisattva, Great Brilliance Bodhisattva, Akṣayamati Bodhisattva, Mind King Bodhisattva, Boundless Mind Bodhisattva, Sun Sound Bodhisattva, Moon Sound Bodhisattva, Beautiful Sound Bodhisattva, Beautiful Voice Bodhisattva, Great Voice Bodhisattva, Solid Vigor Bodhisattva, Ever Solid Bodhisattva, and Solidly Generated Bodhisattva.

There are also: Adornment King Bodhisattva, Ever Compassionate Bodhisattva, Never slighting Bodhisattva, Dharma Superior Bodhisattva, Dharma Mind Bodhisattva, Dharma Joy Bodhisattva, Dharma Leader Bodhisattva, Dharma Accumulation Bodhisattva, Generator of Vigor Bodhisattva, Wisdom Bodhisattva, Pure Awesome Virtue Bodhisattva, Nārāyaṇa Bodhisattva, Good Meditation Bodhisattva, Dharma Meditation Bodhisattva, Bhadrapāla Bodhisattva, Dharma Benefit Bodhisattva, Lofty Virtue Bodhisattva, Lion Traveler Bodhisattva, Joyous Faculties Bodhisattva, and Supreme Jewel Moon Bodhisattva.

There are also: Virtue Free of Falseness Bodhisattva, Dragon Virtue Bodhisattva, Mañjuśrī Bodhisattva, Wonderful Sound Bodhisattva, Cloud Sound Bodhisattva, Supreme Mind Bodhisattva, Illuminating Brilliance Bodhisattva, Brave Assembly Bodhisattva, Supreme Assembly Bodhisattva, Awesome Deportment Bodhisattva, Lion Mind Bodhisattva, Superior Mind Bodhisattva, Beneficial Intentions Bodhisattva, Augmented Mind Bodhisattva, Precious Brilliance Bodhisattva, Wisdom Summit Bodhisattva, Peak of Eloquence Bodhisattva, Possessed of Virtue Bodhisattva, Avalokiteśvara King Bodhisattva, and Dhāraṇī Mastery King Bodhisattva.

There are also: Great Sovereign Mastery King Bodhisattva, Sorrowless Virtue Bodhisattva, Not Seen in Vain Bodhisattva, Beyond the Wretched Destinies Bodhisattva, Universally Brave and Strong Bodhisattva, Dispeller of Darkness Bodhisattva, Merit Jewel Bodhisattva, Floral Awesome Virtue Bodhisattva, Gold Necklace Brilliant Virtue Bodhisattva, Beyond the Aggregates and Hindrances Bodhisattva, Unimpeded Mind Bodhisattva, Pure in All Actions Bodhisattva, Equal Vision Bodhisattva, Unequaled Vision Bodhisattva, Wandering Joyfully in Samādhi Bodhisattva, Sovereign Mastery in Dharma Bodhisattva, Dharma Marks Bodhisattva, Brilliant Adornment Bodhisattva, Great Adornment Bodhisattva, and Jeweled Summit Bodhisattva.

There are also: Jeweled Mudrā Hand Bodhisattva, Ever Raised Hand Bodhisattva, Ever Lowered Hand Bodhisattva, Ever Piteous Bodhisattva, Ever Joyful Bodhisattva, Joy King Bodhisattva, Possessed of Eloquent Voice Bodhisattva, Sound of Thunder in Space Bodhisattva, Upholder of the Jeweled Torch Bodhisattva, Valiant Giving Bodhisattva, Imperial Net Bodhisattva, Horse Light Bodhisattva, Empty and Unimpeded Bodhisattva, Jeweled Supremacy Bodhisattva, Celestial King Bodhisattva, Demon Crusher Bodhisattva, Lightning Virtue Bodhisattva, Sovereign Mastery Bodhisattva, Summit Sign Bodhisattva, and Beyond Transgressions Bodhisattva.

And there are also: Lion's Roar Bodhisattva, Cloud Shade Bodhisattva, Able to Conquer Bodhisattva, Mountainous Marks Banner Bodhisattva, Fragrant Elephant Bodhisattva, Great Fragrant Elephant Bodhisattva, White Fragrant Elephant Bodhisattva, Ever Vigorous Bodhisattva, Never Resting Bodhisattva, Sublime Birth Bodhisattva, Floral Adornment Bodhisattva, Avalokiteśvara Bodhisattva, Mahāsthāmaprāpta Bodhisattva, Water King Bodhisattva, Mountain King Bodhisattva, Indra's Net Bodhisattva, Jewel Giving Bodhisattva, Crusher of Demons Bodhisattva, Adorner of Lands Bodhisattva, Golden Topknot Bodhisattva, and Pearl Topknot Bodhisattva.

One should bear in mind all such bodhisattvas and bow down to them in reverence as one seeks to attain the ground of the *avaivartika.*

The End of Chapter Nine

Part One Endnotes

1. These *ślokas* correspond to *ślokas* 24–28 of Nāgārjuna's *Bodhisambhāra Śāstra*. In my English translation of that entire text with its Indian commentary, they read as follows:

   So long as he has not generated great compassion or the patiences,
   even though he may have gained an irreversibility,
   the bodhisattva is still subject to a form of "dying"
   which occurs through allowing negligence to arise.

   The grounds of the *śrāvaka* disciples or the *pratyekabuddha*s,
   if entered, become for him the same as dying
   because he would thereby sever the bodhisattva's
   roots of understanding and awareness.

   Even at the prospect of falling into the hell-realms,
   the bodhisattva would not be struck with fright.
   The grounds of the *śrāvaka* disciples and the *pratyekabuddha*s, however,
   do provoke a great terror in him.

   It is not the case that falling into the hell realms
   would bring about an ultimate obstacle to his bodhi.
   The grounds of the *śrāvaka* disciples and the *pratyekabuddha*s, however,
   do create just such an ultimate obstacle.

   Just as is said of he who loves long life,
   that he becomes fearful at the prospect of his own beheading,
   so too, the grounds of the *śrāvaka* disciples and *pratyekabuddha*s
   should bring about a fearfulness of just this sort.

2. The first two quatrains correspond to the *Bodhisambhāra Śāstra*'s *śloka* numbers 22 and 23 which read as follows:

   In the bodhisattva's striving for bodhi,
   so long as he has not yet gained irreversibility,
   he acts as urgently as the person whose turban has caught fire.
   Thus one should take up just such intensely diligent practice.

   Thus it is that those bodhisattvas,
   when striving for the realization of bodhi,
   should not rest in their practice of vigor,
   for they have shouldered such a heavy burden.

3. These last two quatrains correspond to the *Bodhisambhāra Śāstra*'s *śloka* numbers 91 and 92 which read as follows:

   Even if one were to take up the vehicle of the *śrāvaka* disciples
   or the vehicle of the *pratyekabuddha*s,
   and hence practiced solely for one's own self benefit,

still, one would not relinquish the enduring practice of vigor.

How much the less could it be that a great man,
one committed to liberate himself and liberate others,
might somehow not generate
a measure of vigor a thousand *koṭis* times greater?

4. I emend here the verse-abbreviated "Three Practices Buddha" reading to "Three *Vehicles* Practices Buddha" to accord with the explanatory text which follows at 42a02–06.

5. See *The Sutra on the Youth Precious Moon's Questions on Dharma* (大乘寶月童子問法經 / T14n0437_p108c01–110a07). The names vary, but the ideas are the same, i.e. sincere mindfulness of ten buddhas in the ten directions can bring irreversibility with respect to one's future attainment of buddhahood.

6. "*Candana*" usually refers to sandalwood, but as noted in MW, it may also be used as a term to refer to anything that is the most excellent of its kind. MW: "mn. sandal (*Sirium myrtifolium*, either the tree, wood, or the unctuous preparation of the wood held in high estimation as perfumes; hence; a term for anything which is the most excellent of its kind."

7. The Chinese translation for this eightieth buddha's name, *guangming fo* (光明佛), "Light Buddha," is duplicated in the name of the ninety-sixth buddha (see next paragraph). Since we do not know the Sanskrit antecedents for these two buddhas' names, I have distinguished them here with slightly variant English translations ("Light Buddha," "Radiance Buddha").

8. The Chinese translation for this ninety-sixth buddha's name, *guangming fo* (光明佛), "Radiance Buddha," is duplicated in the name of the eightieth buddha (see previous paragraph). Since we do not know the Sanskrit antecedents for these two buddhas' names, I have distinguished them here with slightly variant English translations ("Light Buddha," "Radiance Buddha").

9. On sensibility grounds, I adopt here the SYMG editions' variant, *hua yuan fo* (華園佛), "Floral Garden Buddha," to correct what seems to be a graphic-similarity scribal error in the *Taisho* edition, *hua chi fo* (華齒佛), "Floral Teeth Buddha."

10. I reconstruct "*aśoka*," lit. "sorrowless" as the name of this bodhi tree as it is a tree that grows throughout India (*Saraca asoca*) and is in fact said to also be the same kind of tree under which the historical Buddha's mother gave birth to him.

11. VB provides the following citation: "See DN II 4: *Sikhī, bhikkhave, bhagavā arahaṃ sammāsambuddho puṇḍarīkassa mūle abhisambuddho.*"

12. The *śirīṣa* tree is identified by MW as *acacia sirissa*.
13. An "*aśvattha*" tree is an ancient name for what is more commonly known in Buddhist texts as the "bodhi" tree (*ficus religiosa*).
14. In the verses below (at 44b07), this Buddha's name is enhanced with an additional character to "Marks of the Sovereign's Canopy" (王幢相).
15. I suspect that there should only be ten buddhas in this list and that this buddha's name may appear here only as a result of an accidental scribal redundancy, this for two reasons:
    a) The Chinese name is identical to that of the previously listed buddha except that the characters are in reverse order (*wangxiang* [王相] versus *xiangwang* [相王]); and
    b) Although the other ten buddhas' names are mentioned in the following praise verses, this buddha's name is not mentioned there at all.
16. This buddha's name is only slightly different in the verses that follow, occurring there (at 44b15) as "Peacefully Established" (安立).
17. I emend the reading of the reading here by preferring the *zi* (自), "personally," of the SYMG editions to the *mu* (目), "eyes" of the *Taisho* text, this to correct an apparent graphic-similarity scribal error.

Nāgārjuna
on
Mindfulness of the Buddha

Part 2: The Pratuyutpanna Samādhi

Nāgārjuna's *Treatise on the Ten Grounds,* Chs. 20–25

As Translated into Chinese by Tripiṭaka Master Kumārajīva
English Translation by Bhikshu Dharmamitra

Part Two
The Pratyutpanna Samādhi

Ch. 20: Mindfulness of the Buddhas

I. Chapter 20: Mindfulness of the Buddhas

A. On Finishing 1st Ground Practices, the Bodhisattva Sees Buddhas

When the bodhisattva dwelling on the first ground
has completed what is to be practiced,
due to the power of his roots of goodness, he will naturally
be able to see several hundred buddhas.[1]

When, in this [above-discussed] manner, the bodhisattva subdues his own mind, he develops a deep love for the path to buddhahood. He then completely fulfills the first-ground practices in accordance with the way he learned them. Then, due to the power of his roots of goodness and merit, he is naturally able to see the present-era buddhas of the ten directions right before his very eyes.

1. Q: Is There Any Other Way to Be Able to See the Buddhas?

Question: Is it solely through the power of roots of goodness and merit that one is then able to see buddhas or is there some other method by which one can do so?

2. A: On Entering the Pratyutpanna Samādhi, One Sees the Buddhas

Response:

There is a deep samādhi that the Buddha
explained for the sake of Bhadrapāla.
If one acquires this samādhi treasure,
one becomes able to see the Buddhas.

Bhadrapāla was a lay bodhisattva well able to practice the *dhūta* austerities. It was for the sake of this bodhisattva that the Buddha spoke the *Pratyutpanna Samādhi Sūtra*.[2] The *pratyutpanna* samādhi is one in which one sees the Buddhas right before one's very eyes. When the bodhisattva accesses this magnificently precious samādhi, even though he might not yet have gained the heavenly eye and heavenly ear, he is nonetheless able to see the buddhas of the ten directions and he is also able to listen to the Dharma of the sutras being taught by those buddhas.

3. Q: How Can One Acquire This Samadhi?

Question: What means should one use to acquire this samādhi?

4. A: Envision the Buddhas with the 32 Marks and 80 Characteristics

Response:

One should bring to mind the Buddhas,
envisioning them as residing in a great assembly,
replete with all thirty-two major marks
and eighty secondary characteristics adorning their bodies.

a. Recollection of the Buddhas' Qualities and Accomplishments

In cultivating this samādhi, the practitioner brings to mind the Buddhas with the thirty-two major marks and eighty secondary characteristics gracing their bodies, with bhikshus close by, with devas making offerings, and with a grand and reverential assembly surrounding them. With focused mind, one envisions each of the major marks of those buddhas.

One also recollects the Buddhas as those who are possessed of great vows, recollects their perfection of the great compassion and the fact that it has not been cut off, recollects their perfection of the great kindness through which they bring profound peace to beings, recollects their practice of the great sympathetic joy and their fulfillment of beings' aspirations, and recollects their practice of equanimity through which they have abandoned aversion and craving and do not abandon beings.

One also recollects their practice of the truthfulness basis of meritorious qualities by which they are never deceptive, recollects their practice of the relinquishment basis of meritorious qualities by which they have rid themselves of the miserliness defilement, recollects their practice of the thorough [quiescence][3] basis of meritorious qualities by which their minds maintain a state of thorough-going quiescence, and recollects their practice of the wisdom basis of meritorious qualities through which they have acquired great wisdom.[4]

One recollects too their perfect practice of *dāna pāramitā* by which they have become the lords of Dharma giving, their perfect practice of *śīla pāramitā* by which their observance of the moral precepts is pure, their perfect practice of *kṣānti pāramitā* by which their capacity for patient endurance is analogous to that of the earth, their perfect practice of *vīrya pāramitā* by which their vigor is preeminent, their perfect practice of *dhyāna pāramitā* by which they have destroyed all hindrances to meditative absorption, and their perfect practice of *prajñā pāramitā* by which they have destroyed all obstacles to wisdom.

b. Recollection of the 32 Marks of the Buddhas

One recollects too:

Their mark of having the wheel insignia on the hands and feet, emblematic of their ability to turn the wheel of Dharma;
Their mark of securely planted feet, emblematic of their standing securely in every dharma;
Their mark of proximal webbing on fingers and toes, emblematic of the extinguishing of all afflictions;
Their mark of seven places of fullness, emblematic of their complete fulfillment of merit;
Their mark of soft and tender hands and feet, emblematic of their harmonious manner of proclaiming the Dharma;
Their mark of slender and long fingers and toes, emblematic of their cultivation and accumulation of every sort of good and sublime dharma during the long night [of previous lifetimes];
Their mark of having broad heels and wide eyes, emblematic of their vast learning;
Their mark of having a large and erect body, emblematic of their proclamation of the great and upright Dharma;
Their mark of having high arches, emblematic of their being lofty in all things;
Their mark of having upwardly spiraling bodily hairs, emblematic of their ability to cause beings to abide in the supreme and sublime dharma;
Their mark of having legs gradually growing in thickness like those of the *aiṇeya* antelope;
Their mark of long arms reaching past the knees, their arms appearing like golden gate bars;[5]
Their mark of the stallion-like retracted male organ, emblematic of their possession of the treasury of Dharma jewels;
Their mark of the golden-hued body emanating light of countless colors;
Their mark of fine and thin skin, emblematic of their proclamation of subtle and sublime Dharma;
Their mark of one hair per hair pore, emblematic of their revealing of the single-mark Dharma;
Their mark of the [mid-brow] white-down tuft adorning the countenance, due to which beings happily and tirelessly gaze at the Buddha's face;
Their mark of a lion-like upper torso, emblematic of the Buddha, like the lion, being one who is fearless;
Their mark of round and large shoulders, emblematic of their ability to make skillful distinctions regarding the nature of the five aggregates;

Their mark of fullness in the sub-axillary region, emblematic of their possession of a full measure of good roots;
Their mark of distinguishing every flavor, emblematic of their having perfectly tasted the flavor of quiescence;
Their mark of having a square-set body, emblematic of having crushed the fear of births and deaths;
Their mark of the fleshy prominence atop the crown, emblematic of their heads never having to be lowered in reverence [to someone superior];
Their mark of the large tongue the color of real coral that is even able to cover the face;
Their mark of the Brahmā-like voice and the physical mark that reaches even to the Brahma Heaven;
Their mark of the lion-like jaw;
Their mark of the broad shoulders, these being emblematic of their ability to demolish [the views held by] non-Buddhist traditions;
Their mark of even teeth, emblematic of their practice of pure *dhyāna* meditation;
Their mark of their teeth being of even height, emblematic of their minds' equal regard for all beings;
Their mark of closely set teeth, emblematic of their abandonment of the desires;
Their mark of having forty teeth, emblematic of their perfection of the forty dharmas exclusive to buddhas;
Their mark of blue eyes, emblematic of their looking on beings with minds imbued with kindness;
Their mark of having eyelashes like those of the royal bull, with the lashes long and in no way disarrayed;
Their obtaining of a rare physical form that beings look on without ever tiring of holding it in their gaze;
Their having bodies adorned with these thirty-two marks;

c. Recollection of Other Qualities of the Buddhas

Their having the eighty minor characteristics like inlaid adornments on their bodies, emanating brilliant radiance;
Their complete fulfillment of merit;
Their transcendently supreme and awesome powers;
Their wide-spread illustrious esteem;
Their bodies' incense-like fragrance produced by purity in observing the moral precepts;
Their invulnerability to being moved by worldly dharmas;
Their ability to remain undefiled by any arising of afflictions;

Their ability to remain unsullied by others' verbal abuse;
Their ability to roam and sport through use of their spiritual powers;
The ability of the Buddhas to be so intensely magnificent in the manifestation of their awe-inspiring powers that no one would dare obstruct them;
Their freely exercised sovereign mastery in using wisdom to proclaim the Dharma that is like the roaring of a lion;
Their ability to dispel the darkness of delusion by marshaling the power of vigor;
Their use of magnificent brilliance to everywhere illuminate the heavens and the earth;
Their utter invincibility in debate;
Their being such that everyone looks up to them and no one can look down on them;
Their constancy in regarding all beings with kindness;
Their possession of mindfulness as vast as the great oceans;
Their meditative absorption that is like Mount Sumeru [in its unshakability];
Their possession of patience comparable to the earth's [ability to endure anything];
Their ability to bring about growth in the merit planted by beings that is analogous [to the growth-enhancing capacity of] water's moisture;[6]
Their ability to bring forth roots of goodness in beings that, in its power, is like the rising of the wind;
Their ability to ripen beings that is like fire's ability to cook things;
Their possession of wisdom as boundless as empty space;
Their universal raining down of the great Dharma [rain] that is like [the rain that pours done from] immense dense clouds;
Their ability to remain unstained by worldly dharmas that is like lotus blossoms' [ability to rise from mud and yet remain unsullied by it];
Their ability, like lions pouncing on deer, to decisively refute [the doctrines of] non-Buddhist masters;
Their ability to bear a heavy burden that is like that of the great king of the elephants;
Their ability to lead a great congregation of followers that is like that of the great king of bulls;
Their possession of a retinue of pure followers that is like [the retinue of] a wheel-turning king;
Their utter supremacy in the world that is like that of the lord of the Mahābrahma Heaven;

Their ability to inspire fondness and delight that is like that of a bright moon in the clear night sky;
Their universal illumination that is able to burn as brightly as the brilliantly shining sun;
Their bestowal on beings of the causes and conditions for peace and happiness that is like [the generosity of] a humane father;
Their acting out of pity toward beings, protecting them in whatever way is appropriate, that is like the actions of a lovingly kind mother;
Their purity of conduct that is like [the purity of] the real gold in the heavens;
Their possession of the power of great strength that is like that of Indra in the heavens;
Their diligence in benefiting those in the world that is like that of a world-protecting lord;
Their ability to cure the disease of the afflictions that is like [the curative power of] a king of physicians;
Their ability to rescue one from disastrous circumstances that is like that of close relatives;
Their ability to accumulate a store of meritorious qualities that is like an immense treasury;
Their possession of immeasurably vast moral virtue;
Their possession of boundless meditative absorptions;
Their ineffable wisdom;
Their unequaled liberation;
Their knowledge and vision of liberation that is the equal of the unequaled;
Their incomparability in all things;
Their supremacy over everyone in the world due to which they are recognized as foremost among men;
And their perfection of great dharmas by which they are recognized as great men.

It is in this way that the bodhisattva engages in recollective contemplation of all buddhas in accordance with their possession of the qualities characteristic of the great men. [So, too, he recollects]:

d. Recollection of More Special Qualities & Abilities of Buddhas

That these buddhas have cultivated these meritorious qualities for a countless, boundless, inconceivable, and incalculable number of hundreds of thousands of myriads of *koṭis* of kalpas during which they have been well able to guard their physical, verbal, and mental karma;

That they are well able to completely sever all doubts with respect to the five categorical repositories of dharmas: past dharmas, future dharmas, present dharmas, unconditioned dharmas, and ineffable dharmas;

That, without falling into any error, they employ the four modes of reply: the definitive reply, the distinguishing reply, the counter-questioning reply, and the reply that sets aside the question;[7]

That they skillfully explain the dharmas of the thirty-seven enlightenment factors, namely: the faculties, the powers, the limbs of enlightenment, the path, the stations of mindfulness, the right efforts, and the foundations of psychic power;[8]

That they are well able to distinguish [each link comprising the chain of] cause-and-effect, namely: ignorance, actions, consciousness, name-and-form, the six sense faculties, contact, feeling, craving, grasping, becoming, birth, and aging-and-death;

That they are free of any attachment to the eye or visual forms, to the ear or sounds, to the nose or fragrances, to the tongue or flavors, to the body or touch, or to the mind or dharmas [as objects of mind];

That they skillfully expound the nine types of passages contained in the Dharma of the sutras, namely: sutras; *geyas*; prophetic teachings or expositions; *gāthās*; *udānas*; *nidānas*; [short] discourses beginning with "Thus [spoke the Buddha]..."; *vaipulyas*; and unprecedented events;

That they are not influenced by any of the negative influences such as: greed, hatred, delusion, arrogance, the view that conceives of the existence of true personhood, extreme views, wrong views, seizing upon views; seizing on rules and regulations, or doubts;

That they are not assailed by such afflictions as absence of faith, absence of a sense of shame, absence of a dread of blame, flattery, deviousness, frivolousness, neglectfulness, indolence, somnolence, animosity, miserliness, or jealousy;

That they have known and seen the truth of suffering, have cut off its origination, have realized cessation, have cultivated the path, have abandoned what is to be abandoned, have seen what is to be seen, have done what is to be done, have utterly destroyed the foes,[9] and have perfectly fulfilled their vows;

That they are venerated in the world, are as fathers to the world, and are lords of the world, are well come, are well gone, are possessed of the well-cultivated mind, are consummately skilled in meditative stillness, are well-realized in the realization of cessation, and are well liberated;

That, as they abide in countless and boundless worlds throughout the ten directions in worlds as numerous as the sands in the

Ganges, [one envisions them] as if they were appearing directly before one's very eyes.

e. Contemplative Recollection of the 80 Secondary Characteristics

The bodhisattva should also envision in contemplation all of the buddhas as graced with their eighty secondary characteristics,[10] recollecting:

That their nails are copper-colored is emblematic of their practice of pure dharmas;

That their nails are prominent and large is emblematic of birth into the great clan;

That their nails are glossy and smooth is emblematic of a deep affection for beings;

That their fingers are round, tapered, and long is emblematic of the depth and duration of their practice;

That their fingers are fully fleshed is emblematic of fully developed roots of goodness;

That their fingers are tapered and long is emblematic of sequential accumulation of all dharmas of a buddha;

That their veins are hidden and invisible, but they do not hide the lineage of [the quality of their conduct in] body, mouth, and mind;

That there are no thick knots in their veins is emblematic of their having broken up the knots of afflictions;

That their ankle bones are flat and inconspicuous is emblematic of their not hiding away the Dharma;

That their feet are not misaligned in their track is emblematic of their liberation of the multitudes who have fallen into deviant conduct;

That their gait is like that of the lion is emblematic of their being the lions among men;

That their gait is also like that of the king of elephants is emblematic of their being the elephant kings among men;

That their gait is also like the king of geese is emblematic of their flying high, like the wild goose;

That their gait is also like the king of bulls is emblematic of their being the most revered of all men;

That, when walking, they turn around to the right, is emblematic of their skillful proclamation of the right path;

That their posture is not hunched or crooked is emblematic of the fact that their minds are never crooked;

That their bodies stand solid and erect in their posture is emblematic of their praise of solidity and durability in upholding the moral precepts;

That their bodies gradually grew large is emblematic of their sequential exposition of Dharma;

That all parts of their bodies are large and majestic is emblematic of their ability to skillfully explain the great and sublime meritorious qualities;

That their bodies are perfectly developed is emblematic of their perfection in the Dharma;

That their strides are of equal length is emblematic of their equal-minded regard for all beings;

That their bodies are pristine in their cleanliness is emblematic of the purity of their three types of karma;

That their skin is fine and soft is emblematic of the naturally pliant character of their minds;

That their bodies remain free of all dust and dirt is emblematic of their good views that have abandoned all defilement;

That their bodies do not shrink through wasting [even in old age] is emblematic of their minds' always remaining unsinkable;

That their bodies are boundless and immeasurable is emblematic of the immeasurability of their roots of goodness;

That the flesh of their bodies is taut and finely textured is emblematic of their eternal severance of [karmically-compulsory] later incarnations;

That all of their joints are smooth in their articulations is emblematic of their skillful explication of the twelve causes and conditions and their perfectly clear distinguishing of each of them;

That the hue of their bodies is not dark is emblematic of their knowledge and vision being free of any darkness;

That their waists are full all around is emblematic of their disciples' possession of fully developed conduct;

That their bellies are clear [of blemishes] and of fresh and immaculate appearance is emblematic of their being well able to completely know the serious faults of *saṃsāra;*

That their bellies do not protrude is emblematic of their having crushed the mountain of arrogance;

That their bellies are flat and do not show is emblematic of the fact that their proclamation of Dharma is directed equally toward everyone;

That their umbilici are round and deep is emblematic of their penetrating comprehension of extremely deep dharmas;

That their umbilici have a rightward swirl is emblematic of their disciples' compliance with instruction;

That their bodies are in every way graceful in their refinements is emblematic of the thoroughgoing purity of their disciples;
That their awesomeness in deportment is utterly immaculate is emblematic of the incomparable purity of their minds;
That their bodies are free of blemishes is emblematic of their being completely free of any black dharmas;
That the softness of their hands is superior even to that of *tūla*-cotton silk is emblematic of the experience of those receiving their instruction who feel as if their bodies have become as light as a wisp of down;
That the lines on their palms form a deep pattern is emblematic of the profoundly dignified nature of their awesome deportment;
That the lines on their palms are long is emblematic of their contemplative regard for the long-term future of those receiving their Dharma teaching;
That the pattern on their palms is lustrous and smooth is emblematic of their relinquishing of the affection of relatives and of their acquisition of the fruits of the great path;
That their countenances remain free of any long-faced expression is emblematic of the presence of exceptional circumstances in the moral precepts they establish;
That their lips are as red as *bimba* fruit is emblematic of their looking on the entire world as merely like an image reflected in a mirror;
That their tongues are soft and pliant is emblematic of their initial use of gentle speech in liberating beings;
That their tongues are thin and wide is emblematic of the purity and abundance of their meritorious qualities;
That their tongues are crimson red is emblematic of their Dharma's ability to cause common people to understand what they find difficult to understand;
That their voices are like thunder is emblematic of their not fearing the boom of a thunderclap;
That their voices are harmonious and gentle is emblematic of their proclamation of soft and gentle Dharma;
That their four central incisors are rounded [in their visible profile] and straight is emblematic of their proclamation of the Dharma of the straight path;
That their four central incisors are all sharp is emblematic of their liberation of those beings who are possessed of sharp faculties;
That their four central incisors are immaculately white is emblematic of their being foremost in purity;

That their four central incisors are evenly and equally set is emblematic of their standing on the level ground of the moral precepts;

That the profile of their rows of teeth gradually taper to those that are smaller [in height] is emblematic of the graduated sequence in their explanation of the dharma of the four truths;

That they have noses that are high and straight-ridged is emblematic of their standing atop the high mountain of wisdom;

That their nasal apertures are clear and clean is emblematic of the purity of their disciples;

That their eyes are wide and laterally long is emblematic of their wisdom's qualities of being vast and far-reaching;

That their eyelashes are not sparse or in disarray is emblematic of their skill in their differential assessment of beings;

That the whites and pupils of their eyes are as fresh and pristine as the petals of a blue lotus blossom is emblematic of their being such that even devas and heavenly maidens are moved to gaze upon them fondly and bow down in reverence before them;

That their eyebrows are high and long is emblematic of the far-reaching spread of their fame;

That the hair of their eyebrows is smooth and glossy is emblematic of their thoroughgoing knowledge of the dharmas of mental pliancy;

That their ears are equal in their appearance is emblematic of the equality of all who listen to the Dharma;

That their faculty of hearing is undamaged is emblematic of their ability to liberate any being possessed of an undamaged mind;

That their foreheads are flat and of fine appearance is emblematic of their having skillfully abandoned all views;

That their foreheads are unrestricted in their wide breadth is emblematic of their having broadly refuted [the claims of] non-Buddhist traditions;

That their heads are in all respects perfectly developed is emblematic of their having thoroughly perfected [the goals of] their great vows;

That their hair is the color of the black bee is emblematic of their having transformed the pleasures associated with the five types of desire;

That their hair is dense and fine is emblematic of their having already put an end to the fetters;

That their hair, so pleasing in its appearance, is soft in texture is emblematic of their pliant and sharp wisdom's ability to know well the flavor of dharmas;

That their hair is not in disarray is emblematic of their words never being disordered;
That their hair is smooth and glossy is emblematic of their always being free of any sort of coarse speech;
That their hair has a marvelous fragrance is emblematic of their use of the fragrant blossoms of the seven branches of bodhi to teach and guide beings in whatever way is appropriate.
That their mark of virtue, peace, and joy appears in their hair.
And that their mark of virtue, peace, and joy also appears on the palms of their hands and on the soles of their feet.

f. Envisioning the Buddhas in an Assembly, Teaching, on the Lion Seat

1) Envisioning the Buddhas as They Sit on the Lion's Seat

It is in this manner that a bodhisattva should envision the Buddhas residing in the midst of a great assembly, speaking on right Dharma, and sitting on the lion seat. The lion seat has feet made from *vaiḍūrya* inset with various jewels, a headrest made from real coral with marvelous red pearls, and a canopy made of hammered gold. It is draped with all sorts of soft, silky, and lustrous heavenly robes and is supported by bejeweled lions whose bodies are made of purple gold. Their eyes are amber and their tails are mother-of-pearl. They have carnelian tongues, four white-diamond tusk-teeth, hair made of real white silver, and long, full manes. That seat rests upon these four lions. They form [the base of] the throne that has armrests made from royal elephant tusks and a footrest made of the many sorts of jewels.

The Buddhas receive there the reverential obeisance of the devas, dragons, *yakṣas, gandharvas, asuras, garuḍas, kinnaras,* and *mahoragas.* The Buddhas appear in this way on this throne. They wear the *saṃkakṣikā*[11] and the *nivāsana,*[12] neither too high nor too low, so that they cover the three regions of the body and are neatly arranged and straight all around. They wear a light-colored *saṃghāṭī* robe,[13] with the strips composing it clearly visible, neither too high nor too low, and not misaligned.

2) Envisioning the Audience as the Buddhas Teach Dharma

They abide in the midst of an audience adorned by the presence of the eight kinds of great *āryas,*[14] surrounded by a great assembly of humans and devas. When in attendance there, the dragons and golden-winged *garuḍa* birds all listen together to the teaching of Dharma, remaining free of any thoughts of mutual hostility.[15]

Everyone in the entire assembly is imbued with a deeply sincere sense of shame and dread of blame as, with reverential affection for the Buddha, they all listen single-mindedly to the discourse of the

Buddha, accept and uphold it, reflect upon it, and practice in accordance with what is taught. Because their minds are focused as they listen and because their thoughts are pure, they are able to block any interference by the hindrances. Everyone in the great assembly gazes insatiably up at the Tathāgata, with all the hairs raised on their bodies, with their eyes filled with tears, with their minds afire with intensity, or with hearts filled with great joy.

Wherever people have become like this, one knows that their minds have become purified. They remain there motionless and silent, serenely still, and as if having entered *dhyāna* absorption. Their minds are free of either love or hatred and remain undistracted by any extraneous matters. They have thoughts of great compassion[16] by which they feel kindness and pity for beings, wishing to rescue them all. Their minds do not descend into flattery or deviousness, but rather have become utterly quiescent and pure as they distinguish what is good from what is bad. They have an immensely strong determination from which they neither fall away or shrink back and they do not regard themselves as superior or others as inferior.

3) Envisioning the Manner in Which They Teach Dharma

The Buddhas are all observed abiding in such great assemblies, teaching Dharma that is easy to understand and easy to completely fathom. [Their audiences] listen with insatiable delight. Their voices are deep, are not subject to fading [even at a distance], are gentle, and are pleasing to the ear. Originating in the belly, through the interaction of the throat, tongue, nasopharynx, dental palate, teeth, and lips, the air is caused to become sounds and sentences that may be soft and pleasing to the ear, may be as powerfully strong as the earth-quaking thunder emanating from huge, dense rain clouds, may be like those fierce winds off the great ocean that drive up the surf, or may be like the voice of the devas in the Mahābrahma Heaven. With voices such as these, they lead forth and guide those beings that are capable of being liberated.

They have abandoned any modes of expression associated with scolding that may involve contortion of the brow, the countenance, or the lips. Their speech is neither deficient in any way nor unnecessarily long and redundant. There is no doubt in what they proclaim and their words will certainly be beneficial. Their speech is entirely free of any deceptive statements, any statements vulnerable to refutation, or any other such statements. It is entirely free of these faults and it is heard equally well by those far and near.

The Buddhas are freely able to answer the four types of challenging questions. They explain the four truths, thereby causing beings to gain the four fruits of the path. They establish points of meaning and make statements supported by reasons. They are completely equipped with all of the methods used in speaking. In the many different sorts of matters that they discuss, their meaning is easy to completely comprehend. Whatever they proclaim is entirely clear and never intentionally cryptic or convoluted. Their speech is neither too fast nor too slow. The beginnings and conclusions of each discourse are mutually compatible and invulnerable to anyone's challenges.

4) Envisioning the Effects of the Buddhas' Teaching of Dharma

With speech such as this, they spread forth and proclaim the Dharma which is good in the beginning, middle, and end, imbued with meaning, beneficial, devoted solely to Dharma, and, in all respects, perfect.[17] It is able to cause beings to gain karmic rewards in in this very lifetime. Their discourse is not meaningful only for a time, is such that one can test it for oneself, and is such that will lead to the fulfillment of one's aspirations. Those possessed of profound and sublime wisdom realize it within themselves. It can extinguish in beings the raging fire set ablaze by the three poisons. It is able to rid one of all karmic offenses committed by body, speech, and mind, and it is also well able to open up and reveal the essence of moral virtue, the meditative absorptions, and wisdom.

It begins with mere naming that in turn provokes realization of meaning that then in its own turn causes one to be filled with joy. From this joy, there then arises bliss, and from this bliss, there then arises meditative concentration. From this meditative concentration, there arises a wise knowing in accordance with reality, and from this wise knowing in accordance with reality, one then develops renunciation. Due to having developed this renunciation, one becomes able to destroy the fetters, and due to having destroyed those fetters, one then gains liberation.

In this very manner, this Dharma is caused to unfold in a sequence whereby:

It is well able to open forth and reveal the four bases [of meritorious qualities]: truth, relinquishment, quiescence, and wisdom;

It is able to reveal for beings the means by which they are caused to perfectly fulfill the *pāramitās* of giving, moral virtue, patience, vigor, meditative concentration, and wisdom;

It is able to cause beings to sequentially enter and proceed through the Ground of Joyfulness, the Ground of Stainlessness, the ground of Shining Light, the Ground of Blazing Brilliance, the Difficult-to-Conquer Ground, the Ground of Direct Presence, the Far-Reaching

Ground, the Ground of Immovability, the Ground of Excellent Intelligence, and the Ground of the Dharma Cloud;
It is able to make clear distinctions with regard to the Śrāvaka Disciple Vehicle, the Pratyekabuddha Vehicle, and the Great Vehicle;
It is able to provoke realization of the fruits of the path gained by the stream enterer, once returner, non-returner and arhat;[18]
And it is able too to cause complete success in gaining wealth and happiness in the realms of humans and devas.

This is what constitutes the treasury of meritorious qualities that provides all of the foremost forms of benefit.

5) Instruction on This Type of Contemplative Mindfulness

It is in this manner that one uses right thought in the recollective mindfulness of all buddhas. One abides in a peaceful and quiet place, rids oneself of sensual desire, ill will, dullness and drowsiness, doubtfulness, regret and agitation, and single-mindedly carries on focused mindfulness in which one refrains from generating thoughts that obstruct or cause one to lose meditative absorption. One employs this sort of mind in one's focused mindfulness of the Buddhas. If one's mind sinks, one should raise it up again. If one's mind becomes scattered, one should draw it back into a focused state. One then sees the entire great assembly as if it were always right before one's very eyes.

6) The Importance of Praising the Major Marks and Secondary Signs

When one has not yet managed to enter concentrated meditative absorption, one should always praise the two types of phenomena that consist of the Buddha's major marks and secondary characteristics, using verses to celebrate the qualities of the Buddhas and to cause one's mind to become well trained in this.

a) Verses in Praise of the Buddhas' 32 Marks

Accordingly, there are these lines of verse as follows:

Referring to the marks and characteristics of the Bhagavats
and the karmic causes and conditions by which they acquired them,
I shall use these marks and their corresponding karmic actions
to set forth the praises of these great *āryas*:

The thousand-spoked wheel mark on the feet
is associated with a pure retinue and with giving.
It is because of these causes and conditions
that the many worthies and *āryas* surround them.

The mark of the stable stance of the feet
arises from upholding without fail all goodness one has taken on.
It is because of this that the legions of Māra's armies
are unable to succeed in destroying them.

Their fingers and toes join with proximal webs
and their bodies have the mark of purple golden coloration.
Because of their skillful practice of the means of attraction,
the great assembly naturally bows in deferential reverence.

Their hands and feet are extremely soft
and the body has the mark of fullness in the seven places.
It is due to giving food that accords with others' wishes
that they are naturally given many offerings.

They have long fingers, broad heels,
and the body has the mark of being large and upright.
This results from abandoning the causes and conditions of killing
and may lead to a lifespan lasting even up to a kalpa in length.

The hairs of the body grow in an upward and rightward spiral
and the feet have the mark of high arches.
By always advancing in good endeavors,
they thereby acquired the dharma of irreversibility.

They have the gradually tapering legs of the *aiṇeya* antelope
due to always delighting in study and recitation of scriptures.
It is through speaking the Dharma for others
that they rapidly realized the unsurpassable path.

As for having long arms that reach below the knees,
this is due to never being miserly in giving
anything one possesses to whoever seeks to acquire them.
Thus they can teach and guide others in ways suited to their wishes.

Genital ensheathment reflects a treasury of meritorious qualities
associated with skillfully reconciling those who are estranged.[19]
As a result, they acquire a great congregation of humans and devas
and use the pure wisdom eye to create their sons.[20]

Their thin skin that radiates golden light
is associated with giving marvelous apparel and halls.
As a consequence, they acquire an abundance of fine robes
as well as pristine quarters, buildings, and viewing terraces.

The single hair in each pore
and the white hair tuft between the eyes
are associated with serving as a supreme protector.
Hence they are revered throughout the three realms of existence.

They have an upper body like that of a lion
with the two shoulders rounded and full.
These result from always using speech that is pleasing to others.
As a consequence, there is no one who opposes them.

The marks of sub-axillary fullness and cognition of all tastes
stem from providing medical care and medicines for the sick.
As a consequence, devas and men all revere and love them
and their bodies remain ever free of disease.

The roundness of the mid-body and the crown's fleshy *uṣṇīṣa* sign
reflect the merit of giving with a harmonious and delighted mind.
As a consequence of exhorting and teaching even the stubborn,
they reign as sovereignly masterful kings of Dharma.

As for the voice like that of a *kalaviṅka* bird,
the broad tongue, and the voice like a Great Brahma Heaven deva,
they are from the speaking of words that are both gentle and true.
They therefore acquire the Great Ārya's eight voice qualities.[21]

Having first brought contemplative thought to bear
and then afterward spoken words of definite truthfulness,
they acquired the lion-like mark.
Hence all who see them trust them and defer to them.

That their teeth are white, straight, and close-set
is because they have always refrained from slighting
those who have previously given offerings.
Hence the minds of those in their retinue are agreeable and unified.

Above and below, they have a total of forty teeth
that, being close-set, have no gaps.
These result from never slandering and not lying.
Hence their disciples' [loyalty] cannot be destroyed.

The pupils and whites of their eyes are clearly delineated
and they have the mark of eyelashes like those of a royal bull.
These are caused by kindly thought and an amicable view of others.
Consequently all observers look on them with a tireless gaze.

Even though a wheel-turning king
who rules over four continents
possesses these major marks and secondary characteristics,
their radiance still cannot compare with that of a buddha.

I pray that the power of the merit from my setting forth praises
of the major marks and the secondary characteristics
may be able to cause everyone
to have purified minds as well as everlasting peace and happiness.

a) Verses in Praise of the Buddhas Secondary Characteristics

The bodhisattva should also engage in contemplative mindfulness of the buddhas by way of their eighty secondary characteristics. Accordingly, there are these lines of verse, as follows:

All buddhas possess the marvelous secondary characteristics,
eighty in number, with which their bodies are adorned.
You should all delight in them
and listen intently as I describe them.

The Bhagavats have round and slender fingers,
nails that are purplish red in hue,
convex in profile, smooth, and glossy,
characteristics of having everything in measureless abundance.

Their veins lie flat, their ankle bones are invisible,
their feet are not skewed in their track,
their gait is like that of the king of lions,
and they are incomparably awe-inspiring to all observers.

When walking, the entire body turns to the right.
They are serene in manner and refined in their deportment.
The parts of their squarely set bodies are orderly in their posture
and their dignified grace inspires fondness and happiness.

Their bodies are firm in tone, but extremely soft.
The articulations of their joints are quite visibly distinct.
When walking, they do not travel in a meandering manner.
All of their sense faculties are fully and perfectly developed.

The flesh on their bodies is extremely taut, finely textured,
freshly radiant, and especially immaculate.
Their physical posture is especially upright, refined,
and devoid of any feature subject to dispraise.

The belly is round, but does not visibly bulge.
The navel, though deep, does not appear to be an orifice.
Its creases manifest as a rightward spiraling swirl.
Their deportment is extremely pure.

The body is free of any blemishes
and the hands and feet are extremely soft.
The lines in the palms are deep and long,
continuous, straight, and lustrous.

The tongue is slender, the face is not too long.
The central incisors are white, rounded, slender, and sharp.
The hue of the lips is like that of the *bimba* fruit.
Their voice is as deep as the king of the wild geese.

The nose is prominent in profile and the eyes are bright and clear.
The eyelashes are close-set and fine, but not in disarray.
The brow is elevated, has eyebrow hair that is soft,
and it is straight and not crooked.

The hair of the brows, being even and straight,
is emblematic of being well aware of the faults in any dharma.
The hair of the brows is smooth and glossy,
a feature emblematic of skillfully liberating and aiding beings.

The ears are full, long, even in shape,
undamaged, and especially pleasing to the eye.
The forehead is broad and straight.
All of the head's features are perfectly formed.

The hair is fine, dense, never in disarray,
the color of the king of the black bees,
clean, pleasantly fragrant, immaculate,
and possessed of three of the marks.

b) Summation on Importance of Such Recollective Contemplation

This has been the description of the eighty secondary characteristics. Because these eighty secondary characteristics are interspersed with and serve to adorn the thirty-two major marks, if one fails to take up contemplative mindfulness of both the thirty-two marks and the eighty secondary characteristics in one's praises of the Buddha's body, then one may lose forever the causal factors conducing to well-being and happiness in the present and future lives.

The End of Chapter Twenty

Ch. 21: Forty Dharmas Exclusive to Buddhas (Part 1)

II. Chapter 21: Forty Dharmas Exclusive to Buddhas (Part 1)

A. Introduction to the Forty Dharmas Exclusive to Buddhas

It is in the above-discussed manner that the bodhisattva uses the thirty-two major marks and eighty secondary characteristics in his contemplative mindfulness of the Buddha's physical body. Now one should proceed to mindfulness of the dharmas exemplifying the Buddha's meritorious qualities, namely:

One should also use the forty exclusive dharmas
in one's contemplation of the Buddhas,
for the Buddhas are their Dharma body
and are not merely associated with their physical bodies.

Although the Buddhas possess countless dharmas not held in common with any other persons, there are forty dharmas that, if borne in mind, will cause one to experience joyful happiness. And why [should one bear them in mind]? It is not the case that the Buddhas are their form bodies, for they are rather to be identified with the Dharma body. This accords with this scriptural testimony: "You should not contemplate the Buddha merely in terms of his form body, for it is on the basis of Dharma that one should carry on such contemplation."

As for the forty dharmas exclusive to the Buddhas, they are as follows:[22]

1) Sovereign mastery of the ability to fly;
2) [The ability to manifest] countless transformations;
3) Boundless psychic powers of the sort possessed by *āryas;*
4) Sovereign mastery of the ability to hear sounds;
5) Immeasurable power of knowledge to know others' thoughts;
6) Sovereign mastery in [training and subduing] the mind;
7) Constant abiding in stable wisdom;
8) Never forgetting;
9) Possession of the powers of the vajra samādhi;
10) Thorough knowing of matters that are unfixed
11) Thorough knowing of matters pertaining to the formless realm's meditative absorptions;
12) The completely penetrating knowledge of all matters associated with eternal cessation;

13) Thorough knowing of the non-form dharmas unassociated with the mind;[23]
14) The great powers *pāramitā;*
15) The [four] unimpeded [knowledges] *pāramitā;*
16) The *pāramitā* of perfectly complete replies and predictions in response to questions;
17) Invulnerability to harm by anyone;
18) Their words are never spoken without a purpose;[24]
19) Their speech is free of errors and mistakes;
20) Complete implementation of the three turnings [of the Dharma wheel] in speaking Dharma;
21) They are the great generals among all *āryas;*
22–25) They are able to remain unguarded in four ways;[25]
26–29) They possess the four types of fearlessness;
30–39) They possess the ten powers;
40) They have achieved unimpeded liberation.

These are the forty dharmas exclusive to the Buddhas. We shall now discuss them more extensively, as below:

B. 1) Sovereign Mastery of the Ability to Fly

As for "sovereign mastery of the ability to fly" all buddhas fly with sovereign mastery, entirely as they wish, and with a manner and speed that are limitless and unimpeded. How is this so? If the Buddha wishes to raise one foot and then the other, walking through space in just such a fashion, then he is immediately able to do so. If he wishes to simply step into space and depart in this manner or if he wishes to simply stand motionlessly in space and depart in this way, he is immediately able to do so.

If he prefers to just sit there peacefully in the full lotus posture and depart like that, then he is also able to leave that way. If he wishes instead to lie down peacefully and then depart, he is able to leave in that way as well.

If he decides to stand upon a precious lotus blossom extending to the very boundaries of empty space, one with a blue *vaiḍūrya* stem, real coral petals, pistils of yellow gold, wish-fulfilling pearls for its pedestal, and countless sorts of surrounding phenomena, one that appears like the sun on first rising—departing in just such a fashion—then he does just that.

Or if, alternatively, he wishes to create through spontaneous psychic transformation a palace like the palaces of the sun or moon, like the supremely marvelous palace of Indra, or like those of the Yāma Heaven devas, the Tuṣita Heaven devas, the Nirmāṇarati Heaven devas, the Paranirmita Vaśavartin Heaven devas, the Brahma Heaven kings, or like the palaces of any of the other devas, and if he then wishes to create any such palaces, sit down within them, and then depart in that fashion [in one of those flying palaces], then he is immediately able to do precisely that.

Then again, if he prefers to use any of the many other means [for flying from one place to another], then he is freely able to depart however he chooses. Hence it is said, "He is able to completely fulfill whatever wishes he makes." Consequently, with but a single step, the Buddhas can pass beyond great trichiliocosms as numerous as the sands of the Ganges.

There are those who claim that the Buddha is able to move beyond some particular number of hundreds of thousands of lands in but a single mind-moment, whereas there are yet others who claim that, if anyone [supposed he could] know that the Buddha could depart such a distance with but a single step and in but a single mind-moment, then that would be [to infer that the Buddha's abilities] could be limited. But the sutras declare that the powers of the Buddhas surpass all limits. One should therefore realize that the sovereign power of the Buddhas to freely fly through empty space is limitless and boundless.

So how is this the case? Given that one of the great *śrāvaka* disciples using his sovereign mastery of the psychic powers is able in a single mind-moment to pass beyond a hundred *koṭis* of Jambudvīpas, Avara-godānīyas, Pūrva-videhas, Uttara-kurus, Four Heavenly Kings Heavens, Trāyastriṃśa Heavens, Yāma Heavens, Tuṣita Heavens, Nirmāṇarati Heavens, Paranirmita Vaśavartin Heavens, and Brahma Heavens—and given that there are a particular number of mind-moments in the wink of an eye and given that one might aggregate enough of these mind-moments to comprise a whole day, seven whole days, a whole month, a whole year, and so forth, on up to a full hundred years, and if in only a single day, such a *śrāvaka* disciple might pass through fifty-three *koṭis* plus two million, nine hundred and sixty-six thousand, that large a number of great trichiliosms, any Buddha would still be able in a mere mind-moment to exceed that number of great trichiliocosms passed through by such a *śrāvaka* disciple in the course of a full hundred years.

Then again, if one were to allow the passage of a single kalpa for each and every grain of sand in the Ganges—and if there was a great *śrāvaka* disciple foremost in psychic powers who, across the course of a lifespan of kalpas as numerous as the Ganges' sands, passed through in each successive mind-moment just such a number of world systems [as described above]—and if he were to do this for a number of mind-moments equivalent to a day, month, or year, doing so with the free exercise of all of his powers even to the exhaustion of such a number of great kalpas—all of those lands passed through by that great *śrāvaka* disciple during that entire time could still be passed through by a buddha in but a single mind-moment. The Buddhas may freely fly from one place to another with just such a speed as this.

In this, they cannot be obstructed by the iron-ring mountains, the ten jeweled mountains, the stations of the Four Heavenly Kings, the stations of the Trāyastriṃśa Heavens, the stations of the Yāma Heavens, Tuṣita Heavens, Nirmāṇarati Heavens, Paranirmita Vaśavartin Heavens, Brahma World Heavens, Brahma Assembly Heavens, Great Brahma Heavens, Lesser Light Heavens, Limitless Light Heavens, Light-and-Sound Heavens, Lesser Purity Heavens, Measureless Purity Heavens, Universal Purity Heavens, Vast Fruition Heavens, Non-Perception Heavens, Not Vast Heavens, No Heat Heavens, Delightful Vision Heavens, Sublime Vision Heavens, or the Akaniṣṭha Heaven.

[Nor can their flight be obstructed by] the great winds, by the great floods, or by the fires that occur at the end of the kalpa. Nor can it be obstructed by any heavenly dragon, *yakṣa, gandharva, asura, kinnara, mahoraga,* deva, Māra, Brahmā, *śramaṇa,* brahmin, or anyone possessed of all the psychic powers. It is therefore said of the Buddhas that they are unimpeded in their ability to fly.

Additionally, by virtue of the sovereign mastery of their flight, they are able to exercise that ability in any manner they wish, by sinking into or emerging from the earth, or by passing through the obstructions presented by stone cliffs, mountains, and such. The Buddha is superior in this ability to any of the other *āryas*. Also, the Buddha is able to make his normal standing body reach in its height on up to the Brahma Heavens. *Śravaka* disciples are unable to match this. There are all manner of differences of this sort.

C. 2) [The Ability to Manifest] Countless Transformations

As for the Buddhas' sovereign mastery in "the ability to manifest transformations," in the matter of manifesting phenomena, they have immeasurable power to do this. The capacity to manifest transformations as possessed by the other classes of *āryas* is both measurable and bounded whereas the Buddhas' capacity to manifest transformations is measureless and unbounded.

The other *āryas* are able, in but a single mind-moment, to manifest a single transformation body whereas the Buddhas are able, in but a single mind-moment, to manifest countless phenomena in whatever way they wish.

This is as described in the *Sutra on the Great Spiritual Powers*: "The Buddha may send forth from his navel a lotus blossom with transformation buddhas sitting atop it that then, in an orderly fashion, fill up all of space on up to the Akaniṣṭha Heaven. The many sorts of transformations created by the Buddhas take all sorts of different forms and all sorts of different shapes and are all created in but a single mind-moment."

Also, *śrāvaka* disciples are able to perform transformations within a thousand lands whereas the Buddhas are able to freely perform transformations within a countless and boundless number of lands and are additionally able to do much more than this, for the Buddhas have gained the solid transformation samādhi. Also, the transformations performed by but one of the Buddhas' bodies are able to occur in worlds as numerous as the sands of the Ganges.

Additionally, a buddha is able in a countless and boundless number of worlds of the ten directions to manifest a buddha being born, taking on a body, dropping to the earth, taking seven steps, leaving the home life, studying the path, defeating Māra's armies, achieving enlightenment, and turning the Dharma wheel. All of these phenomena are created in but a single mind-moment. All of these transformation buddhas are themselves also able to carry out the work of the Buddhas. And the transformation-generated phenomena created by all of those buddhas are themselves countless and boundless.

D. 3) Boundless Psychic Powers of the Sort Possessed by Āryas

Also, the Buddhas have "boundless psychic powers of the sort possessed by *āryas*." As for "the psychic powers possessed by *āryas*," this refers to phenomena such as: radiating light from their bodies that may manifest as raging fire and also pouring forth rains; transforming their length of life however they wish, either lengthening it or shortening it; being able in a single thought to go to the Brahma Heaven; being able to perform transformations of various phenomena, being able to shake the great earth whenever they wish; or being able to ceaselessly radiate light capable of illuminating countless worlds.

Also, "psychic powers possessed by *āryas*," are referred to as such because they are incomparably different from those possessed by common people, because of their being boundless, and because of their going beyond all limits. Although common people may possess some ability to perform transformations of various phenomena, their power to do so is so minor as to be beneath mention here.

A *śrāvaka* disciple may be able to split a thousand lands and then cause them to join back together again, may be able to lengthen his lifespan to a kalpa or somewhat less than a kalpa in duration and then be able to shorten it, but after having shortened it, he will be unable to make it long again. He may be able in a single mind-moment to go to the brahma worlds associated with a thousand lands, may be able to freely perform transformations in a thousand lands, may be able to shake the earth in a thousand lands, may be able to ceaselessly radiate light from his body that can illuminate a thousand lands, and, even if his body is destroyed, he may retain the presence of his spiritual powers and their ability to perform transformations just as before, doing so in a thousand lands.

The lesser *pratyekabuddha* is able to perform a myriad transformations in a myriad lands. The middling *pratyekabuddha* is able to perform a million transformations in a million lands. A great *pratyekabuddha* is able to perform the sorts of transformations cited above, doing so throughout all lands in a great trichiliocosm.

The Buddhas, the Bhagavats, are able to perform transformations in worlds more numerous than the Ganges' sands wherein they send forth fire and water from their bodies. They are even able to grind to fine dust worlds as numerous as the Ganges' sands and then cause them to be restored. They are able to abide for a lifespan of countless kalpas, are able to shorten that lifespan, and having shortened it, they are then able to lengthen it again. They are able to abide for an immeasurably long period of time. They are able to freely perform transformations such that, in the space of but a single mind-moment, they are able to go to countless and boundless worlds as numerous as the sands in the River Ganges.

They are able to cause their usual body, when standing, to reach all the way up to the Brahma Worlds. They are also able to perform a transformation whereby countless and boundless *asaṃkhyeyas* of worlds are all caused to be transformed into gold, or into silver, or into *vaiḍūrya,* coral, mother-of-pearl, or carnelian. To sum up the essential point, they are freely able in accordance with their wishes to cause them to be transformed into a countless number of precious things.

They are also able in accordance with their wishes to transform the waters of the great oceans in worlds as numerous as the Ganges' sands into milk, ghee, yogurt, or honey. They are also able in but a single mind-moment to transform incalculably many mountains into real gold.

They are also able to shake the heavenly palaces of the desire realm and form realm heavens of countless and boundless worlds. They are also able in but a single mind-moment to cause gold-colored radiance to so universally illuminate an immeasurably great number of worlds that the light from all those suns and moons and heavenly palaces of the desire-realm and the form-realm no longer appear at all.

Although a buddha may have already passed into nirvāṇa, afterward, he is still freely ever able in all those worlds to remain for however long he wishes, ceaselessly implementing his spiritual powers.

E. 4) Sovereign Mastery of the Ability to Hear Sounds

As for "sovereign mastery in the ability to hear sounds," the Buddhas have sovereign mastery in their ability to hear sounds however they please. Even if there were countless hundreds of thousands of myriads of *koṭis* of musical sounds being simultaneously played and hundreds of thousands of myriads of *koṭis* of beings simultaneously speaking—whether those sounds are far or near, the Buddhas are freely able to hear whichever sounds they please.[26]

If one were to cause all beings in great trichiliocosms as numerous as a Ganges' sands to simultaneously create any given number of hundreds of thousands of myriads of *koṭis* of kinds of music that filled up all those worlds, and if at the same time all beings in worlds as numerous as a Ganges' sands were to fill up all those worlds with the voice of Brahmā, if any buddha wished to hear only one single sound from among all those sounds, then that buddha would be freely able to hear that single sound while not hearing any other sound.

In the case of the sounds heard by *śrāvaka* disciples, if someone possessed of great spiritual powers were to block any given sound, then they would not be able to hear it. In the case of sounds heard by buddhas, even though there might be someone possessed of great spiritual powers seeking to block their hearing some sound, the Buddhas are nonetheless able to hear it.

A *śrāvaka* disciple may be able to hear any sound within a thousand lands. The Buddhas, the Bhagavats, are able to hear even the most subtle sounds even from a distance spanning countlessly and boundlessly many world systems.

A *śrāvaka* disciple possessed of great spiritual powers and abiding in the Brahma World Heavens is able to issue such a great sound that it is capable of pervasively filling a thousand lands. As for the Buddhas, the Bhagavats, it matters not whether they are abiding here or in the Brahma World Heaven, or are instead in yet some other place—their voices are still able to fill up countlessly and boundlessly many world systems. If they wish to cause a particular being to hear the most subtle sound across a distance of countlessly and boundlessly many worlds, they can cause him to hear it and if they wish to prevent someone from hearing a sound, then that person will indeed be unable to hear it at all. Consequently, it is only the Buddhas who have gained sovereign mastery with regard to the hearing of sounds.

F. 5) Immeasurable Power of Knowledge to Know Others' Thoughts

As for "measureless power of sovereign mastery in the ability to know others' thoughts," the Buddhas, the Bhagavats, are completely aware of all the thoughts of all beings of the present existing throughout countlessly and boundlessly many worlds. Others may develop the ability to know someone else's thoughts, but only as represented by the words [contained in others' thoughts]. The Buddhas, however, know others' thoughts in terms of the associated meanings of the words [contained in others' thoughts].

Moreover, others remain unable to know the thoughts of beings in the formless realm, but the Buddhas are able to know them. Although others may possess the ability to know someone else's thoughts, if anyone possessed of great powers wishes to block that ability, then they will no longer be able to know others' thoughts.

Supposing that all beings had developed psychic powers to the same degree as Śāriputra, Maudgalyāyana, or a *pratyekabuddha*. Now suppose that they used all of their collective spiritual powers to block anyone from knowing someone's thoughts. In such a case, a buddha would still be able to break their spiritual powers and would still succeed in knowing that person's thoughts.

Additionally, a buddha is able to use his spiritual powers to completely know any being's superior, middling, and inferior thoughts, his defiled thoughts, and his pure thoughts. Moreover, he is able to know with regard to each thought, the condition taken as the object of that thought, is able to know also the sequential progression of each thought as it moves from one objective condition to another, and is able to comprehensively know all of the conditions associated with any given thought. Also, he is able to know any being's thoughts in accordance with their true character.

It is on these bases that the Buddhas are acknowledged to have immeasurable powers to completely know the thoughts of others.

G. 6) Sovereign Mastery in [Training and Subduing] the Mind

As for the Buddhas' "*pāramitā* of being foremost in training and subduing the mind," they well know all of the *dhyānas*, samādhis, and liberations and well understand entry into them, abiding in them, and emerging from them. Whether a buddha is immersed in meditative absorption or not, should he wish to focus his mind on a single object, then he is freely able to focus upon it for however long he wishes and then is able to change from this object to focusing on some other condition, freely abiding in that focus for however long he wishes.

If the Buddha, abiding in his normal thoughts, wishes to cause others to remain unaware of his thoughts, then they would be unable to know them. Even if all beings had perfected the ability to know others' minds to a degree comparable to the ability to know others' thoughts as possessed by a king of the Great Brahma Heaven, a great *śrāvaka* disciple, or a *pratyekabuddha,* and they all then caused a single person to acquire their collective abilities in this, and this person then wished to know the normal thought of a buddha, so long as that buddha did not permit it, that person would still be unable to acquire that knowledge.

This is as described in the *Sutra on the Seven Expedients*: "The practitioner:

Well knows the signs of meditative absorption;
Well knows the signs of abiding in meditative absorption;
Well knows the signs of emerging from meditative absorption;
Well knows the signs of stable and secure meditative absorption;
Well knows the signs of the stations of practice in meditative absorption;
Well knows the signs of the development of meditative absorption;
And well knows what is and is not appropriate to the dharmas of meditative absorption."[27]

This is what is meant by the Buddhas' "*pāramitā* of being foremost in training and subduing the mind."

H. 7) Constant Abiding in Stable Wisdom

As for the Buddhas' "constant abiding in stable wisdom," the Buddhas' stable wisdom is constant and unshakeable and their mindfulness is always maintained in their minds. And why is this the case? It is because they first know and then act, because they freely dwell on whichever object they choose while having no doubt in their actions, because they have cut off all afflictions, and because they have gone utterly beyond the realm[28] of movement itself.

This is as the Buddha told Ānanda:

> The Buddha, in this one evening, gains *anuttarasamyaksaṃbodhi* and proceeds then to teach the path to the ending of suffering to everyone in the world, whether they be a deva, Māra, Brahmā, a *śramaṇa,* or a brahmin, and then, in the end, finally enters the nirvāṇa without residue.
>
> During the interim, the Buddha, with respect to every feeling, is aware of its arising, is aware of its abiding, is aware of its birth and

is aware of its cessation. With respect to all perceptions,[29] all tactile contact, all ideation, and all mental discursion, he is aware of their arising, aware of their abiding, aware of their birth, and aware of their cessation.

Māra the Evil One,[30] constantly and without resting, followed along after the Buddha both day and night for seven years yet was never in all that time able to come upon any shortcomings of the Buddha and was never able to observe an instance of the Buddha's mindfulness not abiding in a state of stable wisdom. This is what is meant by the Buddha's constant abiding in the practice of stable wisdom.

I. 8) Never Forgetting

As for the dharma of "never forgetting," because the Buddhas have gained the dharma of irreversibility, have reached a penetrating understanding of the five categorical repositories of dharmas,[31] and have acquired the unsurpassable Dharma, the Buddhas never forget.

With respect to all that the Buddhas have realized beneath the bodhi tree and have then subsequently acquired up to the time when they enter the nirvāṇa without residue, no matter whether it be a deva, Māra, Brahmā, a *śramaṇa*, a brahmin, or some other *ārya*, there is no one who is able to cause the Buddhas to forget anything at all.

This is as described in the *Sutra on the Seal of Dharma*: "As for that which is realized at the *bodhimaṇḍa*, this is known as the genuine realization and there is no dharma superior to it."

This is also as described in the *Horripilation Sutra*: "Śāriputra. If anyone could claim truthfully that they do not have any aspect of Dharma that they forget, I would be the one who could make that claim. How is this so? I alone do not forget anything whatsoever."

This is what is intended when it is said that the Buddhas never forget Dharma.

J. 9) Possession of the Powers of the Vajra Samādhi

As for "the vajra samādhi," the vajra samādhi of all the Buddhas, the Bhagavats, is one of the exclusive dharmas, [so named]:

Because it cannot be destroyed by anything;
Because there is no place where it can be obstructed;
Because it is associated with right and universal knowledge;
Because it destroys all hindrances to Dharma;
Because it is able to equally penetrate [all dharmas];
Because it brings about the power to acquire the benefit of all meritorious qualities;
And because it is the most supreme of all *dhyāna* samādhis.

As for its being called "the vajra samādhi" because there is nothing that can destroy it, it is like the precious vajra gem that cannot be crushed by anything at all. This samādhi is just like this. There is no dharma capable of destroying it. It is therefore known as "the vajra samādhi."

Question: Why is it that it cannot be destroyed?

Response: This is because there is nothing anywhere that obstructs it. It is just as with Indra's vajra that meets no obstruction anywhere. This samādhi is just like that.

Question: Why is this samādhi said to have nothing anywhere that obstructs it?

Response: Because it possesses a right and utterly penetrating comprehension of all dharmas. All buddhas, abiding in this samādhi, are able to utterly penetrate all of the dharmas subsumed within the five categorical repositories of dharmas: all dharmas of the past, of the present, of the future, those that transcend the three periods of time, and those that are ineffable dharmas. It is for this reason that it is said to meet with no obstruction anywhere.

If it were the case that, while abiding in this samādhi, all buddhas still did not have an utterly penetrating comprehension of all dharmas, then that would be a case of still having obstructions. But, in truth, this is not the case. It is therefore said to not be obstructed by anything whatsoever.

Question: How is it that this samādhi brings about a penetrating comprehension of all dharmas?

Response: It is because this samādhi is able to open up all obstructive dharmas, namely the obstacle of the afflictions, the obstacles to meditative absorption, and the obstacles to knowledge. Because it is able to open up all obstructions, it is therefore said to bring about an utterly penetrating comprehension of all dharmas.

Question: How is it that this samādhi is able to open up all obstructions whereas other samādhis remain unable to do so?

Response: This samādhi is well able to penetrate three[32] dharmas:

> Because it is able to destroy the mountain of afflictions so that nothing remains of them;
>
> Because it brings about the right and universal comprehension of all dharmas;
>
> And because it brings about the thorough-going attainment of the liberation of the indestructible resolve.

It is for these reasons that this samādhi is said to be able to open up all obstructions.

Question: How is it that this samādhi is able to equally penetrate these three dharmas?[33]

Response: This is because, when one abides in this samādhi, one gains the power by which one is then able to acquire every sort of meritorious quality. None of the other samādhis possess this sort of power. It is for this reason that this samādhi is able to "equally penetrate" [all dharmas].

Question: How is it that, abiding in this samādhi, one gains the power by which one is then able to acquire every sort of meritorious quality?

Response: This samādhi is the foremost among all meditative absorptions. It is because of this that, abiding in this samādhi, one is able to gain every sort of meritorious quality.

Question: How is it that this samādhi is foremost among all samādhis?

Response: This samādhi is foremost among all meditative absorptions because it is produced through the possession of measurelessly and boundlessly many roots of goodness.

Question: How is it that this samādhi is produced through the possession of measurelessly and boundlessly many roots of goodness?

Response: This samādhi is possessed only by those who are equipped with all-knowledge. It has not been acquired by anyone else. Hence it is known as "the vajra samādhi."

The End of Chapter Twenty-One

Ch. 22: Forty Dharmas Exclusive to Buddhas (Part 2)

Challenges to the Reality of Omniscience

III. Chapter 22: Forty Dharmas Exclusive to Buddhas (Part 2)

A. Q: Your Claim That Omniscience Exists Is False for these Reasons

Question: You claim that only those possessed of all-knowledge possess the vajra samādhi and no one else has it. If this samādhi was only possessed by someone who has all-knowledge and no one else possessed it, then this samādhi does not even exist. Why? Because there is no one who possesses all-knowledge.

And why is this? It is because the dharmas that might be known are measureless and boundless whereas the knowledge that might know them is measurable and bounded. It should not be the case that this measurable and bounded knowledge could know measurelessly many phenomena.

For instance, on the present-day continent of Jambudvīpa, the number of beings dwelling in its waters and on its lands are beyond count. Also, consider the three categories of beings, whether male, female, or neither male nor female, those still in the womb, the children, the young and strong, the frail and old, and also the dharmas associated with their suffering, happiness, and so forth. Also, consider all of the mind and mental dharmas of the past, future, and present, as well as all good and bad karmic actions accumulated in the past, present, and future, all the karmic retributions undergone in the past, present, and future, all the births and deaths of the myriad creatures, and also all of Jambudvīpa's mountains, rivers, springs, ponds, grasses, trees, dense forests, roots, stems, branches, leaves, blossoms, and fruit. The things that can be known are limitlessly many.

The same is true for the other three continents. And just as this is the case with these four continents, it is also the case throughout all of the worlds of the great trichiliocosm. And just as this is the case with all of the worlds of the great trichiliocosm, so too is it also the case for all things that can be known in all other worlds.

As for the number of the worlds, that matter alone is measureless, boundless, and difficult to know. How much the more so is this the case for all of the sentient and insentient beings and all other categories of things on the Jambudvīpa continents in all those worlds.

For these reasons, one should realize that the things that can be known are countless and limitless and, because of that, it cannot be that there is anyone at all who is possessed of all-knowledge.

Suppose that one were to claim that the knowledge [of someone who is omniscient] is possessed of such great power that, because it is unimpeded with respect to those dharmas it cognizes, it is able to pervasively know all those dharmas in just the same manner as empty space is able to reach everywhere in its universal pervasion of all things. Suppose too that one were to claim that, because of this, it ought to be the case that there truly is such a thing as an omniscient person. If one were to make such a claim, this still could not be so, for even if knowledge could possess such a great power as this, even such great knowledge as this would still remain unable to know itself in just the same way that one's fingertip remains unable to touch itself. Therefore, there is no such thing as all-knowledge.

If, [in response to this], one were to claim that there is yet some other knowledge possessed of the capacity to know this knowledge, this could not be the case, either. And why not? That is because this proposition would then fall into the fallacy of infinite regression. Knowledge either knows itself or is known by something other. They cannot both be true.

If, as you say, this knowledge is somehow possessed of measureless power, because of the fact that it still remains unable to know itself, one really cannot claim that it is possessed of measureless power. Therefore there is no such thing as some knowledge possessed of the ability to know all dharmas.

If there is no such thing as some knowledge possessed of the ability to know all dharmas, then there could not be anyone possessed of all-knowledge. And why is this the case? It is because anyone possessed of all-knowledge [could only be so by] availing himself of just such a [non-existent] knowledge that knows all dharmas.

Furthermore, the dharmas that can be known are measureless and boundless. Even if one were to employ the combined knowing capacity of a hundred thousand myriads of *koṭis* of wise men, they would still be unable to exhaustively know them all. How much the less could a single person do so. Therefore there is no such thing as any single person who is able to know all dharmas and there is no such thing as "all-knowledge."

If one were to claim that it is not on the basis of comprehensively knowing every mountain, river, being, or non-being that we speak of someone possessed of all-knowledge, but rather it is simply on the basis of exhaustively knowing all scriptures that one speaks of someone possessed of all-knowledge, this is also wrong. How so? It is because, within the sphere of the Buddha's Dharma, one does not speak of the concepts treated in the Vedas and other such scriptures. If the Buddha really were, [in this sense of the term], a man possessed of all-knowledge, then he should make use of the Vedas and other such scriptures, but in truth, he does not use these, and so, because of this, the Buddha is not an all-knowing man.

Moreover, the scriptures comprising the four Vedas are themselves measurable and limited in their scope and, even so, there is not even anyone capable of exhaustively knowing those scriptures, how much the less could there be anyone who exhaustively knows all the scriptures in existence. Therefore there is no such thing as a person possessed of "all-knowledge" [even in this limited sense of the term].

Moreover, there are scriptures that are able to cause the proliferation of desire and that devote themselves to such things as dance and music and such. If a person possessed of all-knowledge were to become knowledgeable with respect to these matters, then he would be subjected to the arising of desire. Scriptures of these sorts constitute the causes and conditions for the arising of desire. Where there is a given cause, there must necessarily be the corresponding result [ensuing from it]. If a person possessed of all-knowledge does not know these matters, then he could not be validly referred to as someone possessed of all-knowledge.

Furthermore, there are scriptures that are able to influence a person to become full of hate and to take delight in deceiving others, specifically such works as those classics concerned with ruling the world. Were one to become knowledgeable about such matters, then one would come to be possessed of hatred. How is the case? It is because, where there is such a given cause, then there must necessarily be the corresponding result ensuing from it. And were one to not know such matters, then one could not be validly referred to as possessed of all-knowledge. One should therefore realize that there really is no such thing as a person who is possessed of all-knowledge.

Additionally, it is not necessarily the case that a buddha could exhaustively know matters pertaining to the future. Take for instance my present challenge to the plausibility of there being anyone who is omniscient. The Buddha has no scriptural record of having predicted that in the future there would be this particular man of this particular caste from this particular clan in this particular place who would on these particular grounds challenge the plausibility of there being anyone who might be omniscient. If one were to claim that the Buddha exhaustively knows such things, why did he not speak of this matter? If he is the one who spoke these scriptures, then those scriptures should have a record of such matters, but he did not speak of these matters. Therefore one knows that he was not omniscient.

Moreover, if the Buddha exhaustively knew future matters, then he should have known in advance that, after Devadatta left home to become a monk, he would then create a schism in the Sangha. If he had knowledge of that, then he should not have allowed Devadatta to become a monk. Also, the Buddha did not know that Devadatta would use a stick to pry loose a boulder [that would roll down and draw blood from the Buddha's foot]. If the Buddha had known of this matter in advance, then he should not have been walking in that place.

Additionally, the Buddha failed to know in advance that Ciñca, the brahmin woman, would slander him by accusing him of having had sexual relations with her. If the Buddha had known of this in advance, then he should have told the bhikshus that, in the future, there would be just such an occurrence.

Also, there was the case of the *brahmacārin* who, because he was jealous of the Buddha, killed a *brahmacārin* woman named Sundarī in another place and then buried her in a trench in the vicinity of the Jeta Grove. The Buddha did not know of this matter. If he had known of this, then he should have sought among the brahmins to [find a way to] see that her life would be saved.

The Buddha went to that place beneath which Devadatta was about to set loose the falling boulder, failed to announce in advance the incidents having to do with the brahmin woman and the *brahmacārin* woman. Because he did not know of these matters, one should realize that the Buddha did not exhaustively know the future. Therefore he could not possibly have been omniscient.

Furthermore, the Buddha once entered a brahmin village seeking food on the alms round but then had to leave with an empty bowl. He was unable then to know in advance that Māra would so turn the minds of the villagers against him that he would be unable to obtain anything to eat. If the Buddha had known of this matter, then he should not have entered that brahmin village. Therefore one knows that the Buddha did not exhaustively know how matters would transpire in the future.

Moreover, because King Ajātaśatru wished to harm the Buddha, he released a drunken elephant used to guard the treasury.[34] Because the Buddha did not know of this matter, he entered the city of Rājagṛha on his alms round. If he had known of this matter in advance, then he should not have gone into the city. Therefore he did not have knowledge of future matters. Because he did not have knowledge of future matters, he therefore could not have been omniscient.

Additionally, the Buddha did not know of the causal circumstances involved in Agnidatta's invitation to the Buddha. Consequently he immediately accepted that invitation and then led the bhikshus to the state of Verañjā. Because this brahmin had forgotten his prior issuance of that invitation, he caused the Buddha to eat only horse fodder. If the Buddha had known of this matter in advance, then he should not have accepted that invitation on account of which he spent the entire three months [of the rains retreat] surviving only on horse fodder. We know therefore that the Buddha did not have knowledge of future matters. Because he did not have knowledge of future matters, he therefore could not have been omniscient.

Also, because the Buddha accepted Sunakṣatra as a disciple, he could not have had knowledge of future matters. This man possessed an obdurately evil mind, made himself difficult to teach, and did not believe the words of the Buddha. If the Buddha had known of this, how could he have accepted him as a disciple? Because he accepted him as a disciple, then he could not have known future matters. Because he did not have knowledge of future matters, he therefore could not have been omniscient.

Furthermore, if the Buddha had been omniscient, then, in order to prevent inevitable future instances of moral transgressions, he would have formulated his moral precepts in advance. Because he had no prior knowledge of the causal circumstances that eventually led to the formulation of each particular moral precept, it was only after someone had committed such a transgression that he then subsequently laid down these moral regulations. This being the case, he could not have known of future matters. Because he did not have knowledge of future matters, he therefore could not have been omniscient.

Moreover, in the Dharma set forth by the Buddha, it is solely on the basis of seniority in years of monastic ordination that, within the community, one sits more toward the front and is accorded reverence and obeisance [by those of fewer years of seniority]. One is not acknowledged as of greater eminence merely on the basis of one's venerable age, one's noble birth, the stature of one's clan, one's meritorious qualities, the level of wisdom one has developed, the degree of learning one has achieved, the particular *dhyāna* absorptions one has entered, the fruits of the path one has gained, the fetters one has cut off, or the spiritual powers one has acquired.

If the Buddha had really been someone possessed of all-knowledge, then he would have accorded eminence, higher priority in the receipt of offerings, and stature in receipt of reverential obeisance on the basis of one's venerable age, one's noble birth, the stature of one's clan, one's meritorious qualities, the level of wisdom one has developed, the degree of learning one has achieved, the particular *dhyāna* absorptions one has entered, the fruits of the path one has gained, the fetters one has cut off, and the spiritual powers one has acquired. If the Buddha had made stipulations of this sort, then that would qualify as having established a well-regulated community.

Regarding the matter of years of monastic ordination seniority, this is the principle by which a practitioner of the path ordained for only five years is enjoined to accord reverential obeisance to a monk ordained for six years.

As for the issue of nobility of birth caste, the world has four classes of beings: *brahmans, kṣatriyas, vaiśyas,* and *śūdras. Śūdras* are enjoined to revere *vaiśyas, kṣatriyas,* and *brahmans. Vaiśyas* ought to pay obeisance to *kṣatriyas* and *brahmans. Kṣatriyas* are supposed to pay reverential obeisance to *brahmans.*

As for the status of clans, there are the artisan clans, the business-and-trade clans, the merchant clans, the clans led by those of senior status, the clans of great officials, royal clans, and so forth. Among them, the members of lesser-status clans are supposed to revere members of the eminent clans. This being the case, when those from poor and base clans leave the home life to become monks, they should be enjoined to pay reverence to monks from wealthy and noble clans.

With respect to meritorious qualities, whoever has broken moral precepts should be enjoined to revere and bow in formal obeisance to those who uphold the moral precepts. Those who strictly observe the moral precepts should not be bowing in reverence to anyone who has broken the moral precepts.

Those who do not practice the twelve *dhūta* austerities[35] should bow in reverence to those who are practitioners of the twelve *dhūta* austerities. Those who are not perfectly complete in their practice of the *dhūta* practices should bow in reverence to those who are perfect in their practice of the *dhūta* austerities.

As for the matter of wisdom, people devoid of wisdom should bow in reverence to those possessed of wisdom. With regard to learning, those of shallow learning should bow in reverence to those who have achieved a high level of learning. Those who do not recite many scriptures should bow in reverence to those who are able to recite many sutras from memory.

As for the fruits of the path, the stream enterer should bow in reverence to the *sakṛdāgāmin* and it should proceed in this fashion on up to [the circumstance where realizers of the first three fruits of the path are enjoined to] bow in reverence to the arhat. As for all of the common people, they should bow in reverence to anyone who has gained any of the fruits of the path.

Those who have severed fewer of the fetters as well as those who have not yet severed any of the fetters should all bow in reverence to those who have severed many of the fetters.

Regarding the matter of spiritual powers, if one has not yet acquired any of the spiritual powers, he should then be bowing in obeisance to whomever has already acquired spiritual powers.

If the Buddha had skillfully set forth such sequentially ranked protocols regarding the making of offerings and the according of reverence, then his proclamations on these matters would be of a superior order. But, in truth, he did not do so. One can therefore know that the Buddha was not omniscient.

Furthermore, the Buddha was not even able to know all matters having to do with the present. If you were to ask me how I know that the Buddha did not have knowledge of present-era matters, then I would now inform you as follows:

There were beings whose fetters were but slight, who had no karmic obstacles, who were free of the eight difficulties, who were capable of practicing deep dharmas, and who were able to be successful in the cultivation of right Dharma, and yet the Buddha did not realize this. After the Buddha had attained enlightenment and was first on the verge of proclaiming the Dharma, he gave rise to the following doubt:

> The Dharma that I have gained is extremely profound, recondite, far-reaching, sublime, quiescent, difficult to know, difficult to comprehend, and such as only the wise might be able to realize inwardly. The beings in this world are attached by their desires to worldly matters. That there might be any among them who might be able to cut off their afflictions, extinguish craving, and develop renunciation—this would be the rarest of possibilities. If I were to expound the Dharma, beings would fail to comprehend it. Such an endeavor would be but a useless experiencing of wearisome hardship.

And so the Buddha generated just such a doubt even though there were in fact beings whose fetters were but slight, who had no karmic obstacles, who were free of the eight difficulties, who were capable of practicing deep dharmas, and who were able to be successful in the cultivation of right Dharma. Because the Buddha was unable to know of the existence of such beings, one should therefore know that the Buddha failed to know matters having to do with the present time.

The Buddha also thought as follows: "Previously, when I was practicing ascetic austerities, the five bhikshus made offerings to me and supported me. It is only appropriate that I first benefit them. Where are they now?"

After he had this thought, a deva informed him: "They are now in Benares, in the place known as 'Deer Park.'"

On account of this, one knows that the Buddha did not even know of matters having to do with the present. If he failed to know of matters having to do with the present, then we can know from this that the Buddha could not have been omniscient.

Furthermore, after he had attained enlightenment, the Buddha accepted the invitation to expound on Dharma and then had this thought, "As I now proceed to proclaim the Dharma, who is it that ought to be the first to hear it?" He then had another thought: "Udraka Rāmaputra—this is a man of sharp wisdom, one who might easily become enlightened."

By this time, that man had already died and yet the Buddha nonetheless went in search of him. A deva then informed him: "His life came to an end just last night." The Buddha thought again and, having reflected, he decided he wanted to liberate Ārāḍa Kālāma. A deva then told him, "This man died seven days ago."

If the Buddha had been omniscient, he should have known beforehand that these men had already died, but in truth he did not know these events had happened. Because the Buddha did not know about past matters, he could not have been omniscient.

The methods employed by an omniscient man would be such that he should strive to bring about the liberation of those capable of achieving liberation while setting aside those incapable of success in this.

Moreover, in place after place, the Buddha spoke in terms revealing the presence of doubts on his part. Take for example the city of Pāṭaliputra that he said was bound to be destroyed by one of three causes: by flood, by fire, or by a conspiracy between insiders and outsiders. If the Buddha had really been omniscient, then he should not have had instances where his speech was marked by the presence of doubts. One knows therefore that he could not have been omniscient.

Additionally, the Buddha inquired of the bhikshus, "What matter have you all come together to discuss?" He asked questions of this sort. If he were omniscient, then he should not have asked about matters of this sort. Because he was compelled to ask others [in order to know of these matters], then he could not have been omniscient.

Also, the Buddha engaged in self-praise while deprecating others. This is as described in the sutras, "The Buddha told Ānanda, 'I alone am foremost, without a peer, unequaled by anyone.'"[36]

He told the bhikshus, "The Nirgranthas and others of that sort are base and evil people who have perfected the five types of deviant dharmas. The Nirgranthas and such have no faith, have no sense of shame, have no dread of blame, and are men of but little learning who are indolent, possessed of only scant mindfulness and shallow wisdom."

He also discussed all manner of impermissible endeavors engaged in by *brahmacārins*, by Nirgranthas, and by the disciples and other followers of the non-Buddhist traditions.

Self-praise and deprecation of others is a behavior of which even common people of the world are ashamed. How much the more so should this be the case for someone who is omniscient. Because the Buddha engaged in behaviors of this sort, he could not have been omniscient.

Furthermore, comparing beginnings and endings, one finds that the Buddhist scriptures are self-contradictory. Take for instance the statements in the sutras wherein, on the one hand, the Buddha claims, "Bhikshus, I am one who has newly discovered the path." Then, on the other hand, he claims: "I have attained that path which has previously been attained by all buddhas of antiquity."

Even wise worldly people abandon any tendency to contradict themselves through chronological inconsistencies. How much the less should it be that a monastic possessed of all-knowledge could stumble into such chronological self-contradictions. Because the Buddha fell into chronological inconsistencies, one should realize that he could not possibly have been omniscient. Therefore your claim that the vajra samādhi is only acquired by omniscient men is wrong, this because there is no such thing as an omniscient person. Nor can one establish any case for the existence of some sort of omniscience samādhi.

B. A: Wrong. As I Shall Now Explain, The Buddha Truly Is Omniscient

Response: You should not speak this way. The Buddha truly is omniscient. And how is this so? In general, all dharmas are comprised of five categorical repositories of dharmas, namely: past dharmas, future dharmas, present dharmas, dharmas that transcend the three periods of time, and ineffable dharmas. It is only a buddha who completely knows all these dharmas in accordance with reality.

I shall now respond to your earlier challenge that asserts, because knowable dharmas are measureless and boundless, there are no omniscient people. Insofar as knowable dharmas might be measureless and boundless, the corresponding knowledge is also measureless and boundless. There is no fault in claiming that it is by means of measureless and boundless knowledge that one may know measureless and boundless dharmas.

As for your earlier assertion that knowing should somehow also involve a knowledge that knows [itself] and that this would entail the fallacy of infinite regress, I shall now respond, as follows:

It should be the case that dharmas are known by one's cognition. This cognition is similar to what is referenced when the world's common people describe themselves in this way: "I am a knowledgeable person," "I am someone with no knowledge," "I am someone possessed of only a coarse type of knowledge," or "I am someone who possesses subtle knowledge."

One should realize from these circumstances that it is with one's own cognitive ability that one knows [the character of one's own] knowledge. This being the case, there is no fallacy of infinite regress involved here. This is just a case of using one's own present cognitive ability to know one's past knowledge. It is in this way that one can exhaustively know all dharmas without any omissions.

Also, this is just like when someone counts others [in addition to oneself], thus reaching [for instance a total of] ten [people in all]. The capacity to know is just like that. For knowing to thereby know both itself and others is thus a concept free of any fault. This is also analogous to when a lamp is able to illuminate both itself and other things as well.

As for your contention that even the aggregated knowing capacity of a hundred thousand myriads of *koṭis* of wise people could not exhaustively know all dharmas, how much the less might a single person be able to know them—this is wrong. How is this so? An omniscient person is able to know the many things. Although there may be some additional multitude of people, if they have no cognitive ability, they won't know much of anything.

This is comparable to a situation in which there was a group of a hundred thousand blind men. [Even together], they still could not get hired as guides, but just one single person with good eyes might well be able to serve as a guide. Consequently, as regards your challenge to [the plausibility of omniscience on the part of] a single person, even in a situation where many knowers might be involved, they would still have no knowledge at all compared to the Buddha's capacities in this regard. Therefore your position as stated is erroneous.

As for your contention that, because the Buddha does not discuss the Vedas and other such non-Buddhist scriptures, he must therefore not be omniscient—I shall now respond to that as follows:

The Vedas are entirely lacking in the dharma of [liberation achieved through] skillful realization of nirvāṇa.[37] They contain only all manner of conceptual elaboration. Since what the Buddhas proclaim is all entirely devoted to the skillful realization of nirvāṇa, even though the Buddha is already well aware of the contents of the Vedas and other such scriptures, the Buddha does not discuss such things because those [Vedic] teachings have no capacity to lead anyone to the skillful realization of nirvāṇa.

Question: The Vedas *do* contain discussions of the skillful realization of nirvāṇa. Before the arising of this world, all was darkness and nothing whatsoever existed. In the beginning there existed a great man who appeared like the rising of the sun. If one was able to see him, then one could be liberated from the difficulty of being subject to dying.

[The Vedas] contain yet more guidance on these matters. They state that, because one's person is but small, then one's spiritual soul is correspondingly small. However, if one's person is great, then one's spiritual soul will be correspondingly great in scope, for the body is the home of the spiritual soul that always abides within it. If one uses wisdom to untie the bonds restraining one's spiritual soul, one will then gain liberation. Therefore one should realize from this that the Vedas *do* contain teachings leading to liberation through attainment of nirvāṇa.

Response: This is simply not so. Why not? The Vedic scriptures are tied up with the four inverted views. The world is impermanent and yet they posit the existence of a separate and permanent world. They claim that only one or two sacrifices to their deva [is insufficient and] conduces to falling away from it, but with a third sacrifice, one will not be subject to falling away from it. This scenario involves the inverted view that falsely ascribes permanence to what is itself impermanent.

The world is a place of suffering and yet the Vedas claim the existence of a sphere of eternal bliss. This is just an instance of the inverted view that falsely ascribes bliss to what is inherently bound up with suffering.

The Vedas also claim that one's soul may transform into one's son and be subject through prayer to an extended lifetime of a hundred years. But a "son" is another person, so how could it constitute a self? This is just an instance of the inverted view that falsely ascribes selfhood to what is not actually a self.

They also claim that one's body is possessed of the foremost level of purity and so incomparable in this respect that not even the purity of gold, silver, or precious gems can approach the purity of the body. This is just an instance of the inverted view that falsely ascribes purity to what is devoid of purity.

If one holds inverted views, then [one's views] are devoid of reality. [If such teachings] are devoid of reality, how could they possess [a path to] nirvāṇa? Therefore the Vedas are devoid of any good methods for attaining nirvāṇa.

Question: The Vedas assert that whoever is able to know the Vedas becomes purified and possessed of peace and security. How then can you state that they have no good methods for attaining nirvāṇa?

Response: Although the Vedas assert that whoever knows the Vedas will gain peace and security, this is not ultimate liberation. Rather, this is but an envisioning of liberation projected onto another body. This claim bases itself on the idea that existence in the long-life heavens constitutes liberation. Therefore the Vedas truly contain no means to achieve liberation.

Furthermore, the teachings in the Vedas generally embody three types of concepts: The first involves chants and prayers. The second involves the utterance of praises. The third involves the principles of their dharma.

"Chants and prayers" refers to praying, "May I be caused to obtain a wife and sons, cows, horses, gold, silver, and precious jewels."

"Utterance of praises" refers to statements such as, "Oh, you, the spirit of fire with your black head, your red neck, and your yellow body—you abide eternally in the five great elements of living beings."

"Principles of their dharma" refers to teachings stating that one should do this and abstain from doing that.

Just as with their [erroneous teaching that] fire was first received from the Pleiades, so too, in truth, their methods of using chants and prayers and utterances of praises are all devoid of [any means to achieve] nirvāṇa's liberation. How is this so? Covetous attachment to worldly pleasures, [offerings of] burning ghee, spells, and incantations—these are all devoid of genuine wisdom. Since these do not cut off the afflictions, how could [the Vedas] have [the means to achieve] liberation?

Question: The dharmas in the Vedas have come forth from antiquity and are deserving of the foremost degree of faith. As for your contention that they have no good methods by which one might reach nirvāṇa, they are therefore not fit to be believed, this is wrong. Why?

Whereas the Buddha's Dharma has only recently emerged into the world, the Vedas have come down from long distant antiquity and have always prevailed in the world. Therefore, given that ancient dharmas are deserving of belief and newly arisen dharmas are not deserving of belief, your claim that the Vedas are devoid of any good methods by which one might realize nirvāṇa—this is wrong.

Response: Their relative antiquity is no justification for faith. Ignorance tends to come first whereas right knowledge comes only later. Erroneous views emerge first whereas right views emerge later. One cannot have faith in ignorance and erroneous views simply because they happened to emerge first nor can one deem right knowledge and right views to be unbelievable simply because they emerged later. This is analogous to there first being mud and only later lotuses, first being disease and only later a cure. Matters of these sorts are not worthy of being valued simply because they happened to appear first. Therefore, as for your contention that, because the Vedas came first and the Buddha's Dharma came later, the latter is unworthy of belief, this is a fallacy.

Furthermore, Dīpaṃkara Buddha and the other buddhas of the past all came into the world earlier. Their Dharma principles emerged in antiquity whereas the Vedas actually came forth only later. If you insist on relying on chronological primacy and long history as your bases for according esteem, then the Buddhas and their Dharma should be most highly valued.

Question: You claim it is because the Vedas have no good methods for reaching nirvāṇa that they are therefore not discussed in the Buddha's Dharma. But if the Buddha had really already known they are unable to lead to nirvāṇa, why did he bother to become knowledgeable about them? If in fact he was not *already* knowledgeable about them, he could not have been omniscient. Both stances are faulty.

Response: Your claim is wrong. The Buddha knew from early on that the Vedas have no good methods for reaching nirvāṇa. It is for this reason that he neither discussed them nor practiced what they teach.

Question: If it really was because the Buddha already knew there is no benefit to be had through the Vedas that he therefore instructed others not to cultivate their teaching, what was the point in his acquiring knowledge about them?

Response: People possessed of great knowledge should thoroughly distinguish between the correct path and the erroneous path. It is because one wishes to cause countless beings to go beyond dangerous and bad paths that one takes up the practice of the right path. This is analogous to a guide who skillfully distinguishes between errant paths and the right path.

The Buddha is just the same in this respect. Since he himself had already succeeded in escaping the dangerous path of birth, aging, and death and also wished to cause other beings to escape from it as well, he knew well the genuine eightfold path of the Āryas and also knew the dangerous and bad paths of the Vedas and other such teachings. It was in order to facilitate others' abandonment of deviant and bad paths and in order to encourage their practice of the correct path that, [with regard to the Vedas], he merely became knowledgeable about them, but did not discuss them.

This is analogous to the situation with farmers who plant their fields and then, with the arrival of autumn, reap a harvest that may also happen to include a few useless weeds. The Buddha is like this as well. For the sake of achieving success in the unsurpassable path, he cultivates assiduously and vigorously and consequently gains the path of bodhi while incidentally gaining knowledge of the Vedas and other such erroneous paths. Hence there is no fault on his part in any of this.

As for your previous statement claiming that no single person can completely know the four Vedas, this challenge of yours is false. People of the world each have the power of memory. There are those who, in a single day, can only recite five verses from memory, whereas others can recite one or two hundred verses from memory. If a particular person who cannot even recite ten verses from memory then holds the opinion that nobody could be able to recite from memory a hundred or more than a hundred verses, this would be an untruthful claim. It is because people such as yourself are unable to completely know the Vedas that you then claim nobody knows them.

If someone observes that some other person was unable to ford a particular river and then claims that nobody can cross that river, this person's statement on the matter does not qualify as correct speech. Why not? It is because there will naturally be some other person possessed of great strength who can indeed cross that river. This case is just like that. Even if one supposes that other [ordinary people] would be unable to entirely know [the Vedas], what fault is there in stipulating that someone possessed of all-knowledge would know them?

Furthermore, the *pisuo*[38] rishis all study the Vedas and ought themselves to be able to reach all-knowledge. Thus if there are these persons who have completely studied the Vedas, how can you say that nobody can have all-knowledge?

I shall now respond to your [above-stated] claim that there are scriptures which [by their explication of the causes and conditions conducing to desire] are capable of causing one to feel desire or hatred. If one wishes to have a long life, he should abandon causes and conditions conducive to death. The Buddha, too, in this same way, wished to influence beings to cut off their desires and hatreds. This required that he know the causes and conditions that initiate the arising of desire and hatred.

Additionally, as for your contention that, if one is able to know the classical texts concerned with generating desire or hatred, one will then become afflicted with desire and hatred—this is a baseless claim. Although the Buddha had knowledge of these texts, because he did not use them or implement their practices, he was without fault in this respect. So too, if a person merely knows the causes and conditions that precipitate death, this does not entail his dying [as a result]. Only if he were to implement the causes and conditions that precipitate death would he then die as a result. This case is just the same as that one.

I shall now address your contention that, if one does not know future matters, then one does not qualify as omniscient. This does not constitute as a valid challenge. We already know of instances involving challenges to the plausibility of omniscience. As stated in the sutras: "The Buddha told the bhikshus, 'The common person bereft of wisdom has three characteristics: He contemplates what he should not contemplate, discusses what he should not discuss, and does what he should not do.'"[39]

Everything of relevance is already comprehensively mentioned in that statement. You common people of this future time are all included in it. As it would have no particular benefit, what would be the point in his having distinguished and mentioned names and such [related to future events]?

If one were to claim [that there is a contradiction] if the Buddha knew there would be these challenges, yet failed to reply to them in advance, there would really have been no need for this, for, in this presently existing fourfold assembly there are already those well able to cut off doubts in their responses to challenges [such as this]. We now already have those well able to refute challenging inquiries. What then would be the point in [the Buddha himself] responding in advance to such things? Right now, among the bhikshus you encounter in the present day, there are already those well able to refute the tenets posited by brahmins. Therefore there is no need [for the Buddha] to have responded in advance to such challenges.

Furthermore, there have already been prior responses to such challenges that are scattered in various places throughout the many sutras. Because people are unable to completely know the Dharma of the Buddha, they do not know where those passages are located.

I shall now address your challenge on the matter of the Buddha's having allowed Devadatta to leave the home life and become a monk. As for your opinion that, if the Buddha allowed Devadatta to leave the home life, he could not have been omniscient, this statement is wrong. When Devadatta left the home life to become a monk, it was not the Buddha who was involved in allowing him to become a monastic.

Question: Even if it was someone else who allowed him to become a monastic, why did the Buddha allow this to happen?

Response: The doing of good and the doing of evil each have the season in which they occur. It was not necessarily the case that, having left home, he would immediately embark on doing evil. After Devadatta left home to become a monk, he had all of the meritorious qualities that are associated with upholding the moral precepts. Therefore there was no fault in [permitting] his leaving the home life.

Additionally, for twelve years, Devadatta was pure in his observance of the moral precepts and also became able then to recite from memory sixty-thousand lines from the treasury of Dharma. The karmic reward from this is such that, in the future, [such cultivation] will not have been in vain. In fact, it will definitely benefit him later on.

I will now reply to your statement regarding Devadatta's prying loose of a boulder [in an attempt to murder the Buddha]. Because all buddhas have already perfected the dharma of not killing, nobody in any world can ever rob them of life.

Question: If the Buddha had actually perfected the dharma of not killing, why did the boulder shatter and [allow a piece of it] to come down [and strike him in the foot]?

Response: The Buddha had planted karmic causes associated with damage to the body for which he was bound to undergo this fixed retribution. He manifested the appearance of having to undergo it in order to demonstrate to beings that karmic retributions cannot be escaped. It was for this reason that he voluntarily came to that place.

I shall now respond to your contention that there was some problem in the Buddha's not having spoken in advance about the incident involving that woman, Ciñcā. There is nothing in that woman, Ciñcā's, disparaging of the Buddha that can serve as a causal basis for impugning his qualification as omniscient. If the Buddha had announced in advance: "In the future, that woman, Ciñca, will come forth and slander me," then that woman, Ciñca, would not in fact have come forth as she did. Furthermore, it was due to the karmic causes and conditions associated with the Buddha's having slandered others in a previous lifetime that he was now definitely bound to undergo [the corresponding retribution]. [40]

I shall now address your challenge as to how it could have been that the Buddha failed to prevent the incident that occurred when Sundarī entered the Jeta Grove.[41] This incident does not constitute a reason for impugning the Buddha's qualification as omniscient. The Buddha does not have some power by which he is able to cause every being's life to be an entirely happy one. Also, the Buddhas have all left behind disputation, do not elevate themselves, and are not attached to [making others] uphold moral precepts, consequently he did not act to prevent this incident.

Additionally, it was because of the ripening of karma from a previous life that he was definitely bound to undergo that seven days of slander. Moreover, when beings observed that the Buddha was neither perturbed over hearing himself slandered nor joyful when his innocence was made clear, they brought forth the resolve to follow the unsurpassable path, uttering this vow, "We too shall acquire just such a pure mind as this." Therefore there was no fault [in the Buddha's having acted as he did].

I shall now respond to your contention that, because the Buddha entered a brahmin village and then left with an empty bowl, he was therefore not omniscient.[42] The Buddha [did not go to that village] for the sake of food and drink, [but rather because] he had contemplated the minds of the people there. It was only after he entered the village that Māra changed the villagers' minds.

Question: This is a matter about which the Buddha should have become aware in advance, thinking, "If I go into this village, Māra will change these peoples' minds."

Response: The Buddha in fact *did* know about this matter in advance [and entered that village anyway] in order to bring great benefit to those beings. It is not solely on the basis of receiving alms food from them that the Buddhas benefit beings and facilitate their liberation. There were those who welcomed him there with pure minds, bowed in reverence to him, and looked up to him with congenial gazes. All of these things already served great benefit. Why should it be an essential requirement that he be given food and drink? There are many different sorts of methods by which he was able to be of benefit to beings. Thus it was not in vain that he entered that village.

I shall now respond to your statement about the Buddha's having gone up the road on which there was a drunken elephant.[43] Although the Buddha already knew of this matter, there was a reason he deliberately went there. It was because this drunken elephant was definitely at a point where he could be brought across to liberation. The Buddha was also intent on preventing his falling into the karmic offense of harming a buddha.

Additionally, this elephant's body had the appearance of a black mountain. When the population there saw this elephant bow down its head in reverence to the Buddha, they all brought forth thoughts of reverence. It was for these reasons that the Buddha deliberately went up that road. Also, there was no error involved in the Buddha's having entered that road to encounter that elephant. Only if some unfortunate incident had transpired would you have a basis for bringing up this challenge.

As for your challenge regarding the Buddha's having gone to Verañjā, that was simply a case of having to undergo retribution for karmic deeds committed in a previous life.[44]

I shall now address your statement on the issue of the Buddha's having accepted Sunakṣatra as a disciple.[45] The Buddha has no need to guard against errors in actions of body, speech, mind, or livelihood.[46] It was because he is utterly without fear that he permitted Sunakṣatra to become a disciple.

Also, because this man always dwelt in close proximity to the Buddha, he was thus able to observe the display of all manner of spiritual powers and also saw the arrival of devas, dragons, *yakṣas, gandharvas, asuras,* kings, and others, all coming to make offerings to the Buddha and to pose respectful questions to him on all manner of extremely profound and essential dharmas. Hence his mind was thereby able to become purified. Because he was able to achieve purification of mind, this was a causal basis for his [eventual] benefit. Therefore, even though he was an evil man, the Buddha nonetheless accepted him as a disciple.

Question: This man had many evil thoughts about the Buddha. Therefore the Buddha should not have permitted him to become a disciple.

Response: Even if the Buddha had not accepted him as a disciple, the man still would have had those evil thoughts. Therefore there was no fault in the Buddha's permitting him to become a disciple.

I shall now respond to your challenge as to why the Buddha did not formulate the moral precepts in advance of [his disciples'] commission of the corresponding transgressions. The Buddha did in fact formulate moral precepts in advance. He set forth the eightfold path of the Āryas that consist of right views, right thought, right speech, right action, right livelihood, right effort, right mindfulness, and right meditative concentration. Because he did describe this path leading to the attainment of nirvāṇa, he in fact had already formulated all of the precepts.

Furthermore, the Buddha described the three trainings wherein one thoroughly trains in moral virtue, thoroughly trains in [focusing] the mind, and thoroughly trains in wisdom. One should then realize from this that he had in fact already set forth all of the moral precepts.

Additionally, the Buddha told the bhikshus that they should definitely not do any sort of evil. Does this not constitute prior formulation of moral precepts?

Also, the Buddha spoke of the path of the ten courses of good karmic action, namely abandoning killing, stealing, sexual misconduct, divisive speech, harsh speech, false speech, frivolous speech, covetousness, ill will, and wrong views. Does this not constitute prior formulation of moral precepts?

Twelve years earlier, the Buddha described in a single verse the *upoṣadha* dharma,[47] namely:

> To refrain from doing any sort of evil deed,
> to respectfully engage in every sort of good deed,
> and to purify one's own mind—
> This is the teaching of all Buddhas.[48]

One should therefore realize that the Buddha in fact *did* formulate the moral precepts in advance.

Also, the Buddha stated that one should abandon even all of the most minor causes and conditions associated with evil, as stated in these lines:

> Abandon all evil actions of the body.
> Also abandon all evil speech,
> abandon all evil actions of the mind,
> and utterly abandon all other forms of evil.

On the basis of statements such as these, one should realize that the Buddha had already formulated the moral precepts in advance. Additionally, the Buddha had already described in advance the dharmas through which one guards against transgressions, as stated in these lines:

> To guard the body is good indeed.
> To be able to guard one's speech is also good.

To guard one's mind is good indeed,
and to guard against all errors is good as well.[49]
The bhikshu guards against all errors
and thereby succeeds in abandoning all evil.

One should realize on the basis of these statements that the Buddha in fact *did* formulate the moral precepts in advance. Moreover, the Buddha also described in advance the characteristics of goodness, as stated in these lines:

Do not allow hands or feet to carelessly commit transgressions.
Restrain your words and take care in actions done.
One should take pleasure in guarding and focusing the mind.
It is on these bases that one is rightfully called a bhikshu.[50]

One should realize on the basis of statements such as this that the Buddha in fact *did* formulate the moral precepts in advance.

Furthermore, because the Buddha described the dharmas by which one is a *śramaṇa*, one should realize he did in fact formulate the moral precepts in advance. There are four dharmas by which one is a *śramaṇa*: First, one does not respond in kind to hate-filled actions. Second, one remains silent in the face of scolding. Third, one is able to endure even being beaten with staves. And fourth, one maintains patience with those who have dealt one harm.

Moreover, the Buddha taught the four stations of mindfulness, namely the contemplation of the body, the contemplation of feelings, the contemplation of thoughts, and the contemplation of dharmas, doing so because they constitute the abode of the path to nirvāṇa. Hence one should realize that he *did* formulate the moral precepts in advance.

The Buddha would not even permit the most subtle form of evil, how much the less would he condone any sort of evil karma in one's physical actions or speech. For reasons such as these, one should realize that he did indeed formulate the moral precepts in advance.

This is analogous to a king's establishment of laws in which one is forbidden to do evil deeds. When, later on, there are transgressions against those laws, it is according to the relative gravity of the crime that corresponding punishments are imposed. The Buddha is just the same in this respect. He first made general statements describing the moral precepts. Later on, when offenses occurred, he described the specific characteristic factors by which the given action constituted an offense.

Where there were those who committed evil deeds, they were instructed and caused to repent. He instructed that, for a given offense, a given corresponding form of penance was to be performed or that either temporary expulsion or complete expulsion was stipulated so that the miscreant could not to dwell together with the community, and so forth. It was only with the establishment of these sorts of cases that we came to have the subsequent formulation of moral precepts.

I shall now address your contention that superior position in the monastic community should be accorded on the basis of age, nobility of birth caste, status of one's clan, and so forth. In the dharmas of the path, issues of age, nobility of birth caste, status of one's clan, and so forth afford no benefit. How is this so? It is on the basis of being born into the Dharma of the Buddha that one qualifies as being born into nobility and into a fine clan. Seniority is determined on the basis of the number of years one has received the higher ordination and this is the rationale for being referred to as an elder.

As for your opinion that those who are merely older in years should be given priority in the receipt of offerings, is it not the case that those who first left the home life and received the ordination precepts are better regarded as of greater eminence?

Furthermore, from the time one receives the ordination precepts onward, there are no longer any distinctions on the basis of one's caste and such. It is only when bhikshus receive the precepts of the higher ordination that they then qualify as having been born into the family of the Buddhas. It is at this point that one loses any name associated with prior birth into a greater or lesser clan and everyone then belongs to this one single family.

As for your statements on upholding the precepts—those who first left the home life to become monastics and who have observed the moral precepts for the longest time and then proceed to uphold those moral precepts for a long time—it is because of their years of seniority in this that they should be accorded a superior position within the monastic community. This is as set forth in the original formulation of the moral precept code.

I shall now address your contention that those who are most strictly observant in their upholding of the moral precepts should not bow in reverence to those who have broken the moral precepts. Those who truly have broken the moral precepts should not even be allowed to dwell together with the community, how much the less should they receive reverential obeisance or offerings.

It is on the basis of their claim to be a bhikshu that one pays reverence to them according to their order of seniority. This is similar to when one bows in reverence before a deity's image made of clay or wood, doing so as a means of bearing in mind that actual deity.

The Buddha decreed that those of fewer years seniority should revere those who are seated in a superior position within the monastic order. It is through according with the Buddha's instructions in this that one acquires karmic merit.

I shall now respond to your statement that the according of reverence should be based on one's practice of the *dhūta* austerities. In this matter of those who take up the *dhūta* practices, there are five general types of practitioners among which it is difficult to make clear distinctions:[51]

First, there are those who are deluded and who, due to an absence of right knowledge, are driven by desire to practice these difficult dharmas;

Second, there are those possessed of only dull faculties who wish to acquire benefits as a result;

Third, there are those with evil intentions focused on deceiving others;

Fourth, there are those who are mentally ill;

And fifth, there are those who [take them up], thinking, "The dharmas of the *dhūta* austerities are praised by all buddhas, worthies, and *āryas* because they accord with the path to nirvāṇa."

Among these five classes of practitioners of the *dhūta* austerities, it is difficult to distinguish which are genuine and which are false.

Now, as for this matter of one's level of learning, just as with the *dhūta* austerities, it is difficult to distinguish clearly among those who have acquired abundant learning. How is this so? It could be that it is on the basis of delighting in the path that one has accrued much learning. Or perhaps it is only for the sake of receiving offerings that one has accrued much learning. It is difficult to make clear distinctions in matters such as these.

Additionally, in the Dharma of the Buddha, it is practice in accordance with one's words that is accorded esteem. One does not accord esteem merely on the basis of having engaged in much study or having become able to recite many scriptures. Also, according to the statements of the Buddha himself, if one practices but a single sentence of Dharma and is thereby able to derive self-benefit from that, this itself qualifies as abundant learning.

So too it is with this matter of wisdom. If one remains unable to implement a level of practice consistent with one's level of discourse, of what use is this wisdom? Consequently, it is not on the basis of one's degree of wisdom that one determines who is accorded a superior position in the monastic order.

This is analogous to the current way of doing things in the world. Although a younger brother may indeed be more learned or more wise, the elder brother is still not enjoined to pay him reverence. Therefore, after this same fashion, it is not on the basis of one's level of wisdom that one gains priority in the receipt of offerings or reverence. So it is then that, even though one may indeed have accrued much learning or wisdom, one should still accord reverence on the basis of who first received the ordination precepts. Were one to accord priority in the receipt of offerings to those of greater learning or a higher level of wisdom, this would inevitably result in discord within the community.

As for the other [criteria you propose for priority in according reverence], namely realization of the *śramaṇa's* fruits of the path, severance of fetters, and acquisition of spiritual powers, those are the most difficult matters to know. Whether or not this person has attained a fruit of the path, whether he has cut off more fetters or fewer fetters [than this other person], and whether or not he has acquired spiritual powers—one cannot use such matters as the basis for superior position in the monastic order. Consider for instance those who have realized the same fruits of the path, cut off the same fetters, and acquired the same spiritual powers. Who among them should be accorded superior position in the monastic order? Consequently, it is by far the best to simply accord with the Buddha's instructions on these matters.

I shall now address your contention that the Buddha himself was beset by doubt about whether he should expound the Dharma.[52] The Buddha had no doubts at all even with regard to the most profound sorts of dharmas, how much the less might he have had doubts with regard to whether or not he should expound the Dharma. The Buddha never said that he would entirely forego his teaching of the Dharma. He merely indicated a preference for continuing to abide in serenity, refraining from becoming involved in numerous endeavors. There was no fault in his having simply waited till later to begin expounding the Dharma.

Also, the non-Buddhist partisans would say, "If the Buddha is such a great *ārya* that he remains silent and declines to involve himself in conceptual elaboration, what use could he have for assembling a following and offering to give teachings?" Then again, once he started teaching, this would inevitably turn into an endless endeavor. It was as if he was weighing the utility of proceeding to teach the Dharma and assemble a group of disciples when this could appear outwardly as if it were a mark of covetous attachment.

Due to these factors, the Buddha reflected, "Though my Dharma is extremely deep, the wisdom and skillful means that might be employed in teaching it would be measureless and boundless. Still, those who are actually amenable to gaining liberation are but few." Consequently, he thought to himself, "It would be better to remain silent." It was also to defend against the potential for mocking deprecation by non-Buddhist partisans that he instead influenced the Brahma Heaven King to [first] request the proclamation of Dharma. The Brahma Heaven King and others then immediately addressed the Buddha, saying, "Beings are surely worthy of pity. There are among them those of sharp faculties and but few fetters who would be easy to teach and bring across to liberation."

Because of this, the Buddha acceded to the request of the Brahma Heaven King and others. It was as if someone who had just found a great treasury of jewels felt he should reveal their presence to others. In this same way, when *āryas* themselves gain the benefits of the Dharma, they feel they should also use it to benefit others.

I shall now address your contention that, because the Buddha expressed a wish to speak the Dharma for Ārāḍa Kālāma and others, not realizing that they had in fact already died, [this contradicts the plausibility of his being omniscient]. The Buddha had not brought to mind the issue of whether or not they had already died, but rather was only considering the fact that, because these men's fetters were but scant, they would be capable of being instructed and brought across to liberation. It is in correspondence with the point upon which one's thought is focused that a corresponding knowledge arises. It was as a consequence of this that the Buddha first said this to himself and a deva then appropriately informed him.[53]

Also, since earlier on, when the Buddha had just abandoned the home life, he had gone to those men, [Arāda Kālāma and Udraka Rāmaputra], and had spent time with them, the devas and other people could have entertained doubts in which they thought the Buddha had perhaps received the sublime Dharma from them and had then become enlightened in another location. Because the Buddha wished to cut off any doubts that they might have had, he immediately exclaimed, "Oh, those men—they have for so long suffered such misfortune as this. How can it be that they have still not heard this sublime Dharma?"

By inferring the implications of this idea, one can deduce the nature of the matter of the five bhikshus. It was because the Buddha had only brought to mind the causes and conditions associated with their capacity to gain liberation that he had not yet considered precisely where they were currently dwelling. Afterward, once he had thought about where they were dwelling, he then knew where they were.

Therefore one should not look upon these issues as refuting the plausibility of there being an omniscient person.

I shall now address your stated doubt with regard to the causes for the destruction of the city of Pāṭaliputra. The precise causes and conditions by which this city would meet its destruction were still unfixed. To make a fixed pronouncement on the unfolding of unfixed causes and conditions would itself be a fault.

Also among the forty exclusive dharmas listed earlier, I stated that all buddhas are thoroughly cognizant of dharmas that are unfixed. In response then, I do not accept this challenge as valid.

I shall now address your contention about the Buddha's querying the bhikshus as to the contents of their conversation by asking, "So, what are you all gathered together to discuss?" It was because the Buddha was about to hold forth on some aspect of Dharma that he initiated the discussion by asking a question of this sort. It could have been that, because he wished to formulate another of the moral prohibitions, he directed them to talk about what they were discussing. Because he took all sorts of such instances as occasions for speaking Dharma, the Buddha's posing a question was free of any fault [in relation to the issue of his omniscience].

Furthermore it is a commonplace in the world, even when one is already well aware of what is happening, for one to go ahead and ask a question. For instance, on observing someone eating, one may ask, "Oh, so you're eating, are you?" Or, for instance, on a particularly cold day, one may ask, "Isn't it cold?"

In this same way, even though he already knew, the Buddha would nonetheless pose a question. Being but a means of conforming to convention, this is entirely free of fault.

I shall now address your judgment that anyone who praises himself and criticizes others could not possibly be an omniscient person. The Buddha entertained no desires with respect to himself and so was not the least bit covetous of receiving offerings. He did not hate other men and was not possessed of overweening pride. As for the reason for his having declared himself to be foremost among everyone in the world, it was because there were beings who were amenable to faith and possessed of acutely sharp faculties who, if they cast aside bad spiritual guides and took the Buddha as their teacher, they could then gain that peace and security that would see them through the long night [of subsequent rebirths]. It was for this reason that the Buddha did in fact praise his own personal qualities.

Additionally, there were those who, although they sought the path to the supreme bliss, were still indolent and unable to bring forth vigorous effort. Consequently the Buddha declared, "In this matter of gaining the most supreme benefit, one must not be indolent. I am the supreme spiritual guide in this world, the one who well proclaims right Dharma. It is only fitting then that you become assiduous and vigorous, for it is only then that you may gain the fruits of the path." And so it was that, for reasons such as these, the Buddha did indeed praise his own personal qualities. It was not out of a wish to be accorded esteem, nor was it out of a wish to slight and deprecate others.

In cases where the Buddha rebuked evil men, it was for the sake of inducing them to get rid of evil dharmas. It was not because he detested other beings. In some cases, there were those seeking to achieve benefit through Dharma, people whose minds were pure and of straightforward character, but who were locked in relationships with bad spiritual guides. In order to induce them to abandon these bad teachers, the Buddha would sometimes criticize and rebuke them. Even before he had achieved buddhahood, [in earlier lifetimes] he even sacrificed his own brain and the very marrow of his bones as gifts to others. How much the less could it be that, once he had already attained buddhahood, he would be inclined to berate and scold others?

I shall now respond to your contention that there were chronologically contradictory tenets in the Buddha's Dharma. There are no contradictions present in the Dharma of the Buddha between what came at the beginning and what followed later on. It is only because you and your cohorts do not understand the concepts involved in the Buddha's Dharma that you have the opinion that it is inherently contradictory.

This path leading to the realization of nirvāṇa had not been either proclaimed or realized by anyone during the entire time between Kāśyapa Buddha's nirvāṇa on forward to the present. It was for this reason that the Buddha declared, "I am he who has newly attained the path." In other places, he also said, "I have attained the ancient path." The path is that which was previously realized by Dīpaṃkara Buddha and the other buddhas of the past, namely the eightfold path of the Āryas that is able to lead one to nirvāṇa. It is because, in all these cases, it is but a single path relying on but a single set of causes and conditions that it is referred to it as "the ancient path." One should realize from this that the Buddha did obtain all-knowledge.

Question: As for the so-called "all-knowledge," precisely what is it that constitutes all-knowledge? Is it really on the basis of knowing absolutely everything that it is referred to as "all-knowledge"?

Response: "All-knowledge" refers to knowing all that can be known. "What can be known" refers to the five categorical repositories of dharmas, namely all past, future, and present dharmas, the dharmas that transcend the three periods of time, and the ineffable dharmas. That which is used in knowing these five categories of dharmas is cognition. Hence it is both cognition and those things that it knows that are referred to as the "all" [in the term "all-knowledge."]

Question: As for this contention that it is both the faculty of cognition and those things it knows that together comprise the "all" [of all-knowledge], this is wrong. How so? This is but a singular dharma, this because that cognition that is capable of knowing is itself knowable as when people of the world speak of this person's cognitive ability as sharp whereas that person's cognitive ability is dull.

Response: Well, if as you state that "all" is itself just a singular entity, then it should be that those polar opposites such as "hot" and "cold" are but one thing. And so too it should be that "bright" and "dark," "suffering" and "happiness," and all polar opposites should in each case be but a single thing. But this is not the case. Therefore, one cannot claim that "all" is but a singular entity.

Question: That idea to which you are clinging is itself possessed of this same fault. If the faculty of cognition is one thing, then [that which it knows, namely] "suffering," "happiness," and so forth—those should all also be but singular entities, but in truth, they are not.

Response: I never claimed that everything that can be known is, [in aggregate], but one single thing. Now that idea to which *you* are clinging is indeed that everything [that can be known] *is* somehow, [in its collective aggregate], but a single thing. Therefore, [what I am saying] is not the same as that faulty concept you are proposing.

Furthermore, since you claim that [both of] these positions are equally at fault, that idea to which you are clinging is faulty. In a case where someone accepts that the idea he is proposing is faulty, his position is thereby refuted. Now, when you understand that the idea to which you have been clinging is faulty, you should not continue to claim that someone else is the party whose position is faulty. Hence, as for your contention that what I have set forth here is somehow possessed of the same fault that characterizes your position—this is wrong.

Moreover, if you claim that the two dharmas consisting of the faculty of cognition on the one hand and that which is known on the other are somehow but a single entity, then one should be able to use any particular knowable dharma to know phenomena like vases and robes and such, but in truth it is solely the faculty of cognition that can be used in the knowing of all things.

If you are going to claim that phenomena like vases and robes and such are no different from the faculty of cognition—this vase and robe and so forth—they are entirely unable to know any phenomenon at all. It immediately follows that it ought to be the case that they are different [from the faculty of cognition] and it is truly the case that one uses the faculty of cognition to know everything.

Because your position is faulty in these ways in place after place, you cannot thus claim that the constituent phenomena forming the "all" of all-knowledge are all collectively but a single thing.

So, again, the faculty of cognition and that which is known, these two things—they are what constitute the "all" of "all-knowledge," this because they together constitute all dharmas. It is because of the Buddha's knowing of all of these dharmas that he is known as the Tathāgata and is renowned as one who is possessed of all-knowledge. This omniscient man became possessed of all-knowledge because of the *vajra* samādhi. Therefore the *vajra* samādhi is indeed something that can be established. As for your initial contentions that the *vajra* samādhi cannot be established and that "all-knowledge" is also not something that can be established, these contentions are both wrong.

The End of Chapter Twenty-Two

Chapter 23:[54] Forty Dharmas Exclusive to Buddhas (Part 3)

IV. Chapter 23: Forty Dharmas Exclusive to Buddhas (Part 3)

A. 10) Thorough Knowing of Matters That Are Unfixed

As for knowing well the unfixed dharmas, the Tathāgata's wisdom has achieved power within the sphere of all dharmas even at that point when they have not yet arisen, have not yet come forth, have not yet reached completion, have not become definitively fixed, and have not yet become clearly distinguishable. This is as stated in the *Sutra on the Buddha's Distinguishing of Karma* wherein it states:

> The Buddha told Ānanda, "There are people who practice good deeds with the body, who practice good deeds through speech, and who practice good deeds with the mind, and yet, when their lives come to an end, they then fall into the hells. There are yet other people who practice evil deeds with the body, who practice evil deeds through speech, and who practice evil deeds with the mind, and yet, when their lives come to an end, they are nonetheless reborn in the heavens."
>
> Ānanda addressed the Buddha and asked, "Why do events occur in this way?"
>
> The Buddha replied, "It may have been that the causes and conditions associated with previous life karmic offenses or meritorious deeds had already ripened, whereas the karmic offenses or meritorious deeds of the present life had not yet ripened. Or, alternatively, when approaching the end of life, they gave rise to either right views or erroneous views that precipitated either wholesome or evil thoughts, this because the power of the thoughts produced as one approaches the moment of death—their power is immense."[55]

Additionally, in the *Śuka Sutra,* it states:

> Śuka, son of a brahmin, addressed the Buddha and asked, "Gotama, why is it that the brahmin laity are in some cases able to cultivate meritorious deeds and roots of goodness in a manner superior to that of some of those who have left the home life and become monastics?"
>
> The Buddha replied, "For these sorts of matters, I do not present a fixed reply. There may be cases in which someone who has left behind the home life does not cultivate goodness and, as a consequence, in this endeavor, he does not equal the efforts of a given

householder. This is a case in which a householder is able to cultivate goodness in a manner superior to that of a particular monastic."

Furthermore, the *Great Nirvāṇa Sutra* states that the city of Pāṭaliputra is bound to be destroyed by one of three circumstances: by flood, by fire, or by a conspiracy between insiders and outsiders.

Also, [another example of an unfixed statement] arose because of a *brahmacārin* named Patikaputra about which the Buddha said:

> As for this naked ascetic, the *brahmacārin* named Patikaputra, if he fails to relinquish this statement, these thoughts, and these wrong views, then it will be impossible for him to come and appear before me. He will either be trapped by a broken rope or prevented from leaving by a broken body. In any case, he will never be able to arrive here in the presence of the Buddha.

Additionally, in the *Sutra on the Analogy of the Raft*, the Buddha said:

> This Dharma of mine is extremely deep. It is by resort to expedients that I enable even those who are shallow to easily reach an understanding of it. If there be anyone possessed of a straightforward mind who is willing to practice in accordance with the teachings, he will gain one of two kinds of benefit from this, either the cessation of the contaminants in this present lifetime or, in the event that he doesn't achieve the cessation of the contaminants, he will still succeed in attaining the path of the non-returner (*anāgāmin*).[56]

Also, in the *Ekottara Āgama*'s *Shejiali Sutra*,[57] the Buddha told Ānanda:

> As for whosoever deliberately undertakes the requisite karmic actions, none among them will fail to gain the karmic rewards and thus achieve success in the path, whether that be through receiving the results of present-life karma in this present life, whether that be through receiving them in the next birth, or whether that be through receiving them in subsequent lives.[58]

In addition, we also have this statement in the *Ekottara Āgama*'s *Afuluo Sutra*:[59] "The Buddha told the bhikshus, 'When evil people die, they may become animals or they may fall into the hells. Good people will be reborn either in the heavens or among humans.'"

Also, in the *Prince Fearless Sutra*, it states:

> Prince Fearless addressed the Buddha, saying, "Does the Buddha not have instances in which what he proclaims is able to cause others to become angry?"
>
> The Buddha replied, "Prince, this is an unfixed matter. It may happen that the Buddha, motivated by pity, will influence someone to become angry with the intended result that they will there-

> by plant the causes and conditions for goodness. This is analogous to a wet-nurse having to use a crooked finger to clear an infant's mouth of some dangerous object. Although it may inflict injury, it is done in order to prevent a calamity."[60]

There is also the statement recorded in the Abhidharma: "Beings fall into three groups. From the [karmically] indefinite group, they may fall into the definitely deviant group or the definitely righteous group."[61]

There are several thousand or even myriads of similar such types of unfixed phenomena that are cited within the four repositories of the Dharma.[62]

Question: If a person's wisdom is unfixed and characterized by indefinite thought that takes a given circumstance to perhaps be this way or perhaps not be this way, then this is not someone who is omniscient. One who is omniscient would not make two different statements [with regard to a single matter], but rather would instead be able to make definitive pronouncements, pronouncements that are utterly clear. Because of this, "thoroughly knowing unfixed matters" cannot be referred to as a dharma exclusive to the Buddha.

Response: Unfixed matters are such that they may either be this way or not this way. It is because they develop in accordance with a multiplicity of causes and conditions that one should not make definite pronouncements about them.

Moreover, were one to offer definite answers regarding indefinite phenomena, then that itself would indicate that one is *not* omniscient. Consequently, in assessing unfixed phenomena, it is essential to employ the knowledge of unfixed matters. Hence there is this exclusive dharma referred to as "the knowledge of unfixed matters."

Additionally, if one were to claim definitive knowledge with respect to all dharmas, then one would fall into the erroneous determinist fallacy. If all dharmas really were already definitely fixed, then all that one does would not require any human effort and skillful means to bring it about. This idea is as set forth here:

> If good or bad experiences were already definitely determined,
> then the character of a person's efforts should be fixed as well.
> There would be no need for any of the causal factors
> involved in the skillful means that one uses in one's cultivation.

Moreover, it is already manifestly clear that if one fails to take care with regard to one's personal behavior, then one will bring about manifold sufferings, whereas, if one is guarded with respect to one's personal behavior, then one will enjoy peace and benefit as a result of doing so.

Also, this is just as in all sorts of endeavors involved in carrying on one's livelihood wherein, on the one hand, one is required to endure a good deal of weariness and suffering to later acquire a reward in the form of all manner of wealth and happiness, whereas, on the other hand, someone else is able to simply remain still and silent in this present life, doing nothing whatsoever, only to then reap karmic rewards. So it is that there are these unfixed circumstances. It is because they are cognizant of these unfixed circumstances that we can know that the Buddhas possess the knowledge of what is unfixed.

Question: Whether or not you personally take care and whether or not you make a direct personal effort, these unfixed circumstances will still occur. On the one hand there are those who skillfully defend against untoward developments and yet still end up being subjected to intense anguish while on the other hand there are those who do not defend against such exigencies at all and yet do not encounter any intense anguish at all. Also, there are those who, in their diligence, undergo much weariness and pain, but still do not obtain the fruits of their efforts, whereas there are others who are not the least bit diligent and make no particular effort and, even so, they still manage to gain fruits [otherwise] associated with making an effort. These matters are all unfixed.

Response: Your statement simply serves to cooperate in the establishment of my position regarding unfixed matters. If these unfixed matters do indeed exist, then this wisdom that is cognizant of whatsoever is unfixed should exist. I never claimed that, if someone failed to guard against untoward events they would always be subjected to suffering. Nor did I ever claim that, without the expenditure of effortful action, one would necessarily be able to enjoy fruitful results. There are those people who, despite making an effort, are still blocked from the enjoyment of happiness by karmic obstacles originating in earlier lifetimes. I never claimed that all cases were necessarily this way. Therefore the challenges that you have posed on this topic are wrong.

This is what is meant [when it is said] with regard to unfixed circumstances that it is the Buddhas alone who possess complete knowledge of what is unfixed.

B. 11) Thorough Knowing of Formless Absorption Phenomena

As for knowing the formless realm stations, *śrāvaka* disciples and *pratyekabuddhas* know a lesser portion of the beings and dharmas associated with the formless realm stations of existence whereas the Buddhas, the Bhagavats, have a perfectly complete knowledge of the beings and dharmas associated with the formless realm stations of existence.

Regarding these formless realm stations of existence, the Buddhas know:

That a certain number of beings are born into this station;

That a certain number of beings are born into that station;

That a certain number of beings are born into the station associated with the first formless absorption;

That a certain number of beings are born into the second station;

That a certain number of beings are born into the third station;

That a certain number of beings are born into the fourth station;

That a certain number of beings have dwelt there for a particular amount of time since they were born there;

That a certain number of beings, after a particular period of time, will fall away from that realm;

That a certain number of beings will enjoy a maximum lifespan of a particular amount of time;

That a certain number of beings will have a definitely fixed lifespan;

That a certain number of beings will enjoy a lifespan the length of which is not definitely fixed;

That a certain number of beings will be born here after their lifetimes in the desire realm have come to an end;

That a certain number of beings will be born here after their lifetimes in the form realm have come to an end;

That a certain number of beings will return to be reborn here after their lifetimes in this formless realm have come to an end;

That a certain number of beings will be born here directly after their lives in the human realm come to an end;

That a certain number of beings will be reborn here directly after their lives in the heavens have come to an end;

That, when the lives of these particular beings end here, they will then take birth in the desire realm, that they will then take birth in the form realm, or that they will then take birth in the formless realm;

That, when the lives of these particular beings end here, they will then take birth in the celestial realm rebirth destiny, that they will then take birth in the human realm rebirth destiny, that they will then take birth in the *asura* realm rebirth destiny, or that they will then take birth in the rebirth destinies of the hell realms, the animal realms, or the hungry ghost realms;

That these particular beings will enter nirvāṇa in that particular place;

That a particular group of beings are all merely common people;
That a particular group of beings are *ārya* disciples of buddhas;
That a particular group of beings are [buddhas'] disciples who are common people [that have not yet become *āryas*];
That a particular group of beings will achieve success in the Śrāvaka Disciple Vehicle;
That a particular group of beings will achieve success in the Pratyekabuddha Vehicle;
That a particular group of beings will all achieve success in the Great Vehicle;
That a particular group of beings will fail to achieve success in the Śrāvaka Disciple Vehicle;
That a particular group of beings will fail to achieve success in the Pratyekabuddha Vehicle and will also fail to achieve success in the Great Vehicle;
That a particular group of beings will develop their practice to the point of reaching nirvāṇa;
That a particular group of beings will fail to develop their practice to the point where they reach nirvāṇa;
That a particular group of beings will pursue a superior level of practice;
And that a particular group of beings are all disciples of a particular buddha.

The Buddhas also know:

That this particular meditative absorption is one in which one is exposed to delectably blissful experiences;[63]
That in this particular meditative absorption there will be no exposure to delectably blissful experiences;
[That this particular meditative absorption] is wholesome or is merely neutral;
That in this particular meditative absorption one may successfully sever a certain number of fetters;
And that this particular meditative absorption is superior, is middling, or is inferior.

To summarize, only the Buddhas, by employing their knowledge of all modes are able to clearly distinguish which of these formless-realm meditative absorptions are greater or lesser, which are deeper or shallower, which involve mental dharmas, which involve dharmas not associated with the mind, which are acquired as resultant effects [of previous karma], which are not acquired as resultant effects [of previous karma], and so forth. This is what is meant when it is said that the

Buddhas thoroughly know the stations of existence corresponding to the formless meditative absorptions.

C. 12) The Knowledge of All Matters Related to Eternal Cessation

As for [the completely penetrating knowledge of all] dharmas pertaining to cessation, the Buddhas possess a penetrating knowledge of the *pratyekabuddhas* and arhats who have entered nirvāṇa either in the past or present eras. This is as recorded in the sutras where it states:

> Bhikshus, ninety-one kalpas prior to this "Worthy Kalpa" (*bhadrakalpa*), Vipaśyin Buddha appeared. After thirty-one kalpas, there followed two more buddhas, the first of whom was Śikhin and the second of whom was Viśvabhū. Then, in this Worthy Kalpa, Krakucchanda, Kanakamuni, and Kāśyapa Buddha emerged.[64]

Just such great knowledge and vision regarding all buddhas of the past should be discussed [more extensively] herein in relation to this sutra.[65] It also reaches to those *śrāvaka* disciples who have entered the nirvāṇa without residue and extends also to the *pratyekabuddha* named "Success," to the one named "Floral Insignia," to the one named "Seer of Dharma," to the one named "Dharma Basket," to the one named "Delightful Vision," to the one named "Stainless," to the one named "Free of Gain," and to the other such *pratyekabuddhas* as well. So it is that the Buddhas possess a completely penetrating knowledge of those who have entered the nirvāṇa without residue.[66]

Additionally, in cases where they have not yet entered final nirvāṇa, but rather still abide in the nirvāṇa with residue, the Buddhas possess a penetratingly comprehensive knowledge with regard to the utter ending of all conditions associated with taking birth. [These matters] also pertain to their penetrating knowledge of [the phenomena associated with] cessation.

This is as recorded in the sutras wherein it states, "The Buddha told Ānanda, 'I entirely know with respect to this person that he no longer has even the slightest darkness. This person has definitely put an end to these particular inward dharmas. When this person reaches the end of this life, he will enter nirvāṇa.'" This too is included in what is meant by "having knowledge of cessation."[67]

Also, regarding other people's penetrating comprehension of the four truths, he is able to know their circumstances. This too is included in what is meant by "having knowledge of cessation."

As it is said in the sutras, "Why should I not simply resort to expedients to cause this person in this very place to gain the liberation associated with ending the contaminants?"

And as the Buddha told Ānanda, "You delight in *dhyāna* concentration and delight in cutting off the fetters." These circumstances too are associated with what is meant by having a completely penetrating knowledge of cessation.

This is also as illustrated in the Buddha's statement to Śāriputra, "I know nirvāṇa, know the path leading to the realization of nirvāṇa, and know those beings who will arrive at the realization of nirvāṇa."[68]

Such sutras as we have cited herein should all be discussed at greater length. The ideas cited above are indicative of what is meant by all buddhas possessing the penetrating comprehension of all matters having to do with cessation.

D. 13) Thorough Knowing of Non-Form Dharmas Unrelated to Mind

As for thorough knowing of the non-form dharmas unassociated with the mind, roots of goodness associated with the moral precepts influence all of those non-form dharmas unassociated with the mind such as the moral regulations requiring wholesome actions and the moral regulations prohibiting bad actions. *Śrāvaka* disciples and *pratyekabuddhas* are unable to possess a completely penetrating comprehension of such matters. The Buddhas, however, are so well able to penetratingly comprehend them that these become as manifestly clear to them as if they were right before their very eyes. This is because they have perfected the foremost power of wisdom with respect to dharmas unassociated with the mind.

Question: Moral regulations requiring wholesome actions and moral regulations prohibiting bad actions are form dharmas. Why do you refer to them as "non-form" dharmas?

Response: Moral regulations requiring wholesome actions and moral regulations prohibiting bad actions are of two kinds, namely those involving actions and those not involving actions. Those involving actions are within the sphere of form dharmas whereas those not involving actions are "non-form" dharmas. As for those non-form dharmas not involving actions, employing his exclusive power of knowing, the Buddha is able to have a clear and present knowledge of them whereas others are compelled to rely upon inferential knowledge to understand them.

Question: Are the Buddhas only able to thoroughly know the non-form dharmas unassociated with the mind while not being able to thoroughly know the dharmas associated with the mind?

Response: If one already possesses a penetrating comprehension of the unassociated dharmas, then there is no need even to bring up the associated dharmas. It is as if we were speaking of an archer able to pierce a single fine feather [floating through the air]. One would have no need in such a case to inquire if his arrow might be able to hit something large.

Furthermore, *śrāvaka* disciples and *pratyekabuddhas* are able to employ their sixth consciousness to know but seven among the seven hundred unassociated dharmas, namely: first, names; second, characteristic marks; third, meanings; fourth, impermanence; fifth, production; sixth, non-production; and seventh, crossing on beyond. The Buddhas, however, are able to employ their sixth consciousness to know every one of them. The Buddhas also know the marks of the four truths as well as the mundane dharmas. It is for these reasons that it is said that the Buddhas thoroughly know the non-form dharmas unassociated with the mind.

E. 14) The Great Powers Pāramitā

As for the powers *pāramitā*, [the Buddhas] gain the power of the knowledge of all modes with respect to all knowable dharmas without exception and are assisted in this by the ten powers, the four fearlessnesses, and the four bases of meritorious qualities. Also, it is due to having gained the ten powers that the Buddhas are therefore able to perfect the powers *pāramitā*. This power is increased in the sixteenth mind-moment [involved in achieving the direct seeing of the path]. All-knowledge is always present in the person of the Buddha until he attains the nirvāṇa without residue. It is because of this that he gains the unimpeded knowledge of all dharmas.

F. 15) The Four Unimpeded Knowledges Pāramitā

As for the *pāramitā* of the [four] unimpeded knowledges (*pratisaṃvid*), they are unimpeded knowledge with respect to: dharmas (*dharma-pratisaṃvid*), meaning (*artha-pratisaṃvid*), language (*nirukti-pratisaṃvid*), and eloquence (*pratibhāna-pratisaṃvid*). [The Buddhas] possess an unlimited penetrating comprehension of these four dharmas that is unimpeded in its implementation. As described in the sutras:[69]

> The Buddha told the bhikshus, "There are four of the Tathāgata's disciples who have perfected the foremost power of mindfulness, power of wisdom, and power of endurance so consummately that they are like a skilled archer who can shoot any single tree leaf without difficulty. Even if these disciples were to all come forth and pose challenging questions on the four stations of mindfulness, setting aside the time required for drink, food, toilet and sleep, I could always and incessantly respond to their questions for a hundred years during which the Tathāgata would always reply with inexhaustible eloquence and wisdom."

Here the Buddha, with his characteristically scant wish to do so, discussed his own implementation of these knowledges. Supposing that there were a number of great trichiliocosms as numerous as all the atoms in all four continents of all worlds in a great trichiliocosm, supposing also that all those world systems were filled with beings all of whom were the likes of Śāriputra and the *pratyekabuddhas*, and suppose too that all of these men employed their perfected knowledges and eloquence to pose difficult questions to the Tathāgata on the four stations of mindfulness, doing so to the exhaustion of lifetimes extending to a number of kalpas as numerous as all the aforementioned atoms—the Tathāgata would still be able to reply to their questions on the meanings involved in the four stations of mindfulness, expounding on their meaning without redundancy and with inexhaustible eloquence.[70]

Now, as for the unimpeded knowledge with respect to dharmas, [the Buddhas] are well able to distinguish all details involved in the designations of dharmas with an unimpededly penetrating comprehension.

As for the unimpeded knowledge with respect to meaning, they are able to bring to bear an unimpededly penetrating comprehension of the meanings associated with those dharmas.

In the case of their unimpeded knowledge with respect to language, the Buddhas are able to accord with the languages and phrases through which the various sorts of beings are caused to understand those meanings, doing so with an unimpededly penetrating comprehension.

Regarding their unimpeded knowledge as it applies to eloquence, during that entire time in which they are answering questions, they are skillful and clever in speaking on Dharma and they are able to carry on in this fashion endlessly. Whatever topic all other worthies and *āryas* are unable to treat exhaustively, it is only the Buddhas who can reach the limits of that topic.

It is on these bases that we speak of the *pāramitā* of the unimpeded knowledges.

G. 16) The Pāramitā of Perfectly Complete Replies and Predictions

Regarding the *pāramitā* of perfection in the answering of questions, the Buddha is well able to answer in all situations involving the posing of difficult questions. And why is this so? It is because, in the four types of responses, he remains utterly free of erroneous or disordered presentations, because he well knows the conceptual meanings, because he has perfected the *pāramitā* of preserving the undamaged meaning, and because he delights in a profound knowing of the natures of all beings, what they themselves practice, and what they themselves find pleasing. This is illustrated by the instance in which Śāriputra addressed the Buddha, saying:

> Bhagavat, when the Buddha discourses on the good Dharma, many are the beings who, upon hearing this, then gain realizations. Having gained such realizations, their minds become free of all craving. And because they become free of all craving, they no longer have anything in the world that they indulge. And once they no longer have anything at all that they indulge, their minds achieve a state of inward cessation.

The Buddha exhaustively knows, without exceptions, the unsurpassable aspects of the good Dharma. There is no one who is superior to him in this regard.

Question: You spoke of the four types of replies. What are those four?

Response:

> First, the definitive reply.
> Second, the distinguishing reply.
> Third, the counter-questioning reply.
> And, fourth, the reply that sets aside the question.

In the case of the definitive reply, this is illustrated by the instance where a bhikshu asked the Buddha, "Bhagavat, is it or is it not the case that there could be some form that is eternal and unchanging? Bhagavat, is it or is it not the case that there could be any feelings, perceptions, formative factors, or consciousnesses that are permanent and unchanging?"

The Buddha replied, saying, "Bhikshu, there is no form that is permanent and unchanging. There are no feelings, perceptions, formative factors, or consciousnesses that are permanent and unchanging."

Cases such as these illustrate the "definitive reply."

The distinguishing reply is illustrated by the instance where Potaliputta,[71] the Brahmacārin, inquired of Samiddhi,[72]asking: [73] "In instances where a person deliberately performs actions of body, speech, or mind, what sorts of karmic retributions ensue therefrom?"

Samiddhi responded with a definitive reply, saying, "In instances where persons deliberately perform actions of body, speech, or mind, they are bound to undergo retributions involving suffering and anguish."

But this should have involved a distinguishing reply. This *brahmacārin* later came and asked the Buddha about this matter, to which the Buddha replied, saying, "Potaliputta, in instances where someone deliberately performs actions of body, speech, or mind, this karma may result in undergoing painful retributions, in undergoing pleasurable retributions, or in undergoing retributions that are neither painful nor pleasurable. Pain-inducing actions result in undergoing painful retributions. Pleasure-inducing actions result in undergoing pleasurable retributions. Actions that are neither pain-inducing nor pleasure-inducing result in undergoing karmic retributions that are neither painful nor pleasurable."

Scriptural passages such as these illustrate instances of the distinguishing reply.

The counter-questioning reply is illustrated by that instance in which the *brahmacārin* named Śreṇika inquired of the Buddha and the Buddha replied, "I shall now return the question to you whereupon you may reply in accordance with your own idea on this matter. Śreṇika, what do you think? Do physical forms constitute the Tathāgata, or not? Or is it that feelings, perceptions, formative factors, or consciousnesses constitute the Tathāgata?"

He replied, "No, Bhagavat. They do not."

[The Buddha then asked him], "Is the Tathāgata apart from form, feelings, perceptions, formative factors, or consciousnesses, or not?"

He replied, "No, Bhagavat. He is not."

These types of passages from scripture should be more extensively discussed. They illustrate what is meant by the counter-questioning reply.

As for the reply that sets aside the question, this applies to the response to questions regarding the fourteen classic erroneous views, namely:

Is the world eternal?
Is the world non-eternal?
Is the world both eternal and non-eternal?
Is the world neither eternal nor non-eternal?
Is the world bounded?
Is the world unbounded?
Is the world both bounded and unbounded?
Is the world neither bounded nor unbounded?
Does the Tathāgata exist after his nirvāṇa?
Does the Tathāgata not exist after his nirvāṇa?
Does the Tathāgata both exist and not exist after his nirvāṇa?
Does the Tathāgata neither exist nor not exist after his nirvāṇa?
Is the body identical with a spiritual soul (*jīva*)?
Is the body different from a spiritual soul?

As stated above, even in an instance where all beings possessed the wisdom and eloquence of the *pratyekabuddha* and they inquired of the Buddha on these four matters, the Buddha would in all cases adapt to their needs in answering their questions, offering replies that are neither excessive nor deficient. It is for these reasons that the Buddhas are said to possess the *pāramitā* of perfection in the answering of questions.

H. 17) Invulnerability to Harm by Anyone

There is no one whatsoever who can harm the Buddha. This is because he has gained that dharma by which one cannot be killed. There is no one who can cut off any part of the Buddha's body. He has sovereign mastery over whether he will live or die. This is as stated in scripture, wherein it states: "Were one to seek some method by which to inflict harm on the Buddha—there simply is no such possibility at all."

Question: Is the lifespan of a buddha fixed or is it unfixed?

Response: There are those who claim that it is unfixed. But if a buddha's lifespan were actually fixed, what difference then would there be between his case and that of all others who have fixed lifespans? Still, in truth, the lifespan of a buddha is not fixed. That there is no one who can harm a buddha—now *that* is extraordinary. There are those who say that the lifespan of a buddha is fixed. However, whereas others whose lifespans are fixed are indeed subject to having hands, feet, ears, and nose sliced off, the Buddha [is unique in that he] is entirely free of any such vulnerability.

Question: How is it that the Buddhas have this exclusive dharma of being invulnerable to being harmed?

Response: The inconceivability of the Buddhas can be understood by resort to analogy. Suppose for instance that all beings throughout the worlds of the ten directions were to have a given amount of power. Now, if a single *māra* could possess a certain amount of power, also suppose that each and every one of those beings throughout the ten directions was caused to possess powers like those of Māra, the Evil One. Even if all of those beings then joined in wishing to inflict harm on the Buddha, they would still be unable to move even a single hair on the Buddha's body. How much the less might they actually succeed in harming the Buddha.

Question: Well, if that is the case, how then could Devadatta have succeeded in injuring the Buddha?

Response: This question was already answered earlier. The Buddha wished to show beings the character of the three poisons. Even though

Devadatta had previously upheld the moral precepts and cultivated goodness, because he was attached to receiving offerings, he committing immensely evil deeds.

[The Buddha] also allowed this to happen in order to cause [beings] to realize that the mind of the Buddha does not vary in the way it regards any human or deva. His having compassion and pity for Devadatta on the one hand and Rāhula[74] on the other was the same as his equal regard for his own left and right eyes.

The Buddha always spoke of the mind of uniformly equal regard for everyone. He revealed his equality of regard at this time. When the devas and people observed this, they were struck by the extraordinary nature of this and thus felt even stronger resolute faith.

In addition, because of this, the devas of the long-life heavens could see that the Buddha was still bound to undergo retribution for bad karmic actions done in previous lives. Had he not undergone it now, they might have thought that bad actions could be free of corresponding karmic retributions. Because the Buddha wished to cut off their wrong views, he thereby revealed his own undergoing of this karmic retribution.

Furthermore, the Buddha's mind is no different in the presence of pain or pleasure. His mind is free of any concept of a self. This is because it is ultimately empty. Because his sense faculties have all been made pliant and imperturbable by change, he has no need to use expedients to separate from pain and enjoy pleasures. This is as described in the Bodhisattva canon where it states: "It was merely as an expedient that the Buddha manifested as subject to this experience." One should infer the broader implications of this.

The above points illustrate what is meant by the Buddha's exclusive dharma of being invulnerable to being killed or harmed.

I. 18) Their Words Are Never Spoken without a Purpose

In speaking on the Dharma, their words are never empty. All words spoken by the Buddhas have a corresponding intended effect. Therefore, when the Buddhas speak on Dharma, their words are never empty. And how is this so? Before the Buddhas begin to speak on Dharma, they first contemplate from root to branch where beings' minds abide and whether their fetters are thick or only scant. Thus they know the origins of their meritorious qualities in previous lives, observe the nature and strength of their karmic roots, and know:

Where and when beings [will encounter] obstacles;
Whether they are susceptible to liberation through gentle teaching methods;

Whether they are susceptible to liberation through harsh teaching methods;
Whether they are susceptible to liberation through a combination of gentle and harsh teaching methods.[75]
Whether they need only a little bit of instigation to gain liberation;
Whether they require extensive distinguishing instructions to gain liberation;
That there are those who gain liberation through [teachings on] the aggregates, the sense bases, the sense realms, or the twelve links of conditioned co-production;
Whether they may gain access [to liberation] through the gateway of faith or through the gateway of wisdom;
That this person should gain liberation through the teaching of a buddha;
That this person should gain liberation through the teaching of a *śrāvaka* disciple;
That this person should gain liberation through some other set of conditions;
That this person should be able to gain success in the Śrāvaka Disciple Vehicle;
That this person should be able to gain success in the Pratyekabuddha Vehicle;
That this person should be able to gain success in the Great Vehicle;
That this person has long practiced habitual greed, habitual hatred, and habitual delusion;
That this person has practiced habitual greed and hatred;
And that this person has practiced habitual greed and delusion.

In this way, they distinguish and determine with regard to each and every situation:

That this person has fallen into an annihilationist view;
That this person has fallen into an eternalist view;
That this person is for the most part attached to the view that seizes on the existence of a real self in association with the body [or any of the other four aggregates];[76]
That this person is most often habitually attached to extreme views;
That this person is most often habitually attached to the views that seize upon either prohibitions or on opinionated views;
That this person is for the most part habitually arrogant;
That this person is for the most part habitually inclined toward feelings of inferiority and the tendency to flattery and deviousness;
That this person's mind is mostly inclined toward doubt and regret.

That this person has developed a fondness for refined literary expressiveness;
That there are those who prize refinement in meanings and principles;
That there are those who delight in profundities;
That there are those who enjoy topics that are merely superficial;
That, in previous lifetimes, this person has accumulated the Dharma provisions requisite to success in the path;
That this person is accumulating the Dharma provisions for the path in this present lifetime;
That this person has only accumulated roots of goodness conducive to enjoying karmic rewards [from previous meritorious actions];
That this person has only accumulated roots of goodness associated with thorough understanding;
That this person should be able to rapidly become enlightened;
And that this person will require a long time before he can become enlightened.[77]

The Buddha first engages in investigative contemplation and assessment of individual circumstances and then, according with whichever approach is appropriate to instigate someone's liberation, he then speaks Dharma for them and thereby brings about their liberation.

It is as a consequence of this that every instance of the Buddha's speaking of Dharma is free of any merely empty discourse. This is as described in a sutra: "The Bhagavat first knows and sees and only then speaks Dharma. It is not the case that he speaks Dharma without first knowing and seeing."

J. 19) Their Speech Is Free of Error

Regarding the absence of errors and mistakes [in their speech], when the Buddhas speak Dharma, they do not commit any errors or make any mistakes. "Absence of errors" refers to there being no instances in which the meaning of what they say is contradictory. "Absence of mistakes" means they make no mistakes with regard to meanings.

It is because they do not make mistakes with regard to causes and conditions as they relate to the path that they are said to not make mistakes. It is because they do not commit errors with regard to causes and conditions as they relate to the fruits of the path that they are said to not commit any error.

It is because they are not deficient that they are said to not make mistakes and it is because they are not excessive that they are said to not commit any error.

This is accomplished through their possession of a penetrating comprehension of the four unimpeded knowledges, through their constant harmonization of mindfulness and stable wisdom, and through their utter abandonment of views associated with annihilationism, eternalism, acausality, erroneous causality, or other such wrong views.

In the Dharma that they speak, there is no cause by which people become perplexed. In whatsoever they say, there are no faults involving inconsistencies between what is set forth in the beginning and in the end.

Scriptures accordant with these concepts should be discussed more extensively herein. As it says in one of the sutras: "Bhikshus. When I speak Dharma for you, it is good in the beginning, good in the middle, and good in the end. The phrasings are good and the meanings are good. It possesses a singular purity free of any debasing admixture and it is perfectly complete in its proclamation of *brahmacarya*."[78]

K. 20) Complete Use of the Three Turnings in Speaking Dharma

As regards the matter of [the Buddha's] speaking of Dharma involving rarities, whomever they undertake to teach is immediately enabled to realize the fruits of the path. This is a rarity.

Whenever they provide a reply or offer a prediction, their statements are always genuine and do not differ [from actual circumstances]. This too is a rarity.

The Buddha has the path as the subject of his discourse. This path as it is proclaimed by the Buddha is not admixed with afflictions and is able to bring about the severance of the afflictions. This too is a rarity.

Whenever the Buddha speaks, benefit ensues from it and it never involves mere empty words. This too is a rarity.

Whenever a person applies mental diligence and vigor to the cultivation of the Buddha's Dharma, he can cut off the unwholesome dharmas and bring about increase in the good dharmas. This too is a rarity.

There are three additional rarities: the rarity of displaying spiritual powers, the rarity of foretelling the content of others' thoughts, and the rarity of being able to accomplish the transformational teaching of others. It is on the basis of these three sorts of rarities in the proclaiming of Dharma that the Buddha's discourse on Dharma is said to be characterized by rarities.[79]

L. 21) They Are the Great Generals among All Āryas

Regarding [the Buddha's] eminence as the most superior spiritual guide among all the Āryas, buddhas know what the minds of beings course in, know what they delight in, know whether their fetters are deep or shallow, know whether their faculties are sharp or dull, and know whether their wisdom is superior, middling, or inferior. It is because they know these matters well and know them with penetrating comprehension that they are the most superior spiritual guides among all the Āryas.

They are also able to well know the characteristics of the four truths, and to well know all the general and specific characteristics of all dharmas.

It is also because, when they speak on the Dharma, their words are not empty and because, when they speak on the Dharma, they commit no errors and make no mistakes that they are therefore the most superior spiritual guides among all the Āryas.

Question: But the other four groups are also able to speak on the Dharma and thus refute the teachings of the non-Buddhists and thereby cause them to enter into the Dharma of the Buddha. Why then does one only speak of the Buddha as the most superior spiritual guide?

Response: This should be explained by an analogy. Suppose all beings possessed the wisdom powers of a *pratyekabuddha*. If all of these beings did not receive the intentional assistance of the Buddha and yet wished somehow to bring about the liberation of but a single person, this would be a complete impossibility. When all of these persons spoke Dharma, they would still be unable to cause the severance of a tiny fraction of even one of the formless realm fetters.

If, on the other hand, the Buddha wished to bring about the liberation of some being and then proceeded to say something, even those burdened with the erroneous views of the non-Buddhists, the dragons, the *yakṣas*, and the various other sorts of beings who do not understand the language of the Buddha—these would all still be caused to understand. Then all of these would in turn be able to teach countless other beings. And so this proceeds even to the point that, today, whenever those within the community of *śrāvaka* disciples cause beings to abide in the four fruits of the path, they are all emblematically representative of the Tathāgata as the most superior of all spiritual guides.

It is for these reasons that the Buddha is known as the most superior spiritual guide, and it is for these reasons that this is regarded as an exclusive dharma not held in common with the other *āryas*.

M. 22–25) They Are Able to Remain Unguarded in Four Ways

As for the four unguarded dharmas, the Buddhas are unguarded in their physical actions, are unguarded in their verbal actions, are unguarded in their mental actions, and are unguarded with respect to the means for sustaining life. And why is this? These four matters are not protected from others' [knowledge]. They do not think, "Regarding my [actions of] body, speech, and mind, and my [means of sustaining] life—I fear that others might come to know about them."

And why is this? This is because, during the long night [of previous lifetimes], they have cultivated every sort of pure karmic deed and have always well seen, well known, and well severed every one of the dharmas associated with the afflictions. And this is because they have perfected every sort of peerless root of goodness, because they have so well practiced whatever dharma is amenable to practice, because they have reached the point where there is nothing about them the least bit worthy of criticism, and because they have utterly perfected the *pāramitā* of equanimity.

Now, on this matter of their "equanimity," when their eyes view form, they relinquish any thoughts of either distress or delight. And so it goes [with the other sense faculties and objects] up to and including the mind faculty's engagement with dharmas [as objects of mind]. In this connection, one would ideally also discuss here citations from such scriptures as the *Poheti* and *Uttara* sutras.[80]

N. 26–29) They Possess the Four Types of Fearlessnesses

Now, as for the four types of fearlessness....

Question: There is a single dharma known as "fearlessness." How is it that we here have four of them?

Response: It is because there are four matters in which there is an absence of doubt or fear that we therefore speak of four of them, as follows:[81]

First, as the Buddha told the bhikshus, "I myself here utter these truthful words: 'I am a man possessed of all-knowledge.' If anyone here, whether he be a *śramaṇa*, brahmin, deva, Māra, Brahmā, or other person possessed of worldly knowledge were to challenge this statement in a manner consistent with Dharma, claiming that I do not indeed possess a direct knowledge of this Dharma, I would not then experience in this challenge even the slightest sign of fearfulness, and it is because of not experiencing any such sign that I have become established in security and fearlessness in this regard." This is the first type of fearlessness. It is a result of exhaustively knowing all dharmas in accordance with reality.

As for the second type of fearlessness, the Buddha said, "I myself here utter these truthful words: 'I have brought all of the contaminants to an end.' If any *śramaṇa*, brahmin, deva, Māra, or Brahmā were to claim that these contaminants have not indeed been brought to an end,

I would not then experience in this challenge even the slightest sign of fearfulness.[82] It is because of not experiencing any such sign that I have become established in security and fearlessness in this regard." This is the second type of fearlessness. It is a result of having thoroughly cut off all afflictions and having also cut off the habitual propensities associated with past afflictions.

As for the third [type of fearlessness], [the Buddha said], "I have proclaimed which dharmas constitute obstacles to realization of the path. If anyone herein, whether he be a *śramaṇa*, brahmin, deva, Māra, Brahmā, or other person possessed of worldly knowledge were to challenge this statement in a manner consistent with Dharma, claiming that, even though one might avail oneself of these dharmas, they would not be able to cause an obstacle to the path, I would not then experience in this challenge even the slightest sign of fearfulness. It is because of not experiencing any such sign that I have become established in security and fearlessness in this regard." This is the third type of the fearlessness. It is a result of having thoroughly known those dharmas that constitute obstacles to the achievement of liberation.

As for the fourth [type of fearlessness, the Buddha said], "Whoever practices the path I have proclaimed, practicing it in accordance with the way I have explained the Dharma, will succeed in reaching the end of suffering. If any *śramaṇa*, brahmin, deva, Māra, Brahmā, or other person possessed of worldly knowledge were to challenge this statement in a manner accordant with Dharma, claiming that, although one might practice a dharma such as this in a manner consistent with the way it has been explained, one would be unable to reach the path that brings about the end of suffering, I would not then experience in this challenge even the slightest sign of fearfulness. It is because of not experiencing any such sign that I have become established in security and fearlessness in this regard." This is the fourth type of fearlessness. It is a result of thoroughly knowing the path leading to the extinguishing of suffering.

All four of these types of fearlessness are referred to as "fearlessnesses" because they all involve leaving behind such characteristic signs as fearfulness, terror, or horripilation. They are also termed "fearlessnesses" because they are able to maintain within the Great Assembly an awe-inspiring power of virtue extraordinary in its excellence. They are also called "fearlessnesses" because they so well know how to respond to all sorts of questions. Here, one should extensively discuss citations from *The Sutra on the Convocation of the Devas*.[83]

Question: If the Buddhas are indeed possessed of all-knowledge, then they should be fearless in relation to all dharmas. Why is it then that we speak only of these four types [of fearlessness]?

Response: These serve to raise the major essential topics in order to introduce the most important instances. All other instances are similar to these.

O. 30–39) They Possess the Ten Powers

As for the ten powers of the Buddha, "power" refers to the inexhaustible energetic strength that assists them and makes them invulnerable to interference by anyone. Although there are ten designations in this regard, in truth, this involves a single type of knowledge that, because it takes ten different circumstances as objective conditions, [these ten exemplary manifestations] are known as "the ten powers."

Because the knowledge of the Buddha takes all things as its objective conditions, it should be that there are countless powers. But it is because these ten powers are adequate to bring about the liberation of beings that we only speak of "the ten powers." Through merely introducing these ten powers, one can then know the others by inference.

1. The First Power

The first power is [the Buddha's] definite and completely penetrating knowledge with respect to all dharmas of what does and does not constitute the cause. This is the first power. [This was the basis for, as cited earlier], the Buddha's having said [in reference to the *brahmacārin* named Patikaputra], "If this crazy person does not relinquish these claims, does not relinquish these perverse views, and does not relinquish these thoughts, then, as for his being able to arrive here in the presence of the Buddha—this is an utter impossibility."

[This is also the basis for] the Buddha's having said to Ānanda:

> "It is utterly impossible that two buddhas might arise in the world at the same time. However, it is indeed possible for a single buddha to come forth into the world."[84] This was said solely with respect to the circumstance of a single buddha emerging in a single world. In truth, in all of the countless and limitless worlds throughout the ten directions, there are countless hundreds of thousands of myriads of *koṭis* of buddhas simultaneously emerging throughout those worlds.
>
> Additionally, the sutras state: "It is impossible that bad physical, verbal, and mental karmic actions might have excellent and desirable results. However, it is indeed possible that good physical, verbal, and mental karmic actions may have excellent and desirable results."[85]

Here one should extensively discuss related scriptural citations from among the five categorical repositories of Dharma.

2. The Second Power

The second power is [the Buddha's] knowing in accordance with reality and with distinguishing clarity the place, the circumstances, and the karmic retributions associated with all past, future, and present karmic deeds along with all the dharmas that are involved in experiencing [those retributions].

If the Buddha wishes to know with regard to any being their past karmic deeds and their past karmic retributions, he is able to immediately know them. So too, he is immediately able to know:

With respect to past karmic deeds, their retribution in the present;
With respect to past karmic deeds, their retribution in the future;
With respect to past karmic deeds, their retribution in the past;
With respect to past karmic deeds, their retribution in both the past and the future;
With respect to past karmic deeds, their retribution in both the past and the present;
With respect to past karmic deeds, their retribution in both the future and the present;
With respect to past karmic deeds, their retribution in the past, the future, and the present;
With respect to present karmic deeds, their retribution in the present;
With respect to present karmic deeds, their retribution in the future;
With respect to present karmic deeds, their retribution in both the present and the future;
And with respect to future karmic deeds, their retribution in the future.

There are all manner of such distinctions regarding the dharmas involved in undergoing karmic retributions. There are four dharmas categorizing such karmic retributions, namely:

Undergoing blissful experiences in the present followed by undergoing suffering in future lifetimes;
Undergoing suffering in the present followed by undergoing blissful experiences in future lifetimes;
Undergoing blissful experiences in the present followed by blissful experiences in the future;
And undergoing suffering in the present followed by undergoing suffering in the future as well.[86]

As regards [the Buddha's knowing] "the place," this refers to his knowing for any karmic deed the time and place [of its occurrence] as well as the precise place in which this retribution will be undergone.

As regards [the Buddha's] knowing "the circumstances," this refers to knowing the corresponding causes and conditions, knowing the three corresponding types of bad karmic roots, knowing whether the deed was primarily performed by oneself, or knowing whether the deed occurred for the most part through the instigation of someone else. The Buddha entirely knows all such causes and conditions associated with good and bad karmic deeds.

As regards [the Buddha's knowing] "the karmic retributions," he knows that all karmic deeds have their corresponding karmic retributions. For instance, good karmic deeds may result in being reborn in a good place or in attaining nirvāṇa, whereas bad karmic deeds may result in being reborn in any of the wretched destinies.

The Buddha knows entirely with respect to all these karmic deeds their roots, their branches, their associated causes and conditions, and whether they were done at one's own behest or at the behest of others. It is because this power of knowledge does not diminish that it is referred to as a "power."

3. The Third Power

The third power is the Buddha's knowing in accordance with reality the *dhyānas,* the meditative concentrations, the liberations, and the samādhis, together with their corresponding marks of defilement and purity.

"Dhyānas" refers to the four *dhyānas.* "Meditative concentrations" refers to the four formless-realm meditative concentrations, the four immeasurable minds, and other such states, all of which are referred to as "meditative concentrations. "Liberations" refers to the eight liberations. As for "samādhis" all of the other meditative concentrations aside from the *dhyānas* and the liberations are referred to as "samādhis."

There are others who claim that the three gates to liberation, meditative concentrations still characterized by initial ideation (*vitarka*) and discursive thought (*vicāra*), meditative concentrations characterized by the absence of initial ideation and the presence of discursive thought, and meditative concentrations devoid of both initial ideation and discursive thought—these may all be referred to as "samādhis."

There are yet others who claim that "meditative concentrations" are relatively minor [meditative states] whereas "samādhis" are relatively major. Therefore, one may refer to all meditative concentrations realized by any buddha or bodhisattva as constituting a "samādhi."

All four of these constituent categories are subsumed within all explanations of *"dhyāna pāramitā."*

As for "defilement," this refers to [meditative states characterized by] the experience of delectably pleasurable (*āsvādana*) sensations whereas "purity" refers here to not indulging delectably pleasurable sensations.

Then again, "defilement" may refer to any meditative concentration still characterized by the contaminants (*āsrava*) whereas "purity" may refer to any meditative concentration characterized by the absence of the contaminants.

As for the distinctions among the samādhis, liberations, and so forth, [the Buddha] knows with distinguishing clarity these sorts of *dhyāna* meditation states.

4. The Fourth Power

The fourth power is [the Buddha's] knowing in accordance with reality the relative superiority or inferiority of the faculties of other beings and other personages.

"Other beings" refers to common persons. "Other personages" refers here to the stream enterer and the other classes of worthies and *āryas*. There may be others who interpret "beings" as a reference not only to common persons, but also even to those practitioners still involved in the learning stages, this because all of these have still not succeeded in putting an end to all of the contaminants. For them, "other personages" is a reference reserved for arhats and such, this because they have utterly ended all afflictions.

Yet others point out that both "beings" and "other personages" are but a single category and it is only the designations themselves that differ.

As for their "faculties," in this context they refer to faith, vigor, mindfulness, concentration, and wisdom and *not* to the sense faculties such as the eye and so forth [as the word might otherwise signify].

"Superior," as it applies to these faculties, refers to faculties that are fiercely sharp and which have the capacity to enable the attainment of enlightenment. "Inferior," on the other hand, refers to [faculties] that are dim, dull, and inadequate to enable one to take up [the practice of] the path.

The Buddha knows the relative superiority and inferiority of these two types of faculties and knows these matters in accordance with reality and in a manner free of any sort of error.

5. The Fifth Power

The fifth power is [the Buddha's] knowing in accordance with reality that in which the minds of other beings and other personages delight. "That in which they delight" refers to whatever endeavors they esteem and are inclined to engage in. For instance, there are those people who esteem wealth and worldly pleasures, whereas there are others who deeply esteem karmic merit and the practice of good dharmas. The Buddha knows all of these matters in accordance with reality.

6. The Sixth Power

The sixth power is the Buddha's knowing in accordance with reality the different types of natures of beings in the world as well as the countless [distinctions among those] natures. "Different types of natures" refers to the myriad variations in these natures. "Countless natures" is a reference to the countless distinctions in each and every one of these types of natures. As for the term "nature," it is because one's mind has always habitually practiced [particular sorts of endeavors] and has always delighted in practicing and cultivating them throughout one's past lives right up until the very present—it is for this reason that they therefore form the basis of one's "nature." The Buddha knows in accordance with reality these two categories of natures, the good and the bad.

7. The Seventh Power

The seventh power is [the Buddha's] knowing in accordance with reality the paths leading to all destinations. As for "the paths leading to all destinations," those are the means by which one may succeed in acquiring all meritorious qualities. These paths are referred to as "the paths leading to all destinations."

These include, for instance, the five-factor samādhi,[87] the five-fold awareness samādhi,[88] the eight-fold path of the Āryas, all dharmas subsumed by the path of the Āryas, or the four bases of psychic power, the latter as cited in a sutra that says: "If a bhikshu cultivates the four bases of psychic power, there is no benefit that he will not acquire."

There are others who claim that this may also refer to the four *dhyānas*, as cited in a sutra that says: "When a bhikshu gains the four *dhyānas*, his mind comes to abide with stability and purity in a single place in which he then succeeds in ridding himself of all afflictions and in destroying all obstacles. It then becomes well-regulated so that it becomes serviceable and no longer subject to movement or distraction."

8. The Eighth Power

The eighth power is the [Buddha's] immediate ability to know past-life matters whenever he chooses to direct his awareness to events from previous lives. If the Buddha wishes to recall any of the countless and limitless lifetimes of either himself or all other beings, he then knows all of these matters entirely. There are no instances in which he is unable to know some particular matter even beyond a number of kalpas equal to the number of sands in the Ganges River.

He knows where this person was born, what his name was, whether he was of noble or lowly caste, what he drank and ate, how he sustained his life, whether he experienced suffering or happiness, the types of endeavors in which he engaged, the karmic retributions that he underwent, what his mind engaged in, and from whence he originally came. He knows all such matters.

9. The Ninth Power

The ninth power is the [Buddha's] ability to see with the heavenly eye purified beyond the power of man's eyes the beings of the six destinies taking on bodies in accordance with their karmic deeds.

A *śrāvaka* disciple possessed of great powers uses the heavenly eye to see the lands contained within a small chiliocosm and also sees when the beings therein are born and when they die.

A lesser *pratyekabuddha* sees the lands of a thousand small chiliocosms and sees when the beings therein are born and when they die.

A *pratyekabuddha* possessed of middling powers sees the lands contained in a hundred myriads of small chiliocosms and sees when the beings therein are born and when they die.

A *pratyekabuddha* possessed of great powers sees the lands contained in a great trichiliocosm and sees the destinies to which they proceed when they die and are reborn.

The Buddhas, the Bhagavats, see a countless, boundless, and inconceivable number of worlds and also see when the beings therein are born and when they die.

10. The Tenth Power

As for the tenth power, it is the [Buddha's] ending of all contaminants, including the contaminant of sensual desire, the contaminant of [craving for] existence, and the contaminant of ignorance, these together with the utter ending of all afflictions or affliction-associated energetic propensities. This is the tenth power.

P. 40) They Have Achieved Unimpeded Liberation

As for unimpeded liberation, there are three types of liberations. The first is the liberation from the obstacles of the afflictions. The second is the liberation from the obstacles to meditative concentration. The third is the liberation from the obstacles to [the knowledge of] all dharmas. Among these, an arhat who has achieved liberation through wisdom gains liberation from the obstacles of the afflictions. Both the doubly-liberated arhat and the *pratyekabuddha* succeed in achieving both the liberation from the obstacles of the afflictions and the liberation from the obstacles to the *dhyāna* concentrations.

It is only the Buddhas who have completely achieved all three of these liberations, namely liberation from the obstacles of the afflictions, liberation from the obstacles to acquisition of the *dhyāna* concentrations, and the liberation from the obstacles to [the knowledge of] all dharmas. It is because he brings together all three of the liberations that the Buddha is designated as having achieved unimpeded liberation. This [unimpeded liberation] always accompanies the mind all the way up to the point of entry into the nirvāṇa without residue.

Q. Summary Discussion of the Dharmas Exclusive to the Buddha

These forty dharmas exclusive to the Buddhas provide a general introduction to an entryway into the dharmas of the Buddha. They are discussed here because this allows beings to thereby acquire an understanding of them. However, those [exclusive dharmas] that remain undiscussed herein are innumerable and boundless. Specifically, these include the following:

1) [The Buddha] never departs from wisdom.
2) He never errs in knowing the right time.
3) He has extinguished all habitual karmic propensities.
4) He has gained the meditative concentration *pāramitā.*
5) All of his meritorious qualities are possessed of extraordinary supremacy.
6) He has perfected the *pāramitā* of always according in his actions with what is appropriate to the circumstances.
7) No one is able to view the very top of [the light rays radiating from] the crown of his head.
8) No one is his equal.
9) No one is able to surpass him.
10) He is superior to all beings in the world.
11) His attainment of the path is not learned from anyone else.
12) He never turns away from the Dharma.
13) Whoever else might claim to be a buddha is forever unable to enter the presence of the Buddha.
14) He has perfected the dharma of never retreating.
15) He has acquired the great compassion.
16) He has acquired the great kindness.
17) He is the foremost among all whose teachings one may accept in faith.

18) He is the foremost among those [who are worthy of] fame and offerings.
19) No guru who is a contemporary of the Buddha is equal to the Buddha.
20) No guru gains a community of disciples equal to that of the Buddha.
21) The supreme refinement of his appearance causes all who see him to be delighted.
22) Whoever is sent forth as an emissary of a Buddha cannot be harmed by anyone.
23) No one is able to injure anyone whom the Buddha has set out to liberate.
24) From the very moment he first brings forth a thought, he is able to sever all thought-related fetters.
25) He never misses the right time [to provide appropriate instruction to] beings who are capable of achieving liberation.
26) In the sixteenth [mind-moment involved in the acquisition of] wisdom, a buddha attains *anuttarasamyaksaṃbodhi.*
27) He is the foremost among the world's fields of merit.
28) He emanates measureless radiant light.
29) His actions differ from those of anyone else.
30) He possesses the [physical] marks that are associated with a hundred-fold generation of merit.[89]
31) He has measureless and boundless roots of goodness.
32) When he enters the womb—
33) When he is born—
34) When he achieves buddhahood—
35) When he turns the wheel of the Dharma—
36) When he relinquishes the possibility of the long lifespan—
37) And when he enters nirvāṇa—[on all these occasions], he is able to cause all the worlds throughout the great trichiliocosm to shake.
38) [On all of the above occasions], he sets quaking the countless palaces of the *māras*, causing them to lose their awesome power and be struck with terror.
39) [When he achieves buddhahood], the world-protecting heavenly kings, Śakra, ruler of the devas, the Yāma Heaven King, the Tuṣita Heaven King, the Nirmāṇarati Heaven King, the Paranirmita Vaśavartin Heaven King, the Brahma Heaven King, the devas of the Pure Abodes, and the other devas—they all simultaneously assemble and request the turning of the Dharma wheel.
40) The Buddha's body is as solid as the body of Nārāyaṇa.[90]

41) When the moral precepts have not yet been formulated, he is the one who first formulates the moral precepts.
42) Whenever he takes up any endeavor, his power in accomplishing this is superior to that of any man.
43) During the entire time the Bodhisattva is residing in his mother's womb, she loses all thoughts of defiling attachment for men.
44) His power is such that he is able to bring about the rescue and liberation of all beings.

There are measurelessly and innumerably many dharmas such as these that are exclusive to the Buddha. Because it would interfere with the explanation of other matters, there is no need to present an extensive discussion of them here. Although these dharmas as found in the Dharma of the Śrāvaka Disciples do resemble dharmas of the Buddha, due to dissimilarities in the degree of superiority or inferiority, there are distinct differences [in how they are described].

Moreover, to summarize, all of the dharmas of the Buddhas are measureless, limitless, inconceivable, of the foremost degree of rarity, and such that no other being is able to have them in common [with any buddha]. Even if all the countless beings in the worlds of all the great trichiliocosms throughout the ten directions possessed wisdom comparable to the king of the Great Brahma Heaven, comparable to a great *pratyekabuddha,* or comparable to Śāriputra, and one were somehow able to collect all this wisdom together in a single person—even if that one person then wished to approach the most minutely small fraction of these forty dharmas exclusive to the Buddhas—this would still be an utter impossibility. He could not even measure up to but one part in a hundred thousand myriads of *koṭis* of parts of just a single one of those dharmas.

The Buddhas possess the power of just such an immeasurable and limitless number of meritorious qualities. And why is this so? It is because they have securely established themselves in the four bases of meritorious qualities for a countless number of great kalpas during which they have deeply practiced the six *pāramitās* and have become well able to completely equip themselves with all dharmas practiced by the bodhisattva. Because [these dharmas] are not held in common with any other beings, so too, the fruits resulting [from their practice] are not held in common with any beings, either.

The End of Chapter Twenty-Three

Ch. 24: Verses Offered in Praise

V. Chapter 24: Verses Offered in Praise

A. The Importance of Praises to Mindfulness-of-the-Buddha Practice

Now that, in this way, we have reached the end of this explanation of the forty dharmas exclusive to the Buddhas, one should take the aspects emblematic of these forty exclusive dharmas and use them in one's own practice of mindfulness of the Buddha. One should also use verses to praise the Buddha, doing so as if one were standing directly before him, speaking to him. If one proceeds in this manner, then one may succeed in entering the mindfulness-of-the-Buddha samādhi. Accordingly, there are verses, as follows:

B. The Praise Verses

1. Verses in Praise of the Forty Dharmas Exclusive to the Buddhas

Oh, greatly vigorous lord of the Āryas—
Now, in the presence of the Buddha,
I shall praise with reverential mind
these forty dharmas possessed only [by buddhas].[91]

As for his supernatural powers and travel through flight,
their power when enacted is utterly limitless.
Among the psychic powers of the other *āryas*,
there are none at all that can equal these.

Among the *śrāvaka* disciples, he holds sway with sovereign mastery,
using his measureless knowledge of others' thoughts.
Thus he is well able to train their thoughts
by according with their minds as he appropriately responds to them.

His mindfulness is as expansive as the great ocean
while also being tranquil and calmly secure.
In all the world, there is no dharma
able to cause him to become perturbed.

The jewel of the vajra samādhi
that is praised by all buddhas—
he has acquired it and it resides within in his heart
just as the Worthies embrace the straightforward mind.

He thoroughly knows the unfixed dharmas
and the matters associated with the four formless absorptions
that are so subtle they are difficult to distinguish.
He exhaustively knows them all without exception.

Regarding whether a being has already died in the past,
dies now in the present, or will die at some point later in the future,
it is solely the Bhagavat, and he alone,
whose wisdom is able to fully comprehend such things.

He knows well all matters related
to the formless dharmas unassociated with the mind
that everyone else throughout all worlds
remains entirely unable to know.

The Bhagavat's great awesome powers,
his measureless meritorious qualities,
and his boundless wisdom
are all unmatched by anyone at all.

In the four types of responses to questions,
he is so preeminent that he has no peer.
As for all the challenging questions that beings present,
he replies to them all with utter ease.

If anywhere in any world
there is someone wishing to harm the Buddha,
this circumstance never comes to pass,
for he has gained the dharma by which he cannot be slain.

If at any point throughout the three periods of time
there is anything that he says,
those words are definitely not set forth in vain,
but rather always bring great fruits as a result.

Of all the dharmas that he proclaims,
none of them are not especially rare.
He is never in error as regards their significance,
how much the less might he ever err in words and phrases.

For the three types of *ārya* disciples
that differ as either superior, middling, or inferior,
and include the eight classes in four pairs,[92] and the others,
he is the foremost great spiritual guide.

In actions of body, speech, and mind, and in sustaining his life,
he is ultimately and always pure
and hence, in all of these,
he never again needs to act in a guarded way.

When he himself proclaims his possession of all-knowledge,
his mind remains utterly free of any doubt or fear
such that he might think, "If someone comes and challenges me,
I fear there may be something I do not know."

When declaring his characteristic of having ended the contaminants,
thus reaching the utmost elimination of the contaminants,
his mind remains utterly free of any doubt or fear
that there might be residual contaminants that are not yet ended.

When proclaiming his knowledge of the obstructive dharmas,
he has no doubt at the prospect of being challenged
that, though one might indulge in these dharmas,
they might not actually then constitute an obstacle.

As for the eight-fold path of the Āryas that he has proclaimed,
his mind is free of any doubt or fear
that someone might rightly claim of this eight-fold path
that it is unable to lead one to reach liberation.

He knows in accordance with reality that this is a cause,
this is its result, and this other factor does not constitute [a cause].
It is for these reasons that he is said to be omniscient
and that his fame spreads immeasurably far.

All actions carried out throughout the three periods of time,
the fixed retribution associated with these actions,
and their unfixed karmic results—
He thoroughly knows all of these different matters.

As for all coarse, subtle, deep, and shallow phenomena
within all of the *dhyāna* absorptions and samādhis,
he is able to entirely know them all.
In the realm of *dhyāna* absorptions, no one is his equal.

He first knows with regard to the faculties of beings,
their distinctions as either superior, middling, or inferior,
knows what they delight in, and knows their individual natures,
whereupon, adapting to what is fitting, he teaches them the Dharma.

He cultivated the path and gained its benefits
while also teaching and guiding others.
It is in this manner that the community of disciples
gains the wholesome benefit that accords with reality.

His knowledge of past lives is measurelessly vast
and the vision of his heavenly eye has no bounds.
Among all humans and devas,
no one is able to know their limits.

He abides in the vajra samādhi,
having extinguished the afflictions and karmic propensities,
and also knows the utter ending of the human contaminants.
Hence this is known as the power of having ended the contaminants.

The obstacle of afflictions, the obstacles to *dhyāna* absorptions,
and the obstacles to the knowledge of all dharmas—
he has gained liberation from all three obstacles
and hence is known as one who has gained unimpeded liberation.

The forty exclusive dharmas
have measureless meritorious qualities
of which no one could present an expansive explanation.
I have hereby now concluded this general explanation.

Even if, for an entire kalpa, the Bhagavat
spoke in praise of these dharmas of the Buddhas,
he would still be unable to completely describe them.
How much the less might I do so in the absence of such wisdom.

2. Verses Praising the Four Bases of Meritorious Qualities

The shade of the Bhagavat's great kindness
has been thoroughly gathered together through countless deeds.
It is because of the four bases of meritorious qualities
that he has gained the Buddha's measureless Dharma.

As for these four supreme bases of meritorious qualities
of which the Bhagavat has spoken with praise—
I shall now return to these
in setting forth praises of the Tathāgata.

He is completely endowed with the thirty-two marks,
each mark of which requires a hundred-fold generation of merit.
As for the eighty marvelous secondary characteristics,
who residing in the three realms could possibly possess them?

Were one to multiply by a hundred all the karmic rewards
produced by the merit created by all the beings
residing within a great trichiliocosm,
each of the marks has just such a quantity of merit [as its cause].

It would require just such a quantity of merit
as well as its associated karmic rewards,
multiplied yet another hundred times
to produce a buddha's mid-brow white hair mark.

It would require for each and every one of thirty marks
all of their corresponding merit and karmic rewards,
multiplied yet again a thousand more times,
to produce the fleshy *uṣṇīṣa* sign atop a buddha's crown.

The meritorious qualities of the Bhagavat
are such that they could never be measured.
Any attempt to do so would be like someone using a ruler
to measure the endless expanse of empty space.

From the moment he brought forth the great resolve
for the sake of bringing about the liberation of all beings,
he persevered for countless kalpas with solid resolve.
It was because of this that he then achieved buddhahood.

Intensely diligent in his zeal to achieve the fulfillment
of such a magnanimous vow,
throughout an immeasurably great number of kalpas,
he has cultivated all the difficult ascetic practices.

Just as with all buddhas of the ancient past
who taught these four bases of meritorious qualities,
only after countless kalpas were they then perfected
so that now he has succeeded in securely abiding within them.

a. Verses Praising the Truth Basis of Meritorious Qualities

Their foundation lies in preservation of the actual truth,
for which he relinquished even his own body and loved ones,
his riches, treasures, and the happiness associated with wealth.
It is through this that he achieved its complete fulfillment.

Throughout measurelessly many kalpas,
in every instance, he has first thoroughly contemplated
the dharmas that are seen, heard, sensed, and known,[93]
and then, afterward, has explained them for the sake of others.

Where others had not observed (some aspect of Dharma) and such,
as well as in situations where they were beset by doubts,
he was then able to explain these matters in accordance with reality.
Those whom he benefited in this way were measurelessly many.

He would not discuss the confidential matters of others.
Even if resented or ridiculed for this, he still refused to betray them.
His thoughts always dwelt in a state of stable wisdom
as he adapted his teachings to lead others to peace and security.

As for the foremost and most genuinely sublime truth,
nirvāṇa is truly supreme,
for all else, in every case, is false.
The Bhagavat has achieved[94] its complete fulfillment.

b. Verses Praising the Relinquishment Basis of Meritorious Qualities

[He made gifts of] beverages, food, bedding, and such,
halls, buildings, marvelous residences, viewing terraces,
highly prized elephants, horses, and vehicles, and also
relinquished female companions of especially fine appearance.

[He gave away] gold, silver, pearls, jewels, and such,
villages, cities, and towns,

entire states, and exalted official positions,
and gave away [his dominion over] the four continents as well.

[He relinquished] cherished sons, beloved wives,
his limbs, his head, and his eyes,
and made gifts by slicing off his flesh, removing bones and marrow,
or even giving away his entire body.

Doing so out of pity for beings,
he gave them all, having none that he continued to cherish.
He did so aspiring to go beyond *saṃsāra*
and not out of some quest to secure his own bliss.

All of the stars and constellations throughout empty space,
and all the grains of sand in this entire earth—
when the Tathāgata was still a bodhisattva,
the number of times he gave in such ways exceeded even these.

He never resorted to actions contrary to Dharma
as he sought out wealth to be used in giving.
He never engaged in giving unaccompanied by knowledge and
never engaged in giving that was invasive or distressing to others.

He never gave bad things as gifts
because he coveted some other fine thing [in return].
He never gave with an ingratiating deviousness
and never engaged in forceful giving because of coveting something.

He never gave with a hate-filled or doubting mind,
never did so with perverse intent or with derisive laughter,
never did so out of disgust or disbelief,
and never gave with the face turned away, or in other such ways.

He had no discriminating mind [by which he judged],
"This one is worthy and that one is unworthy."
Because he only relied on the mind of compassion,
it was with equal regard for everyone that he practiced giving.

He did not slight other beings,
considering them to not qualify as fields of merit.
On seeing *āryas,* his mind was reverential.
On seeing those who have broken the precepts, he felt pity for them.

He did not elevate himself above others,
treat others as mere inferiors,
engage in giving for the sake of praise,
give in expectation of rewards, or give in other such ways.

He never gave with regrets or with worry-filled misgivings
and never gave with thoughts of disdain or disrespect.

He never gave with a mind affected by irritability or hostility
and never gave simply as a protocol-dictated formality.

He never gave with a disrespectful mind,
never gave by simply tossing the gift on the ground,
never gave deliberately seeking to cause distress,
and never gave out of a jealousy-driven struggle for supremacy.

He would never tease a supplicant,
never failed to present a gift with his own hands,
did not slight the recipient with a merely paltry gift,
and did not give excessively in order to enhance his own esteem.

His giving was never motivated by intentions associated with
either the Śrāvaka Disciple Vehicle or the Pratyekabuddha Vehicle.
His giving was never limited to concern for only a single lifetime
and he never engaged in giving done at the wrong time.

For countless kalpas, the Bhagavat
practiced every form of rare giving,
always doing so for the sake of the unsurpassable path
and not merely in order to seek his own happiness.

Throughout the duration of all buddhas' Dharma,
he became a monastic, practiced renunciation,
cultivated the Dharma of all buddhas,
and proclaimed the Dharma for the sake of all humans and devas.

He taught just such a dharma of giving as this
that is supreme among all types of giving,
just as, among all the stars and the moon,
it is the light of the sun that is supreme.

Such supremacy in the relinquishment basis [of meritorious qualities]
surpasses that of any deva or human,
just as it is the Bhagavat
who is superior to everyone in the world.

He was therefore able to perfect
such supreme practice of the relinquishment basis.
His fame shall endure for countless kalpas,
flowing on and spreading ceaselessly.

c. Verses Praising the Quiescence Basis of Meritorious Qualities

For countless kalpas, the Bhagavat
preserved and upheld the precepts of moral purity
and opened the gates of the *dhyāna* absorptions
for the sake of acquiring the deep quiescence basis.

He began by abandoning five characteristics[95]
and later practiced the eight liberations.
He entered and purified the three samādhis,
and also dwelt in the three liberations.

The Bhagavat well distinguishes
the sixty-five kinds of *dhyānas*.
There is no *dhyāna* whatsoever
that he has not formerly produced.

Even when abiding in these meditative absorptions,
he did not indulge in their delectably pleasurable states.
Due to the various meditative absorptions,
the Bhagavat gained three types of spiritual superknowledges.

He used these in the liberation of beings
and so became supreme in all things.
For countless kalpas, with a mind of equal regard,
the Bhagavat widely spread his kindly transformative teaching.

An *asaṃkhyeya* of beings
was thereby caused to abide in the Brahma World Heavens
because he was able to use skillful means
in thoroughly teaching the *dhyāna* absorptions.

While still a bodhisattva, the Bhagavat
for incalculably many lifetimes, always
remained free of any entanglement in the affliction of covetousness.
Thus he was able to come and go in the world.

Of those who succeeded in encountering him in the past,
countless such beings thereby achieved rebirth in the heavens.
As for that quiescence that
all bodhisattvas of the past were able to practice,

when still a bodhisattva, the Bhagavat
also practiced, doing so in a manner no different from theirs.
Thus, as regards the realization of quiescence,
that supreme basis [of meritorious qualities], it was entirely fulfilled.

d. Verses Praising the Wisdom Basis of Meritorious Qualities

All those forms of wisdom
possessed by the Bhagavat while he was still a bodhisattva—
He relied on such wisdom in his quest for bodhi
so that, as a karmic result, he has now developed this wisdom.

Just as people rely on the earth for the production
of all the food that it supplies,
[so, too], as in life after life, the Bhagavat
relinquished the ten courses of dark and bad actions

and always practiced the path of the ten good actions,
these [deeds] were all due to the power of wisdom.[96]

He renounced the five desires and the five hindrances
and thus acquired all the various *dhyāna* absorptions.
He accomplished this for the number of lifetimes in countless kalpas
and did not acquire this from others.
This is excellent indeed, O Great Honored One of the Āryas.
All of this was due to the power of wisdom.

It is because of the Bhagavat that beings,
countless in number, have taken rebirth in the six heavens.
So too has he enabled them to reach the Brahma World.
All of this was due to the power of wisdom.

Throughout the course of his births and deaths, the Bhagavat,
even when confused and perturbed by sufferings and pleasures,
never lost the resolve to attain bodhi.
All of this was due to the power of wisdom.

Throughout the course of *saṃsāra,* the Bhagavat
did not delight [in worldly existence] and yet still always remained.
He delighted in nirvāṇa, yet did not seize on its [final] realization.
All of this was due to the power of wisdom.

When sitting peacefully there in the *bodhimaṇḍa,*
he overcame Māra and his armies
and proceeded to liberate all the classes of beings.
All of this was due to the power of wisdom.

When he originally strove in quest of bodhi,
he accumulated countless provisions for the path.
If merely hearing of them causes one to be confused and perturbed,
how much the less might one be able to take on their practice.
That the Bhagavat was able to patiently endure such things
was in every case due to the power of wisdom.

That, in lifetime after lifetime, he was able to naturally know
the classic texts as well as all the arts and skills
while also being able to teach them to others
was in every case due to the power of wisdom.

He drew close to countless buddhas
and from them all drank the sweet-dew nectar of their teachings,
He consulted them and inquired about the many different topics
and then also pursued additional distinguishing [clarifications].

He was never the least bit miserly
with the wisdom of the sutras' Dharma,

but rather offered it even to servants, youths, and menials,
allowing them to freely receive his fine explanations.
Because of this, [the fame of] the Bhagavat's
supreme wisdom basis [of meritorious qualities] spreads on afar.

Throughout his former lifetimes, as the Bhagavat
pursued his quest for the realization of bodhi,
he practiced the great kindness and compassion
toward all beings.

Relying on the foremost wisdom,
he always marshalled his great strength
to take up and do all the countless kinds
of rare and difficult endeavors.

3. Concluding Praise Verses

In all of the many worlds,
he exhaustively contributed all his efforts for countless kalpas.
One could never come to the end of them through verbal description,
nor could one even reach it through mathematical calculation.

All of his endeavors of such sorts
surpass those done by any human or deva.
Even in all the many worlds,
there is nothing comparable to his extraordinary marvels.

The fruits reaped through such great deeds
reach complete fulfillment in the realization of all-knowledge.
He is the king of those able to destroy *saṃsāra*
and dwells securely in the place of the Dharma king.

The End of Chapter Twenty-Four

Ch. 25: Teachings to Aid the Mindfulness-of-the-Buddha Samādhi

VI. Chapter 25: Teachings Aiding Mindfulness-of-the Buddha Samādhi

A. Initial Instructions on the Mindfulness-of-the Buddha Samādhi

The bodhisattva should rely on these
forty exclusive dharmas
in his mindfulness of the Buddhas' Dharma body,
for the Buddhas are not their form bodies.

These [preceding] verses have sequentially and summarily explained six categories of meanings associated with the forty exclusive dharmas.[97] In doing so, the practitioner therefore first takes up the mindfulness of the Buddha's form body and then takes up the mindfulness of the Buddha's Dharma body.

Why is this the case? The bodhisattva who has only recently brought forth the resolve [to attain buddhahood] should first take up the practice of mindfulness of the Buddha in reliance on the thirty-two marks and eighty secondary characteristics [of the Buddha's form body], doing so in the manner described earlier.

Then, as one's practice progressively penetrates more deeply, one will develop a middling degree of strength in that practice. One should then rely on the Dharma body in his mindfulness of the Buddha.

Then, as one's mind progressively penetrates yet more deeply, one will then achieve a supreme degree of power in the development of this practice. At that point, one should then take up mindfulness of the Buddha in accordance with the true character of [all dharmas][98] and remain free of any sort of attachment in doing so.

One must not become deeply attached to the form body.[99]
One also refrains from becoming attached to the Dharma body.
One should thoroughly realize that all dharmas
are as eternally quiescent as empty space.

As this bodhisattva develops a superior degree of power [in this practice], he refrains from developing a deep attachment to the Buddha on the basis of either the form body or the Dharma body. Why not? Through one's resolute belief in the dharma of emptiness, one understands that all dharmas are like empty space.

Empty space is defined by the absence of obstruction. The causal circumstances associated with obstruction include phenomena like

Mount Sumeru, Yugaṃdhara Mountain, the rest of the ten jeweled mountains, the Iron Ring Mountains, Black Mountain, Stone Mountain, and the others. There are all sorts of other such causal bases for the existence of obstructions.

Why is this [a point at issue]? Because this person has still not yet gained the heavenly eye, if he brings to mind buddhas abiding in the worlds off in the other directions, the various mountains will block them from his view. Consequently, The bodhisattva who has only recently brought forth the resolve [to attain buddhahood] should use the sublime characteristics described by the ten names as bases for his mindfulness of the Buddha. This is as described in these lines:

> The bodhisattva who has only recently brought forth the resolve
> uses the sublime features described by the ten names
> in practicing mindfulness of the Buddhas that is free of fault,
> seeing them just as if they were images in a mirror.

As for "the sublime features described in the ten names," those ten names are:

Tathāgata;[100]
Worthy of Offerings;
The Right and Universally Enlightened One;
Perfect in the Clear Knowledges and Conduct;
Well Gone One;
Knower of the Worlds;
Unsurpassable Trainer of Those to Be Tamed;
Teacher of Devas and Humans;
Buddha;
Bhagavat.

As for "free of fault," the phenomena that one contemplates are beheld as empty and like space itself. Thus [one's contemplation] is free of any fault with regard to the Dharma. And how is this so? It is because all dharmas, from their very origin on forward to the present, have been unproduced and quiescent. Just as this is true [with respect to these dharmas], so too is this also true of all other dharmas.

By taking these names as the object [of his contemplation], this person develops his practice of the dharma of *dhyāna* meditation. Having done so, he is then able to take these characteristic signs themselves as the object of his contemplation.

At this time, this person then immediately acquires these signs in his practice of the dharma of *dhyāna* meditation and experiences what is referred to as the direct personal experience of an especially extraordinary bliss. One should realize that when this occurs, one has acquired the *pratyutpanna* samādhi. Because of developing this samādhi, one is then able to see the Buddhas.

As for "as if they were images in a mirror," once the bodhisattva has developed this samādhi, it is as if one is seeing one's own face in a clean, brightly-lit mirror or like seeing the image of one's own body in a clear, still pool of water.

Initially, whichever buddha one first brings to mind, it is that very image that one sees. After one has seen this image, if one wishes to see buddhas in other regions, then, in accordance with whichever region one brings to mind, one obtains an unimpeded vision of those very buddhas. Hence, regarding this person:

> Although he does not yet possess the spiritual superknowledges
> by which he could fly to visit them,
> he is nonetheless able to see those buddhas
> and has an unimpeded ability to listen to their Dharma.

For this bodhisattva who has only recently brought forth the resolve [to attain buddhahood], neither Mount Sumeru nor any other mountain can present an obstacle and, even though he has not yet acquired any of the spiritual superknowledges, the heavenly eye, or the heavenly ear, and even though he has not yet developed the ability to fly from this country to that country, through the power of this samādhi, even while still abiding in this country, he is able to see the Buddhas, the Bhagavats, abiding in the other regions and is able to hear the Dharma as they are speaking it. Through always cultivating this samādhi, he becomes able to see all of the buddhas throughout the ten directions just as they really are.

B. Four Dharmas Capable of Bringing Forth This Samādhi

Question: Through which dharmas is one able to bring forth this meditative absorption and how can one acquire it?

Response:

> One draws close to the good spiritual guide,
> brings forth non-retreating vigor,
> develops extremely solid and durable wisdom,
> and develops the power of unshakeable faith.

It is through utilizing these four dharmas that one is able to bring forth this samādhi.

As for "drawing close to the good spiritual guide," someone able to instruct a person in the acquisition of this samādhi qualifies here as "the good spiritual guide." One should bring forth reverential respect and assiduous diligence and, in drawing close [to the good spiritual guide], one must not allow any indolence, diminishment in motivation, or relinquishing of effort to take place. If one acts accordingly, one will then be able to hear the teaching of the deep meaning of this samādhi.

Sharp wisdom, wisdom characterized by penetrating comprehension, and undiminishing wisdom are what qualify as "solid and durable" [wisdom]. One's faculty of faith is deeply and firmly established, so much so that, no matter whether it be a *śramaṇa* or a brahmin or a celestial *māra* or Brahmā or anyone else in the world—none of them could cause it to quaver even slightly. This is what is meant by an unshakeable power of faith. It is these very four dharmas described here that are able to bring forth this samādhi.

C. Four More Dharmas Capable of Bringing Forth This Samādhi

Furthermore:

> With a sense of shame, dread of blame, cherishing reverence,
> and offerings to those who proclaim the Dharma
> presented as if they were given to the Bhagavats themselves,
> one thereby becomes able to bring forth this samādhi.

As for "with a sense of shame, dread of blame, and cherishing reverence," one brings forth a profound sense of shame and dread of blame in relation to those who teach the Dharma. With sincere reverence and affectionate delight, one makes offerings to them as if they were the Buddhas themselves. In this way, these four dharmas are able to produce this samādhi.

D. Four More Dharmas Capable of Bringing Forth This Samādhi

Another preliminary set of fourfold dharmas is as follows:

First, for a period of three months, one strives to refrain from sleeping and, with the exception of using the toilet and eating and drinking, one refrains from sitting down;

Second, for that period of three months, one avoids, even for the duration of a finger snap, indulgence in any thought seizing on the existence of a self;

Third, for that entire three months, one strives to always walk and never rest;

Fourth, for that entire three months, when also engaged in the giving of Dharma, one refrains from seeking offerings from others.

These are the four. There are four more such dharmas, as follows:

E. Four More Dharmas Capable of Bringing Forth This Samādhi

First, one becomes able to see the Buddhas;

Second, one reassures and encourages others to listen to the teaching of this samādhi;

Third, one is never envious or jealous of anyone who is putting the resolve to attain bodhi into practice;

Fourth, one is able to accumulate the dharmas of the bodhisattva path.

These are the four. There are four more such dharmas, as follows:

F. Four More Dharmas Capable of Bringing Forth This Samādhi

First, one makes buddha images that may also include painted images;

Second, one should carefully write out copies of the sutra that discusses this samādhi and then encourage others who have a resolute faith in it to study and recite it aloud once they have obtained it;[101]

Third, teach those of overweening pride[102] to abandon their overweening pride[103] and then influence them to pursue the attainment of *anuttarasamyaksaṃbodhi;*

Fourth, one should devote oneself to the protection and preservation of the right Dharma of all buddhas.

These are the four. There are four more such dharmas, as follows:

G. Four More Dharmas Capable of Bringing Forth This Samādhi

First, one avoids speaking;

Second, both lay and monastic practitioners are to refrain from dwelling together with others;

Third, one always anchors one's mind on the characteristic sign that has been chosen as the object of one's mental focus;[104]

Fourth, one delights in dwelling far apart from others, in a location that is vacant, serene, and silent.

These are the four. The first of the five-fold sets of associated dharmas is as follows:

H. Five More Dharmas Capable of Bringing Forth This Samādhi

First, abiding in the unproduced-dharmas patience (*anutpattika-dharma-kṣānti*), one renounces all conditioned dharmas, does not delight in any of the destinies of rebirth, refuses to accept any of the non-Buddhist dharmas, and remains so disgusted with all worldly desires that one does not even bring them to mind, how much the less might one draw physically close to them;

Second, even as one's mind always cultivates and practices countless dharmas, it remains in a state of one-pointed concentration;

One remains free of the obstacle of hatred toward any being and one's mind always accords with the practice of the four means of attraction;

Third, one becomes able to perfect kindness, compassion, sympathetic joy, and equanimity while also refraining from exposing others' transgressions;

Fourth, one becomes able to accumulate a multitude of dharmas proclaimed by the Buddha while also being able to carry them out in accordance with the way they were taught;

Fifth, one purifies one's physical, verbal, and mental actions as well as one's views.

These are the five. There are five more associated dharmas, as follows:

I. Five More Dharmas Capable of Bringing Forth This Samādhi

First, one delights in according with the practice of giving as praised in the sutras, doing so without miserly thoughts. One delights in speaking on profound dharmas, withholds nothing due to stinginess, and also remains able to dwell in those very dharmas oneself;

Second, one abides in patience, mental pliancy, and delight when abiding in close proximity to others and, if subjected to harsh speech, scolding and cursing, whippings, beatings, being tied up, or other such experiences, one simply attributes it to one's own karmic conditions and does not hate others for doing this;

Third, one always delights in listening to teachings that explain this samādhi, in reading and reciting them, in thoroughly understanding them, in explaining them for others, and in causing them to circulate and spread ever more widely even as one diligently practices and cultivates [this samādhi];

Fourth, one's mind remains free of any jealous feelings toward others, one refrains from elevating oneself and looking down on others, and one strives to rid oneself of the hindrance of drowsiness;

Fifth, one maintains a mind of pure faith in the Buddha Jewel, the Dharma Jewel, and the Sangha Jewel, offers up deeply sincere service to those of senior, middling, and lower station, always remembers and never forgets even the smallest kindnesses of others, and always abides in truthful speech.

These are the five. In addition, there are the following lines:

J. The Guidelines for Lay and Monastic Cultivation of This Samādhi

As for those samādhi dharmas
in which monastic bodhisattvas train,
householder bodhisattvas
should also know these dharmas.

1. Twenty Guidelines for Lay Cultivators of This Samādhi

If a householder bodhisattva wishes to cultivate this samādhi, [he should observe the following twenty guidelines]:

1) One should proceed with a mind of deep faith;
2) One should not seek any sort of karmic reward;
3) One should give up all personal and extra-personal things;
4) One should take refuge in the Three Jewels;
5) One should uphold the five moral precepts purely and in a manner free of any transgression or deficiency;
6) One should perfect the practice of the ten courses of good karmic action while also influencing others to abide in these dharmas;
7) One should cut off all sexual desire;
8) One should repudiate the five types of desire;
9) One should refrain from any feelings of jealousy toward others;
10) One should not nurture an affectionate attachment for either one's spouse or one's children;
11) One should always maintain an aspiration to leave the householder's life to become a monastic;
12) One should always take on and observe the layperson's precepts of abstinence;[105]
13) One's mind should delight in the opportunity to abide within the precincts of a temple;[106]
14) One should be well possessed of a sense of shame and a dread of blame;
15) One should bring forth thoughts of reverential respect toward bhikshus who are pure in upholding the moral precepts;
16) One should not act in a miserly way with the Dharma;
17) One should maintain a mind of deep affection and reverence toward those who teach the Dharma;
18) One should think of teachers of Dharma as if they were one's father, mother, or great teaching master;
19) One should respectfully present all manner of delightful gifts as offerings to the Dharma teaching masters;
20) One should feel gratitude for the kindnesses that have been bestowed upon one and one should repay those kindnesses accordingly.

If a householder bodhisattva abides in meritorious qualities such as these, he will then be able to learn this samādhi.

2. Sixty Guidelines for Monastic Cultivators of This Samādhi

As for [the guidelines appropriate to] a monastic bodhisattva's cultivation of dharmas pertaining to this samādhi, they are as follows:

1) One remains free of any defect as regards observance of the moral precepts;
2) One maintains uncorrupted observance of the moral precepts;
3) One maintains unsullied observance of the moral precepts;
4) One maintains pure observance of the moral precepts;
5) One maintains undiminished observance of the moral precepts;
6) One does not seize on the moral precepts themselves [as constituting the very essence of moral virtue];
7) One does not rely on the moral precepts [alone as the sole component of one's practice];
8) One realizes that the moral precepts cannot finally be apprehended at all [as inherently existent entities];
9) One never retreats from one's observance of the moral precepts;
10) One upholds the moral precepts in the manner that is praised by the Āryas;
11) One upholds the moral precepts in the manner that is extolled by the wise;
12) One accords with the *prātimokṣa* precepts;
13) One perfects the bases for the awe-inspiring deportment;
14) One remains immensely fearful of committing even the most minor transgression of the precepts;
15) One purifies the actions of body, speech, and mind;
16) One maintains purity in right livelihood;
17) One completely upholds all of the moral precepts;
18) One maintains resolute belief in the extremely profound dharmas;
19) One is able to patiently acquiesce in the dharma of the non-apprehension [of any dharma whatsoever] and is able to not be frightened even by the dharmas of emptiness, signlessness, and wishlessness;
20) One remains diligent in bringing forth vigor [in one's practice];
21) One always maintains ever-present mindfulness;
22) One maintains a mind of solid faith;
23) One is well possessed of a sense of shame and a dread of blame;
24) One does not covet offerings;
25) One remains free of jealousy toward others;
26) One abides in the meritorious qualities associated with practicing the *dhūta* austerities;
27) One abides in the subtleties of Dharma practice;
28) One takes no delight in speaking the coarse language of the world;

29) One avoids gathering in groups for [idle] conversation;
30) One knows to repay kindnesses one has received;
31) One acknowledges those who bestow kindnesses and those who repay kindnesses;
32) Toward one's monastic preceptors and monastic Dharma teachers, one brings forth thoughts of sincere reverence and appreciation for the rarity of being able to encounter them;[107]
33) One does away with any arrogance one might be harboring;
34) One overcomes the self-cherishing mind;
35) Because a good spiritual guide can only rarely be encountered, one strives with diligence to look after his needs;
36) With regard to the source from which one first learned about this Dharma, whether by obtaining a sutra text from someone or by hearing someone recite it, one thinks of them with the same regard as one would maintain for one's own father or mother, one's good spiritual guide, or a great teaching master, and with regard to them, one also feels a sense of shame, dread of blame, affection, and reverence;
37) One always delights in dwelling in a forest hermitage;
38) One does not delight in dwelling in a city or village;
39) One does not covet the opportunity to frequent the homes of benefactors[108] and good spiritual friends;
40) One does not maintain a stinting covetousness for one's own physical survival;
41) One remains ever mindful of death;
42) One does not hoard offerings;
43) One does not indulge any defiling attachment for possessions.
44) One remains free of cravings;
45) One guards and preserves right Dharma;
46) One is not attached to one's robes or bowl;
47) One does not hoard leftover things;
48) One prefers to eat only food that has been obtained on the alms round;
49) On the alms round, one moves along seeking alms according to the proper sequence;[109]
50) One always maintains a sense of shame and dread of blame and always feels remorse [for one's past transgressions];
51) One refrains from hoarding gold, silver, precious jewels, or money and also avoids indulging in unwholesome remorsefulness;[110]
52) One's mind remains free of entangling defilements;
53) One always puts the mind of kindness into practice;

54) One cuts off all feelings of anger;
55) One always puts the mind of compassion into practice;
56) One cuts off affectionate attachments;
57) One always seeks ways to benefit and bring peace to the entire world;
58) One always feels pity for all beings;
59) One always delights in [meditative] walking;
60) One does away with lethargy and sleepiness.

The monastic bodhisattva who abides in dharmas such as these should cultivate and practice this samādhi. Additionally:

3. Fifty Dharmas Supporting Cultivation of This Samādhi

One should also train in this same manner
in the other dharmas pertaining to the cultivation of samādhi.

In order to be able to bring forth this *pratyutpanna* samādhi, one should also cultivate the other supportive dharmas. And what are these? They are:

1) One takes the Buddha's kindness as one's objective focus and always mindfully contemplates him as if he were directly before one;
2) One does not allow one's mind to become scattered;
3) One anchors one's attention directly before one;
4) One guards the gates of the sense faculties;
5) With respect to food and drink, one is easily satisfied;
6) One always cultivates samādhi in both the first and last watches of the night;
7) One abandons the obstacle of the afflictions;
8) One brings forth all of the *dhyāna* absorptions;
9) In one's practice of *dhyāna* meditation, one does not indulge in the delectably pleasurable meditation states;
10) One demolishes through separation the appearance of attractive forms;[111]
11) One acquires the sign of unloveliness;[112]
12) One does not desire the five aggregates;
13) One does not become attached to the eighteen sense realms;
14) One does not indulge any defilement in relation to the twelve sense bases;
15) One does not presumptuously rely on one's [superior] caste origins;
16) One destroys any arrogance;
17) One's mind always remains empty and quiescent in relation to all dharmas that one encounters;

18) One imagines all beings as one's close relatives;
19) One does not seize on the moral precepts themselves [as constituting the very essence of moral virtue];
20) One does not make discriminating distinctions regarding the meditative absorptions;
21) One should diligently pursue abundant learning;
22) One does not become arrogant because of this abundant learning;
23) One remains free of doubts with respect to any of the dharmas.
24) One does not oppose the Buddhas;
25) One does not act in a manner that is contrary to the Dharma;
26) One does not do anything that contributes to the destruction of the Sangha;
27) One always goes to pay one's respects to worthies and *āryas*;
28) One distances oneself from foolish common people;
29) One delights in discussion of world-transcending topics;
30) One cultivates the six dharmas of mutual harmony;[113]
31) One always cultivates the five bases of liberation;[114]
32) One rids himself of the nine bases for generating the affliction of anger;[115]
33) One cuts off the eight dharmas associated with indolence;[116]
34) One cultivates the eight types of vigor;[117]
35) One always contemplates the nine signs [of the deterioration of the corpse];[118]
36) One has realized for himself the eight realizations of great men;[119]
37) One perfects all of the *dhyāna* concentrations and samādhis;
38) One has no covetous attachment to these *dhyāna* concentrations and realizes they have no apprehensible reality;[120]
39) When listening to Dharma, one does so with a focused mind;
40) One demolishes the perception of the five aggregates [as inherently existent phenomena];
41) One does not abide in the perception of phenomena [as inherently existent];
42) One is deeply fearful of *saṃsāra*'s births and deaths;
43) One contemplates the five aggregates as like enemies;[121]
44) One contemplates the sense bases as like an empty village;
45) One contemplates the four great elements as like venomous serpents;
46) One brings forth the contemplation of nirvāṇa as quiescent, secure, and happy;[122]
47) One contemplates the five desires as worthy of being spat upon and one's mind delights in escaping from them;

48) One never opposes the teachings of the Buddha;
49) One has no disputes or quarrels with any other being;
50) In teaching beings, one influences them to dwell securely in all of the meritorious qualities.

K. The Benefits of Cultivating This Pratyutpanna Samādhi

In addition:

The bodhisattva should understand
the benefits that result from such a samādhi.

The bodhisattva should also understand the benefits that result from practicing this *pratyutpanna* samādhi.

Question: What are the resulting benefits gained by cultivating this samādhi?

Response: One obtains the resulting benefit of becoming irreversible with respect to the unsurpassable path. Additionally, as for what the sutra says about these resulting benefits, we have the following:[123]

The Buddha told Bhadrapāla Bodhisattva, "By way of analogy, suppose there was a person who was able to crush to dust all the earth in all worlds in a trichiliocosm and was also able also to crush to dust all the grasses, trees, flowers, leaves, and everything else throughout all of the worlds in a great trichiliocosm.

"Bhadrapala, let us consider now that each and every one of those motes of dust were to constitute one world in which a single buddha dwells and suppose then that one filled to overflowing just such a number of worlds with sublimely marvelous precious jewels and presented all of these jewels as an offering to them.

"Bhadrapāla, what do you think? By performing such an act of giving, would this person gain a great deal of merit or not?"

"Indeed, O Bhagavat, he would reap a great deal."

The Buddha said, "Bhadrapāla, I will now tell you truthfully that if there was a son of good family who heard of this samādhi in which all buddhas appear before one and he were then to be neither startled nor frightened by hearing of it, the merit he would reap from that alone would be immeasurably vast. How much the more so would this be the case if he were to have faith in it, accept it, uphold it, read [teachings in which it is explained], recite them, and explain them for others. How much the more so yet would this be the case if he were to actually cultivate it with concentrated mind even for the time it takes to tug a single squirt of milk from the udder of a cow.

"Bhadrapāla, let me tell you: Even this person's merit would surpass one's ability to measure it. How much the more so would this be so in the case of someone who was actually able to succeed in acquiring this samādhi."

The Buddha continued, telling Bhadrapāla, "If a son or daughter of good family who receives, upholds, reads, recites, and explains [teachings on this samādhi] for others were on the verge of falling into the fires arising at the end of the kalpa, those fires would immediately become extinguished.

"Bhadrapāla, whosoever sustains this samādhi—supposing that he were to encounter some difficulty with officialdom, or supposing that he were to encounter hostile thieves, lions, tigers, wolves, fearsome beasts, fearsome dragons, any of the venomous serpents, or any other such threat, whether from *yakṣas, rākṣasas, kumbhāṇḍas, piśācis,* and such, or from humans, non-humans, or any other sort of entity—that any of those entities might succeed in physically harming him, taking his life, or causing him to break the precepts—this would be an utter impossibility.

So too would this also be the case with respect to those who might be reading, reciting, or teaching this to others. In those cases too they would remain free of any destructive affliction, with the sole exception of instances where they were already bound to undergo compulsory karmic retributions.[124]

"Furthermore, Bhadrapala, when a bodhisattva accepts, upholds, reads, or recites the sutra on this samādhi, if he happens to contract some sickness of the eye, ear, nose, tongue, mouth, or teeth, some disease instigated by wind or cold, or any other such disease, that he might then lose his life because of any of these diseases would be an utter impossibility with the sole exception of instances where he was already bound to undergo compulsory karmic retributions.

"Also, Bhadrapāla, if a person were to accept, uphold, read, or recite the sutra on this samādhi, the devas themselves would protect him. So too would he be protected by the dragons, *yakṣas, mahoragas,* humans, non-humans, the Four Heavenly Kings, Śakra, ruler of the devas, the Brahma Heaven King, and the Buddhas, the Bhagavats. They would all join in remaining protectively mindful of this practitioner.

"Furthermore, this person would be one of whom the devas would all be affectionately mindful, and so too would this be so for other such beings up to and including the Buddhas themselves who would also remain affectionately mindful of this practitioner.

"Additionally, this person would be one whom the devas praise, and so too, he would be one whom other beings up to and including all buddhas would praise as well.

"Also, this bodhisattva would be one whom the devas would all wish to see coming to visit them, and so too with the others on up to the Buddhas themselves who would all wish to see him coming to visit them.

"Furthermore, the bodhisattva who accepts and upholds the sutra on this samādhi will naturally become able to hear whichever other sutras he has not yet heard.

"Additionally, this bodhisattva who gains this samādhi will become able to acquire all of these beneficial experiences even in his dreams.

"Bhadrapāla, were I to attempt to describe the merit of this bodhisattva who accepts, uphold, reads, and recites the sutra on this samādhi, doing so even for an entire kalpa or somewhat less than a kalpa, I would still be unable to come to the end of it. How much the less would this be possible in the case of someone who actually succeeds in perfecting this samādhi.

"Bhadrapāla, if some man with strong body and speed like the wind ran for a hundred years without resting, always proceeding to the east, south, west, north, the four midpoints, above, and below, what do you think? Would anyone be able to know the number of miles he traveled in all those regions throughout the ten directions?"

Bhadrapāla replied, "That would be an incalculable number. Except for the Tathāgata, someone like Śāriputra, or an *avaivartika* [bodhisattva], nobody would be able to know such a number."

"Bhadrapāla, suppose that, on the one hand, there was a son or daughter of good family who filled up with real gold all the area traveled by that man and then give it all away as gifts. Suppose too that, on the other hand, there was someone who merely heard of this samādhi and then engaged in four types of rejoicing and dedication of merit to *anuttarasamyaksaṃbodhi* and the constant pursuit of abundant learning, [doing so by reflecting as follows]:

> Just as all buddhas of the past when practicing the bodhisattva path rejoiced in this samādhi, so too do I now rejoice in it;
>
> Just as the bodhisattvas of the present now rejoice in this samādhi, so too do I now rejoice in it;
>
> Just as all future buddhas during their practice of the bodhisattva path shall rejoice in this samādhi, so too do I now rejoice in it;
>
> And in just that fashion as this samādhi was practiced by all past, future, and present bodhisattvas, so too do I now also rejoice in all of that, and just as they all did so for the sake of pursuing abundant learning [essential to the path], so too do I now rejoice in this samādhi for the sake of the quest for such abundant learning.

"Bhadrapāla, if one were to attempt to compare the previously described merit with the merit from this rejoicing, it could not approach a hundredth part or even one part in a hundred thousand myriads of *koṭis* of parts. The futility of this comparison simply could not be adequately described through any form of calculation or analogy. The benefits resulting from this samādhi are just so immeasurable and boundless as this."

L. This Samādhi's Various Stations and Levels of Cultivation

In addition:

> As for the stations in which one may abide in this samādhi
> as well as the distinctions pertaining to lesser, middling, and greater,
> the many different characteristics such as these
> should all be taken up for a discussion of their meaning.

The stations in which one may abide in this samādhi as well as its lesser, middling, and greater characteristics—all such things should be distinguished and known and these matters should then be explained.

Regarding "the stations in which one may abide in it," this samādhi may be acquired in the first *dhyāna*, the second *dhyāna*, the third *dhyāna*, or the fourth *dhyāna* and one may acquire strength in it while in the first *dhyāna*.

It may be that someone who is "lesser" is able to bring forth this samādhi. Here, "lesser" may refer to the fact that a person is possessed of only a lesser degree of strength [in this practice]. "Lesser" may also refer to abiding [in the samādhi] for a shorter period of time. "Lesser" may also refer to the practitioner's seeing a relatively smaller number of buddha worlds. Distinctions regarding "middling" and "greater" may be made in just the same way.

M. Various Qualitative Variations in How This Samādhi Manifests

In discussing this samādhi, one may speak of it as:

Sometimes involving the presence of ideation (*vitarka*) and the presence of discursion (*vicāra*);
Sometimes involving the absence of ideation and the presence of discursion;
Sometimes involving the absence of ideation and the absence of discursion;
Sometimes involving the presence of joy (*prīti*);
Sometimes involving the presence of bliss (*sukha*);
Sometimes involving neither suffering nor bliss;
Sometimes involving the presence of breathing;
Sometimes involving the absence of breathing;
Sometimes definitely being of a wholesome nature;
Sometimes involving the presence of the contaminants;
Sometimes involving the absence of the contaminants;

Sometimes connected with the desire realm;
Sometimes connected with the form realm;
Sometimes connected with the formless realm;
Sometimes not connected with the desire realm;
Sometimes not connected with the form realm;
And sometimes not connected with the formless realm.

N. Various Abhidharmic Classifications of This Samādhi

This samādhi;

Is a mental dharma;
Is [a dharma] associated with the mind;
Is a dharma that occurs along with the mind;
Is a non-form [dharma];
Is a non-manifest [dharma];
Is able to take an object;
Is not karma [*per se*];
Is associated with karmic activity;
Is coexistent with karmic activity;
Is not the result of karmic actions from a previous life except when it is the result of a particular cause;[125]
Can be cultivated, can be known, and can be realized;
Can be realized both with the body and by means of wisdom;
Can be subject to severance or may be invulnerable to severance;
Should be severed when contaminants are present;
And is invulnerable to severance when free of the contaminants.

Similar distinctions of this sort may also made with respect to the knowledge and vision associated with this samādhi. Also, it is not necessarily conjoined with the seven limbs of enlightenment.[126] Ideally, all of these distinctions should be discussed herein.

O. The Practitioner's Offerings, Roots of Goodness, and Teaching

Furthermore, it is through the cultivation of this samādhi that one may succeed in seeing the Buddhas. Accordingly, it is said that:

After one has succeeded in seeing the Buddhas,
one proceeds with diligent resolve to present offerings [to them].
As one's roots of goodness are thus able to grow,
one becomes able to rapidly teach beings.

"Making offerings" refers to having a pure mind imbued with reverence and delight as one brings to mind the countless meritorious qualities of the Buddha. When one praises him in various ways, this constitutes the making of verbal offerings. When one makes formal reverential bows and presents flowers, incenses, and other such things, this constitutes the making of physical offerings.

Because of these actions, one's karmic merit grows ever greater just as a seed starts to grow when it is planted in earth and receives moisture from the rain. "Rapidly teaching" refers to influencing beings to abide in the Three Vehicles. It is in this way that the bodhisattva brings about the growth of his roots of goodness.

P. The Practitioner's Use of the Four Means of Attraction

Through availing oneself of the first two dharmas of attraction,
one is able to attract beings [to the Dharma].
One resorts to the latter two dharmas of attraction
for those not yet fully able to believe and accept [Dharma teachings].

"The first two" refers to "giving" and to "pleasing words" whereas "beneficial actions" and "joint endeavors" constitute "the latter two dharmas" [of the four means of attraction]. Because this bodhisattva who abides on the first ground is as yet unable to completely comprehend everything, [there may be certain aspects of the teaching] that he can only accept on faith.

Q. The Practitioner's Dedication of Roots of Goodness

He then takes all of his roots of goodness
and dedicates them to the realization of buddhahood.
This is comparable to when others smelt gold
and then refine it, whereupon it thereby becomes amenable to use.

It is through being smelted by the fire of wisdom that, in all the endeavors undertaken by the bodhisattva, his roots of goodness ripen and then finally become amenable to use.

The End of Chapter Twenty-Five

Part Two Endnotes

1. Although the arrangement of the *Taisho* text does not make this clear, it is obvious that these first four five-character phrases form a quatrain upon which the following paragraph comments. Hence I have formatted the text accordingly.
2. This most likely refers to "The Pratyutpanna Samādhi Sūtra" preserved in the *Taisho* Canon as the *Banzhou Sanmei Jing* (般舟三昧經 / T13.no. 0418.902c23–919c05). Paul Harrison has produced a translation of this text for the BDK English Tripitaka.
3. I emend the reading of the text here (but still keep the emendation in brackets since there are no supporting variants in any of the other editions), this to correct an obvious scribal error wherein the name of the third of these "four bases of meritorious qualities" is missing from this sentence. The missing "basis" here is *mie* (滅), "quiescence" (*upaśamādhiṣṭhāna*).
4. These four bases of meritorious qualities (四功德處: 諦, 捨, 滅, 慧; *satyādhiṣṭhāna, tyāgādhiṣṭhāna, upaśamādhiṣṭhāna, prajñādhiṣṭhāna*; truth, relinquishment [generosity], quiescence, and wisdom) are brought up repeatedly in this and other Nāgārjunian treatises, sometimes in slightly varying order and sometimes, as in the present case, with the Chinese translation using slightly variant terminological choices for one of the four list components.
5. "Arms appearing like golden gate bars" is a rather obscure simile that I have never encountered. The SYMG editions have *chan* (鋋) which would be the equally obscure "like golden spears."
6. To correct an apparent graphic-similarity scribal error, I emend the reading of the *Taisho* text here by preferring the SYMG editions' *sheng* (生), "growth," to the *Taisho* edition's *zhu* (主), "ruler."
7. The "reply that sets aside the question" is one of polite refusal to provide an answer, not because the answer is not known, but because the question involves a false premise making the query absurd on the face of it, because providing the answer would only promote endless frivolous and fruitless speculation on the part of the questioner (as with the fourteen imponderables), or because providing an answer would in no way serve the goal of spiritual liberation.
8. More specifically, the component lists comprising the thirty-seven wings of enlightenment are: the five faculties, the five powers, the seven limbs of bodhi, the eight-fold path, the four stations of mindfulness, the four right efforts, and the four foundations of psychic power.

9. "Foes" refers here to the three poisons, i.e. the afflictions. An arhat has completely destroyed them. VB points out that this pronouncement references the word play in the word *"arahant"* where it is explained that they are those who are enemy (*ari*) destroyers (*hanta*).
10. Perhaps due to corruption of the manuscript at some point in its long history, the following list contains only 74 of the 80 secondary characteristics.
11. The *saṃkakṣikā* is the monastic's robe that is worn over the left shoulder and under the right arm.
12. The *nivāsana* is the monastic's skirt-like inner robe.
13. The *saṃghāṭī* is the monastic's outer robe.
14. "Eight kinds of *āryas*" usually refers to those eminences who reside at the four candidate stages and the four realization stages on the Śrāvaka Vehicle path. The first is candidate for stream-entry and the eighth is the fully realized arhat.
15. *Garuḍa* birds prey on young dragons, hence the mention that, at least when attending Dharma teachings by buddhas, they manage to remain uncharacteristically free of any mutual hostility.
16. Although the *Taisho* text has *xiang* (相), "appearance," here it is as an often-encountered and more-or-less standard short-form abbreviation for *xiang* (想), "thought."
17. VB notes that this is a stock description of the Buddha's teaching of the Dharma as found in the *suttas* of the Nikāyas, as for example: *"ādikalyāṇaṃ majjhe kalyāṇaṃ pariyosāne kalyāṇaṃ sātthaṃ sabyañjanaṃ,* etc.," and *"sandiṭṭhiko akālika ehipassiko opanayako paccattaṃ veditabbo viññūhi."*
18. KJ transliterated rather than translated these fruits of the path (*srota-āpanna, sakṛdāgāmin, anāgamin*) that, with the exception of *"arhat,"* I have elected to translate.
19. The emendation proposed by the 2009 edition of CBETA ([和>知]) involving a supposed graphic-similarity scribal error is itself erroneous and irrelevant. This verse simply restates an idea clearly articulated late in Chapter 18: "Through not allowing estrangement to occur among other beings or among one's relatives, and through being able to cause those who have become estranged to be reunited, one acquires the mark of male genital ensheathment. Due to having [planted the karmic causes that result in] this mark, one acquires many disciples." See 65b18-20: 能善調人不令眾生親里遠離。若有乖離還令和合故得陰藏相。有是相故多得弟子。
20. "Genital ensheathment" of course also associates with transcendence of sensual desire and, as an incidental implication, that there

may therefore be no biological sons via which the patrilineal lineage might continue on.

Here, the metaphoric interpretation points out that it is the pure wisdom eye (pure by virtue of an absence of attachments) that leads to the continuance of the lineage of the Buddhas, this because it is a buddha's wise teachings flowing from his possession of the wisdom eye that beget "the sons of the Buddha," i.e. the bodhisattvas who will themselves become the buddhas of the future who carry on his Dharma lineage.

21. These are eight voice qualities possessed only by the Buddhas: 1) Extremely fine; 2) Gentle; 3) Appropriate; 4) Possessed of venerable wisdom; 5) Non-feminine; 6) Unmistaken; 7) Deep and far-reaching; and 8) Inexhaustible. These are discussed at length in Section 59 of "A Sequential Explanation of the Initial Gateway into the Dharma Realm" (法界次第初門 / T46n1925_p0697a15–b20) composed by the famous meditation master and immensely prolific Tiantai hermeneutic school exegete Zhiyi (沙門釋智顗, a.k.a. 陳隋國師智者大師).

22. Because the received text's listing of these 40 exclusive dharmas presents them in a somewhat different order than occurs as they are actually presented and discussed in the text, I reorder and renumber them here to follow the actual order of their presentation. I do so based on the usually factual assumption that the section titles and preliminary lists in translations of Sanskrit texts are for the most part *not* part of the original text, but rather are added by the Sanskrit-to-Chinese translator to assist the reader, or, in this case, perhaps by the editors and scribes in Kumārajīva's translation bureau. For those interested in the erroneously ordered and numbered list found here in the received text, it is as follows:

    1) Sovereign mastery of the ability to fly;
    2) [The ability to manifest] countless transformations;
    3) Boundless psychic powers of the sort possessed by *āryas*;
    4) Sovereign mastery of the ability to hear sounds;
    5) Immeasurable power of knowledge to know others' thoughts;
    6) Sovereign mastery in [training and subduing] the mind;
    7) Constant abiding in stable wisdom;
    8) Never forgetting;
    9) Possession of the powers of the *vajra* samādhi;
    10) Thorough knowing of matters that are unfixed
    11) Thorough knowing of matters pertaining to the formless realm's meditative absorptions;
    12) The completely penetrating knowledge of all matters associated with eternal cessation;

13) Thorough knowing of the non-form dharmas unassociated with the mind;
14) The great powers *pāramitā;*
15) The [four] unimpeded [knowledges] *pāramitā;*
16) The *pāramitā* of perfectly complete replies and predictions in response to questions;
17) Perfectly complete implementation of the three turnings in speaking Dharma;
18) Their words are never spoken without a purpose;
19) Their speech is free of error;
20) Invulnerability to harm by anyone;
21) They are the great generals among all *āryas;*
22–25) They are able to remain unguarded in four ways;
26–29) They possess the four fearlessnesses;
30–39) They possess the ten powers;
40) They possess the unimpeded liberations.

23. VB notes: "This is a category in Sarvāstivāda Abhidharma (not in the Theravāda Abhidharma), which indicates the author is familiar with the Sarvāstivāda system."

24. "Without a purpose" here is literally "empty" (in the sense of "in vain" or "fruitlessly").

25. VB notes: "See Anguttara Nikaya 7:58. The four are: conduct of body, speech, and mind, and livelihood."

26. To correct an apparent graphic-similarity scribal error, I emend the reading of the *Taisho* text here by preferring the SYMG editions' *neng* (能), "able to," to the *Taisho* edition's *suo* (所), "that which."

27. VB notes: "See *Anguttara Nikaya,* Sevens, no. 40 (see, too, Sixes, no. 24):

 'Bhikkhus, possessing seven qualities, a bhikkhu exercises mastery over his mind and is not a servant of his mind. What seven? Here, (1) a bhikkhu is skilled in concentration; (2) skilled in the attainment of concentration; (3) skilled in the duration of concentration; (4) skilled in emergence from concentration; (5) skilled in fitness for concentration; (6) skilled in the range of concentration; and (7) skilled in resolution regarding concentration. Possessing these seven qualities, a bhikkhu exercises mastery over his mind, and is not a servant of his mind.'"

28. This appears to be yet another instance of KJ's use of *xing* (性), usually translated as "nature," as a translation for *dhātu* which is more ordinarily translated into Sino-Buddhist Classical Chinese as *jie* (界), "realm."

29. VB notes: "In the above [passage: '諸相諸觸諸覺諸念亦知起知住知生知滅'], 相 is clearly another instance of the confusion between 相 and 想

so common in Chinese texts. The Pali part parallel has *saññā*. See the end of Majjhima Nikāya 123, where the Buddha says he knows the arising, persistence, and passing away of *vedanā*, *saññā*, and *vitakka*."

30. In response to my earlier draft translation of *emo* (惡魔) here as "an evil demon," VB notes: Here there is no doubt that 惡魔 is none other than the infamous Māra, a particular individual, not just any "evil demon." See *Samyutta Nikāya* 4:24 "Seven Years of Pursuit":

"On one occasion the Blessed One was dwelling at Uruvelā on the bank of the river Nerañjarā at the foot of the Goatherd's Banyan Tree. Now on that occasion Māra the Evil One had been following the Blessed One for seven years, seeking to gain access to him but without success....

"Then Māra the Evil One, in the presence of the Blessed One, recited these verses of disappointment:

"There was a crow that walked around
A stone that looked like a lump of fat.
'Let's find something tender here,' [he thought,]
'Perhaps there's something nice and tasty.'

But because he found nothing tasty there,
The crow departed from that spot.
Just like the crow that attacked the stone,
We leave Gotama disappointed."

31. These five are: past dharmas, present dharmas, future dharmas, unconditioned dharmas (referred to below as "those that transcend the three periods of time"), and ineffable dharmas.

32. I emend the text here to correct an apparent graphic-similarity scribal error, preferring SYMG's *san* (三), "three," to the *Taisho* text's *er* (二), "two." The rationale for the emendation is evident in the paragraph's discussion of "three" dharmas that are "strung together," not merely "two."

33. I have made the same emendation here as in the immediately previous note.

34. VB notes that this incident involving the elephant named Nālagiri is described in the Vinaya, Cūlavagga, II 194 foll. of PTS Pali edition.

35. As described later in the text, "The twelve *dhūta* austerities" are:

Adopting the dharma of dwelling in a forest hermitage;
Obtaining one's food through the alms round;
Wearing robes made of cast-off rags;
[Taking one's daily meal in but] a single sitting;
Always sitting to sleep, [never lying down];

Having taken the meal, not accepting food or drink at the wrong times;
Possessing only a single set of three robes;
Wearing only an animal-hair robe;
Laying out one's sitting mat wherever one happens to be;
Dwelling at the foot of a tree;
Dwelling out in the open (lit. "on empty ground");
Dwelling in a charnel field.

36. VB notes: "In the Pali these are laid out as parallel descriptive terms. The Pali actually has nine synonymous terms. See AN 1:174."

37. Based on VB's very sensible suggestion that "quiescent cessation" (寂滅) is probably here as elsewhere simply a somewhat opaque sounding sino-Buddhist translation of "*nirvāṇa*," I have gone ahead and rendered it as such throughout this entire passage as well as in other places throughout the text where the context demands it.

38. I have been unable to find a Sanskrit antecedent for this Chinese transliteration of a type of rishi, a "*pisuo*" (脾娑) rishi. VB suggests that this may be a transliteration of *viśvarśi* (*viś ṛṣi*).

39. VB notes that one can find approximate Pali Canon parallels at MN 110.4, MLDB p. 892, and AN 3:3.

40. VB notes: "The story of Ciñcā the brahmin girl occurs in the Dhammapada Commentary, commenting on verse 176. See Burlingame, *Buddhist Legends* III 19 foll."

41. VB notes: "In the Pali Canon, this incident is referred to in Udāna Section 38."

42. VB notes: "The incident is at SN 4:18 (PTS ed. I 113–14)."

43. VB notes: "The story is in the Pāli Vinaya in Cullavagga, chapter 7; PTS ed II 194–96."

44. VB notes: "This [story] is at the beginning of the Pārājika chapter of the Vinaya."

45. VB notes: "His departure from the Sangha and denunciation of the Buddha are mentioned at the beginning of MN 12. MN 105 is spoken to him, and his arguments with the Buddha about arahants are at DN 23."

46. VB notes: "See AN 7:58: Four things that the Tathāgata does not have to guard: conduct of body, speech, and mind, and livelihood."

47. "The *upoṣadha* dharma" is a reference to spiritual purification, in particular the two days of the month when monastics recite the precepts and the days of the month in which pious lay people voluntarily take on a semi-monastic level of moral precept observance.

48. This is verse 183 of the *Dhammapada*.
49. The first four lines here correspond to *Dhammapada* 361.
50. This corresponds to verse 362 of the *Dhammapada*.
51. VB notes: "See AN 5:181 foll.: 'Bhikkhus, there are these five kinds of forest dwellers. What five? (1) One who becomes a forest dweller because of his dullness and stupidity; (2) one who becomes a forest dweller because he has evil desires, because he is driven by desire; (3) one who becomes a forest dweller because he is mad and mentally deranged; (4) one who becomes a forest dweller, [thinking]: "It is praised by the Buddhas and the Buddhas' disciples"; (5) and one who becomes a forest dweller for the sake of fewness of desires, for the sake of contentment, for the sake of eliminating [defilements], for the sake of solitude, for the sake of simplicity. The fifth is pronounced the best.'"
52. VB notes: "I think the author here is referring to the Buddha's hesitation, immediately after his enlightenment, about going out and teaching the Dharma. See MN 26.19, SN 6:1, etc."
53. VB notes: "This is at MN 26.22–23. Interestingly the author here takes a similar perspective on *sarvajñatā* as the Theravāda commentaries, that knowledge arises when the Buddha directs his attention to some issue (*āvajjanapaṭibaddhaṃ buddhassa bhagavato ñāṇaṃ*), in contrast to the later Mahāyāna view that the Buddha perpetually knows everything simultaneously."
54. The second part of the Chinese text's title, "Forty Dharmas Exclusive to Buddhas: The Exclusive Dharma of Thoroughly Knowing What is Unfixed," is misleading because "the exclusive dharma of thoroughly knowing what is unfixed" only describes the first few pages of this long chapter that in fact discusses all of the remaining exclusive dharmas (nos. 10–40). I have therefore dropped this misleading phrase from the chapter title. One should be aware that these chapter titles almost certainly do not originate with Nāgārjuna but rather with Kumārajīva's translation team.
55. VB notes: "The above corresponds to Majjhima Nikaya no. 136."
56. Commenting on the corresponding passages as preserved in the Pali canon, VB notes: "The Pāli sutta with the simile of the raft mentions all four fruits (MN 22; see the end). But the proposition about one of two fruits occurs in a number of other suttas, such as the Satipaṭṭhāna Sutta (see end of MN 10)."
57. Regarding this "*Ekottara Āgama*'s *Shejiali Sutra*" (舍迦梨經), I have so far been unable to locate the Sanskrit for its title.

58. VB comments: "The above corresponds to Anguttara Nikāya 10:217 (also 10:218). Note that there are three modes in which the karmic results may be received, both in Pāli and Chinese versions: in the present life (現受報), upon rebirth (that is, the next life; 生受), or in a subsequent life (after the next one; 後受). Here is the Pāli followed by my rendering:

    217. *"Nāhaṃ, bhikkhave, sañcetanikānaṃ kammānaṃ katānaṃ upacitānaṃ appaṭisaṃviditvā byantībhāvaṃ vadāmi. Tañca kho diṭṭheva dhamme upapajje vā apare vā pariyāye. Na tvevāhaṃ, bhikkhave, sañcetanikānaṃ kammānaṃ katānaṃ upacitānaṃ appaṭisaṃveditvā dukkhass'antakiriyaṃ vadāmi."*

    "Bhikkhus, I do not say that there is a termination of volitional kamma that has been done and accumulated so long as one has not experienced [its results], and that may be in this very life, or in the [next] rebirth, or on some subsequent occasion. But I do not say that there is making an end of suffering so long as one has not experienced [the results of] volitional kamma that has been done and accumulated."

59. Again, I have so far been unable to find the Sanskrit name for this transliterated title.

60. VB notes: "The Pāli parallel is *Majjhima* 58: *Abhayarājakumāra Sutta*."

61. These "three groups" refers to the *tri-skandha* (三聚) as that term is used to categorize the karmic destinies of beings. Those who are "definitely deviant" or "erroneous" are definitely bound to be unsuccessful in reaching enlightenment whereas those who are "definitely righteous" or "correct" are definitely bound to succeed in becoming enlightened. In his Mppu, in commenting on a passage in the Great Perfection of Wisdom Sutra that brings up the topic of these three groups, N points out that it is the ability or inability to destroy the inverted views that is pivotal in determining one's position in this threefold categorization. It is those who may or may not encounter the karmic conditions enabling the destruction of these inverted views who are categorized as "indefinite." (See T25.n1509.647c27–648a01.)

62. These four "repositories of Dharma" (*dharma-piṭaka*) are identified by Nāgārjuna in his Mppu as: 1) the Sutra Piṭaka; 2) the Vinaya Piṭaka; 3) the Abhidharma Piṭaka; and 4) the Kṣudraka-piṭaka (T12; No. 1509; 143c23–25).

63. These are "delectable absorptions" (*āsvādana-samādhi*) which are characterized by the arising of extremely pleasurable meditation states to which the unskilled or unwise meditator is vulnerable to becoming attached.

64. VB notes: "The Pāli parallel is the opening passage of Dīgha Nikāya no. 14, almost verbatim the same."

65. I emend the reading of the *Taisho* text here by preferring on sensibility grounds the SYMG editions' *ci jing* (此經), "this sutra," to the *Taisho* edition's *jing ci* (經此), "sutra this."

    The sutra to which this text refers is obviously the Ten Grounds Sutra upon which Nāgārjuna's SZPPS comments. This topic of the expansiveness of the Buddha's knowledge and vision is treated at great length in the sutra itself.

66. VB notes: "The names of *pratyekabuddhas* are mentioned in MN 116. I would posit the following equivalents [for a few of the *pratyekabuddhas* mentioned here]:

    無垢 = Ariṭṭha
    華相 = Tagarasikhī
    喜見 = Piyadassī

67. VB notes: "Parallel to the above is AN 6:62 Section 6: (6) 'Then, Ānanda, having encompassed his mind with my own mind, I understand some person thus: "Wholesome qualities and unwholesome qualities are found in this person." On a later occasion, having encompassed his mind with my own mind, I understand him thus: "This person does not have even a mere fraction of a hair's tip of an unwholesome quality. This person possesses exclusively bright, blameless qualities. He will attain *nibbāna* in this very life."'"

68. VB notes: "[This passage is found] in MN 12."

69. VB notes: "The following passage comes toward the end of MN 12."

70. This long paragraph (beginning with "Supposing…") has the appearance of language quoted from a sutra. However, having failed to locate it, I frame it here as simply Nāgārjuna's amplification of the meaning of the immediately preceding passage that VB recognized as having a Pali analogue in MN 12.

71. This is the name as recorded in the Pali canon. I'm not sure about the Sanskrit for this name.

72. Ibid.

73. VB notes that the following passage is found in the beginning of MN 136.

74. Rāhula was the Buddha's son whereas Devadatta was someone intent on killing the Buddha.

75. VB suggest that this passage may be alluding to AN 4:111, "Kesi the Horse Trainer."

76. This refers to *satkāyadṛṣṭi*.

77. Again, although in these last two cases, the Chinese is literally "gain the path" (得道), per Hirakawa (p. 451, column 2) this corresponds to: *"bodhi, abhisaṃbuddha, saṃbodhi-prāpta."* Edgerton in turn suggests "becoming perfectly enlightened" for *abhisambuddhana* (Page 58, column 2).

78. Although *"brahmacarya"* (梵行) generally refers to celibate spiritual practice, it may just as well be thought of as "the holy life" or "the spiritual life. VB notes that this scriptural quote "is found in many places in the Nikāyas: e.g., beginning of MN 148: *"Bhagavā etadavoca – 'dhammaṃ vo, bhikkhave, desessāmi ādikalyāṇaṃ majjhe kalyāṇaṃ pariyosānakalyāṇaṃ sātthaṃ sabyañjanaṃ, kevalaparipuṇṇaṃ parisuddhaṃ brahmacariyaṃ pakāsessāmi.'"*

79. VB notes: "In the Pali suttas, the second wonder is being able to declare another person's thoughts. For the three wonders, see AN 3:60: "There are, brahmin, these three kinds of wonders. What three? The wonder of psychic potency, the wonder of mind-reading, and the wonder of instruction (*iddhipāṭihāriyaṃ ādesanāpāṭihāriyaṃ anusāsanīpāṭihāriyaṃ*; also at DN 11.3–8, I 212–14). The second is explained thus: There is one who … declares: 'Your thought is thus, such is what you are thinking, your mind is in such and such a state.' And even if he makes many declarations, they are exactly so and not otherwise."

80. I have been unable to locate either the Sanskrit or Pali antecedents for the titles of these scriptures. VB also notes: "I'm not sure of the references here. Perhaps the former is the Potaliya Sutta, MN 54, but I'm not sure."

81. VB notes: "[The Pali canon analogue for] the following is at MN 12 and AN 4:8."

82. I emend the reading of the *Taisho* text here by preferring on sensibility grounds the SYMG editions' *wei wei* (微畏, "slightest fear," to the *Taisho* edition's *shi* (是), "this."

83. VB notes that the analogue passage in the Pali canon is found at DN no. 20.

84. VB notes: "See MN 115 and AN 1:277."

85. VB notes: "The above, too, is in MN 115 and AN 1:284 foll."

86. VB notes: "On this, see MN 45, 46."

87. VB notes: "This may be an allusion to AN 5:28."

88. VB notes: "This may be an allusion to AN 5:27."

89. This is a concept with numerous similar alternative explanations, most of which refer to the immense amount of merit and time required to acquire the thirty-two marks and eighty minor characteristics of a

buddha's body and finally achieve buddhahood. This is discussed in greater detail in Nāgārjuna's commentary on the Great Perfection of Wisdom Sutra. See T25.1509.57b05–27.

90. Nārāyaṇa is a powerful celestial eminence regarded as a Dharma protector in Buddhism.

91. As is quite common with the syntax of multi-line Classical Chinese verses, this quatrain has require the rearrangement of its lines to produce a sensible and naturally flowing statement in English.

92. "Eight classes in four pairs" (四雙八輩) refers to the four preliminary phases and four fruition stages on the individual-liberation path of the *śrāvaka* disciples.

93. VB notes: "見聞覺知 = Pāḷi *diṭṭhaṃ, sutaṃ, mutaṃ, viññātaṃ,* where mutaṃ is explained as things sensed through the other three sense faculties: smell, taste, and touch."

Hence, in "seen, heard, sensed, and known," (per Hirakawa's BCSD: *dṛṣṭa-śruta-mata-jñāta* or *dṛṣṭa-śruta-mata-vijñāta*) "sensed" (*mata*) refers to the sensory function of the olfactory, gustatory, and tactile sense faculties. Therefore this series is intended to refer to the functions of all six sense faculties and their corresponding consciousnesses.

94. To correct an apparent scribal error very likely originating in homophony, I emend the reading of the text here, preferring on sensibility grounds the homophonous *de* (得), "achieved" of the SYMG editions to the *Taisho* text's *de* (德), "qualities."

95. "Five characteristics" here is slightly ambiguous. It could refer particularly to the five types of desire which together constitute the first of the five hindrances (visible forms, sounds, smells, tastes, and touchables, or wealth, sex, fame, food, and leisure). Alternatively, it may be intended to refer to all five of the "five hindrances" that must be eliminated to access deep states of meditation (desire, ill will, lethargy-and-sleepiness, excitedness-and-regretfulness, and afflicted doubtfulness).

96. To correct an apparent graphic-similarity scribal error, I emend the reading of the *Taisho* text here by preferring the SYMG editions' *li* (力), "power," to the *Taisho* edition's *fen* (分), "portion."

97. I am not sure precisely what Nāgārjuna intended by "the six categories of meanings associated with the forty exclusive Dharmas," set forth in his preceding praise verses.

98. The Sanskrit antecedent of *shixiang* (實相) in KJ translations is usually *dharmatā,* i.e. the true nature of all dharmas, i.e. *śūnyatā,* i.e. the utter absence of inherent existence in any and all phenomena.

99. To correct an apparent graphic-similarity scribal error, I emend the reading of the *Taisho* text here by preferring the SYMG editions' *shen* (深), "deep" or "profound," to the *Taisho* edition's *ran* (染), "defiled." Nāgārjuna's discussion of this line corroborates the correctness of the emendation.

100. When translated into Chinese, "Tathāgata" means "Thus Come One."

101. Again, this most likely refers to "The Pratyutpanna Samādhi Sūtra" preserved in the *Taisho* Canon as the *Banzhou Sanmei Jing* (般舟三昧經 / T13.no. 0418.902c23–919c05).

102. "Overweening pride," *zeng shang man* (增上慢), corresponds to the Sanskrit *adhimāna*.

103. To correct an obvious graphic-similarity scribal error, I emend the reading of the *Taisho* text here by preferring the SYMG editions' *zeng* (增), "increase," to the *Taisho* edition's *zeng* (憎), "detest."

104. "Characteristic sign" refers here to any of the signs associated with three sequential levels of practice described at the very beginning of this chapter:

    1) The thirty-two marks and eighty secondary characteristics of a buddha's form body;
    2) The Dharma body of the Buddhas;
    3) The true character [of all dharmas], i.e. "emptiness of inherent existence" (*śūnyatā*). This "emptiness of inherent existence" is evidenced by: a) their being merely composite constructs of subsidiary conditions; b) their being merely evanescently transient states in a chain of serial causality; and c) their being mere names attached to a) and b) to which one falsely imputes individual reality.

105. To correct an obvious graphic-similarity scribal error, I emend the reading of the *Taisho* text here by preferring the SYMG editions' *zhai* (齋), "ritual purification," to the *Taisho* edition's *qi* (齊), "uniform."

    Also, "Precepts of abstinence" refers here to the *aṣṭāṅgasamanvāgataṃ upavāsaṃ*, the laity's formal acceptance and observance of the practice of upholding the eight precepts that include celibacy and not eating after midday. One observes this enhanced level of lay precept practice either continuously or on the eighth, fourteenth, fifteenth, twenty-third, twenty-ninth, and thirtieth days of each lunar month.

106. This reference to laypeople staying in a monastery probably refers most usually to the not uncommon practice of allowing laypeople to live in separate quarters on monastery grounds when they are continuously training in these eight lay precepts for a predetermined period of time.

107. I translate here as "monastic preceptor" and "monastic Dharma teacher" what the KJ text retains in transliteration as *"upādhyāya"* and *"ācārya"* respectively.

108. KJ retained the Sanskrit term for "benefactor" (*dānapati*) which I have opted to translate here.

109. VB notes: "This is the practice of seeking alms at every door, without skipping over houses where the people do not give or give poor quality food." The rationale for observing this "proper sequence" is that, since providing alms to monks and nuns produces karmic merit, one would not want to deny that opportunity to anyone.

110. Lest "unwholesome remorsefulness" seem somewhat opaque, this would refer first and foremost to regretting having done something good or regretting not having done something bad.

111. "Demolishing through separation" most likely refers to the "deconstructive analysis" involved in such contemplations as the contemplation of the thirty-two (or 36) parts of the body, the nine stages of the decomposition of a rotting corpse, the white-boned skeleton contemplation, etc. All of these contemplations serve as powerful antidotes to sensual desire.

112. This attainment of the sign of unloveliness refers to directly perceiving the unloveliness of sensually attractive physical forms so completely that the image of their unloveliness is retained even in the absence of the initially contemplated meditation object. This is often accomplished by deeply practicing the contemplations of the parts of the body, the stages of decomposition of a rotting corpse, or the white-boned skeleton.

113. Hirakawa gives the Sanskrit as: *"saṃrañjanīyaṃ dharmam."* These six dharmas refer to mutual harmoniousness, respect, equality, and fairness in matters pertaining to: body, speech, mind, precepts, views, and benefits received (food, robes, shelter, etc.).

114. These five bases of liberation (Skt. *vimukty-āyatanāni*) are five different circumstances under which, with or without the advantage of correct teaching from a qualified Dharma teacher or fellow practitioner, a practitioner may come to engage with and find success in cultivation, establish his mind in concentration, and then finally achieve liberation. VB refers us to AN 5:26 for the precise canonical explanation.

115. VB refers us to AN 9:29.

116. VB refers us to AN 8:80.

117. VB refers us to AN 8:80, noting that this is found in the second part of that sutta.

118. These are the *navasaṃjñā* for which VB refers us to AN 9:16.
119. VB refers us to AN 8:30.
120. "No apprehensible reality" (無所得) refers to emptiness of inherent existence, i.e. there is nothing in or about these *dhyāna* absorptions that can be gotten at as ultimately real.
121. VB notes: "Items 43-45 are at SN 35:238, 'The Simile of the Vipers.'"
122. VB notes: "This may also be in SN 35:238: 'The further shore, which is safe and free from danger': this is a designation for Nibbāna."
123. This appears to be a quotation from the "Pratyutpanna Samādhi Sūtra."
124. "Compulsory karmic retributions" most likely refers here to heinous karmic offenses that entail immediate retribution during or at the end of this very life such as: patricide, matricide, killing an arhat, drawing the blood of a buddha, or causing a schism in the monastic sangha.
125. This statement seems contradictory. As such, I am not particularly confident that this sentence is not corrupted or that I have interpreted its intent correctly.
126. The immediately preceding abhidharmic analytic categories are in some cases phrased so tersely in the Chinese as to be mildly obscure. Hence I may not have rendered all of them with definitively precise accuracy.

Nāgārjuna
on
Mindfulness of the Buddha

Part 3: Recollection of the Buddha

Nāgārjuna's *Exegesis on the Mahāprajnāpāramitā Sūtra*
Chapter 1, Part 36-1

As Translated into Chinese by Tripiṭaka Master Kumārajīva
English Translation by Bhikshu Dharmamitra

Part Three
Recollection of the Buddha[1]

Nāgārjuna on Recollection of the Buddha

I. Recollection of the Buddha

A. The Purpose of the Practice

The Buddha told the bhikshus: "If one is engaging in contemplations in a forest hermitage,[2] an empty building, a charnel ground, the mountains, the forests, or the desolate wilderness, and if one becomes so fearful that the hairs on one's body stand on end, at just such a time, one should engage in recollection of the Buddha, recalling that the Buddha is a *tathāgatha,* an *arhat, samyaksaṃbuddha,* and so forth until we come to a *bhagavat.*[3] One's fearfulness will then disappear."[4]

B. Explanation of the Practice

Question: What is meant by "recollection of the Buddha"?

Response: The practitioner single-mindedly recalls that the Buddha has gained the wisdom which accords with reality and also possesses perfectly realized great loving-kindness and great compassion. Thus he is said to be free of mistakes or errors. There is nothing about him which is not genuine, regardless of whether it be concerned with the gross, the subtle, the manifold, the few, the deep, or the shallow.

C. The Ten Names of the Buddha

Because in every case he accords with reality, he is referred to as "*tathāgata*" (the "Thus Come One"). Also, just as all buddhas of the ten directions throughout the past, future, and present, in the midst of beings, give rise to the mind of great compassion, practice the six perfections, realize the true character of all dharmas, and come forth to arrive at *anuttura-samyak-saṃbodhi* ("the utmost, right, and perfect enlightenment"), so too is this case with this Buddha. This is what is meant by "*tathāgata.*"

Just as the bodies of all buddhas of the three periods of time throughout the ten directions radiate great brilliant light which pervasively illuminates the ten directions, breaking up all darkness, just as their minds put forth the brilliant light of wisdom that dispels the darkness of beings' ignorance, and just as the fame of their meritorious qualities everywhere fills the ten directions as they go forth to nirvāṇa, so too does this Buddha also go forth in the same manner. It is for this reason that he too is referred to as "the *Tathāgata*" ("the Thus Come One").

Because he possesses merit such as this, he is worthy to receive the most supreme offerings from all gods and people of the World. Hence he is referred to as *"arhat"* ("Worthy of Offerings"). If someone were to ask why it is that it is only the Buddha who speaks in accordance with reality, it is because he is "thus" in his coming and "thus" in his going. He is worthy to receive the most supreme offerings because the Buddha has realized the right and universal awakening.

"Right" refers to all dharmas' mark of unshakability and indestructibility. "Universal" refers to not being limited in scope to just one or two dharmas. Thus, because in his complete knowing of all dharmas, there are none not included and none not exhaustively known, he is referred to as *"samyaksaṃbuddha"* ("Of Right and Universal Enlightenment"). This right and universal wisdom is not acquired without a cause, nor is it realized in the absence of conditions. Here it is in reliance upon the perfection of wisdom and observance of moral precepts that he acquires this right and universal wisdom.

"Wisdom" refers to the bodhisattva's wisdom from the time of first generating the resolve [to attain buddhahood] on up to the acquisition of the *vajra* samādhi. "Upholding the moral precepts" refers to the bodhisattva's bodily actions and verbal actions which are pure and corresponding to his intentions from the time of first generating the resolve on up to the acquisition of the *vajra* samādhi. He is therefore known as *"vidyā-caraṇa-saṃpanna"* ("Perfect in Practice of Cognition").[5]

In his practice of these two practices, he achieves the state of being "well gone." This is just as when a cart that is possessed of two wheels is said to be one which is "well gone." The Buddha also goes to those places to which the former buddhas have gone. Hence he is referred to as *"sugata"* ("the Well Gone One").

There may be those who claim, "The Buddha cultivated his own dharma. However, he is unaware of the endeavors of people such as ourselves." For the sake of these, [it may be explained that] he knows the World, knows the causes in the World, knows the cessation of [the dharmas of] the World, and knows the path to the cessation of [the dharmas of] the World. Hence he is referred to as *"lokavid"* ("the World Knower").

Having already understood the World, he is able to train and guide beings. Among all teachers he is the most unsurpassed. It is for this reason that he is referred to as *"anuttaraḥ-puruṣa-damya-sārathiḥ"* ("the Unsurpassed Guide of Men to be Tamed").

He is able to employ the three kinds of paths to extinguish the three poisons and thus causes beings to practice the path of the

Three Vehicles. It is for this reason that he is referred to as *"śāstā devamanuṣyāṇām"* ("the Teacher of Gods and Men").

Suppose someone were to ask, "Because of what endeavor is he able to create incalculable self benefit while also being able to create incalculable benefit for others?" It is because of having perfected comprehensive wisdom which utterly knows everything in all the worlds of the past, future, and present, knowing them whether [those objects of knowledge] are already ended or not, and knowing them whether they abide in a state of flux or not. It is on this basis that the Buddha is known as *"buddha"* ("the Enlightened One").

Having acquired these nine types of names, he is possessed of a great reputation which extends everywhere throughout the ten directions. It is because of this that he is referred to as *"bhagavat"* (the "Venerated One").

In the scriptures, the Buddha himself indicated that one should employ these names in one's recollection of the Buddha.

D. The Illustrious Lineage and Marvelous Birth of the Buddha

Also, all of the various sorts of meritorious qualities are exhaustively present in the Buddha. The Buddha belongs to the lineage of the wheel-turning sage king at the very beginning of the kalpa, Mahāsaṃmata. He is from the wise and awesomely virtuous Śākyans, born in the noble house of Gautama.

When he was born, brilliant light everywhere illuminated the worlds of the great trichiliocosm. Brahmā, king of the gods, held a jeweled canopy [over him]. Śakra Devānām Indra received him with a jeweled cloak. The dragon king Anavatapta and the dragon king Sāgara bathed him with marvelously scented waters. When he was born, the earth moved and shook in six ways. He walked seven steps, peaceful and stable as the king of elephants, gazed contemplatively at the four quarters, and roared the lion's roar, declaring, "This is my very last incarnation. I am destined to liberate all beings."

E. The Physical Characteristics of the Buddha

Asita, the Rishi, examined [the Buddha's] physiognomy and told Pure Rice King, "This person possesses the thousand-spoked wheel mark on the bottom of his feet and the mark of webbing between [the bases of] his fingers. He is one who is destined to stand, peacefully and evenly, within the Dharma, remaining immovable and unrefuted by anyone.

"His hands are adorned with the signs indicating virtue and with proximal webs [at the base of his fingers]. He is destined to use these hands to bring comfort to beings and cause them to be free of fear.

He possesses signs such as these up to and including the "flesh cowl" mark [atop his head] which is like a blue pearl at the summit of a mountain. The blue-colored light emanates from its four sides. The summit mark in the middle of his head is such that no one is able to see to the top of it. Whether one be a god or a man, there are none who are superior to him.

"He is possessed of the white hair-tuft mark placed between his brows, the white light from which surpasses that of crystal. He has pure eyes which are wide and broad and which are purple-blue in color. His nose is prominent, straight, and fine in a way which is extremely attractive and pleasing. His mouth contains forty teeth which are white, pure, sharp, and fine. His four front teeth are supremely white and possessed of the most superior brilliance.

"His upper and lower lips are equal, being neither large nor small nor long nor short. His tongue is thin and yet large. It is red in color like a heavenly lotus blossom. His brahman voice is deep and far-reaching. Those who hear it are delighted by it and never grow weary of listening to it. The color of his body is fine and marvelous, superior in hue to that of Jāmbu River gold. A great light surrounds his body, displaying all manner of varied colors. It is marvelous, fine and incomparable.

"He is complete with thirty-two marks of this sort. Before long, this person will leave behind the home life, realize all-knowledge and attain buddhahood."

The physical qualities of the Buddha's body are such as this. One should [contemplate them] in one's recollection of the Buddha.

Moreover, it is a quality of the Buddha's body that his physical strength is superior to that of one hundred thousand precious perfumed white elephants. This is [just] the physical strength passed on to him by his parents. As for the power which is a quality arising from the spiritual superknowledges, it is incalculable and unlimited.

The body of the Buddha is adorned with the thirty-two marks and the eighty subsidiary characteristics. Because, internally, he is possessed of the incalculable number of meritorious qualities of the Buddha Dharma, one gazes upon him tirelessly. One who looks upon the Buddha's body forgets the five desires of the World and does not bear in mind any of the myriad matters. If one looks at any single place on the body of the Buddha, one experiences fondness and bliss, never feels that one has seen enough, and remains unable to avert one's gaze. The meritorious qualities of the Buddha's body are of such as this. Hence one should take up the practice of mindfulness of the Buddha.

F. The Buddha's Accumulation of Moral Precepts

Also, the Buddha is pure in his perfection of the upholding of the moral precepts. From the very time he first brought forth the resolve [to attain bodhi], he cultivated the moral precepts and increased his accumulation of an incalculable number [of excellent qualities]. In his extending [toward beings] a mind imbued with pity, there is never any seeking after any resulting reward. He never tends toward the path of the Hearers or the Pratyekabuddhas. There is never any admixture of any of the fetters.

He is only concerned that his own mind be pure and free of anything which might be distressing to beings. In life after life, he upholds the moral precepts. It is on account of this that, when he gains the Buddha Path, his observance of the moral precepts has achieved perfection. One should take up mindfulness of the Buddha's accumulation of the precepts in just this way.

G. The Buddha's Accumulation of Meditative Absorptions

Furthermore, the Buddha's accumulation of the meditative absorptions is entirely perfect.

Question: As for his upholding of precepts, one is able to know of this because of the purity of his bodily and verbal karma. As for his wisdom, one is able to know of it because of his making of distinctions in his explanations of Dharma and through his ability to dispel the doubts of beings. But, as for the meditative absorptions, one is not even able to know about this in the case of other persons, how much the less would one be able to know about it in the case of the Buddha?

Response: Because his great wisdom is perfect, one should know that his *dhyāna* absorptions must be entirely perfect. This is analogous to when one sees a lotus blossom which is huge: One necessarily knows that the pool [in which it grew] must also be very large. It is also just as when there is a lamp whose brightness is great. One necessarily knows that it must also contain a lot of *perilla* lamp oil. Also, because the powers of the Buddha's superknowledges and spiritual transformations are incalculable and incomparable, one knows that the power of his *dhyāna* absorptions is also entirely complete. This is also just as when one sees a result which is grand, one therefore knows that the cause must be great as well.

Furthermore, there are times when the Buddha himself has explained this matter for the sake of others, saying, "The qualities of my *dhyāna* absorptions are extremely profound." This is just as set forth in the scriptures where it is stated:

> The Buddha was once in the country of Ādumā, sitting beneath a tree in the forest, having entered into *dhyāna* absorption. There arose at that time a huge rainstorm attended by crashing thunder and lightning bolts. A team of four bull oxen and two plowmen all died from fright on hearing the sound, after which, in a just a brief moment, the sky became clear again. The Buddha arose and began to walk about.
>
> There was a layman who, having bowed reverently at the feet of the Buddha, followed on along behind the Buddha and addressed the Buddha, saying, "World Honored One, there was just now such a crashing of thunder and flashing of lightning bolts that a team of four bull oxen and two plowmen all died from fright on hearing the sound. Did the World Honored One hear it or not?"
>
> The Buddha said, "I did not hear it."
>
> That layman continued, "Was the Buddha sleeping during this time?"
>
> The Buddha replied, "I was not sleeping."
>
> The layman next asked, "Was he entered into the no-thought absorption?"
>
> The Buddha said, "No. I was possessed of thought. It was just that I had entered into absorption, that's all."
>
> The layman said, "This is an unprecedented event."

The greatness of a Buddha's *dhyāna* absorption is extremely profound. He may be possessed of thought and be abiding in *dhyāna* absorption, whereupon there occurs such a great sound as this which, even while entirely awake, he nonetheless does not hear.

This is just as described in yet another scripture:

> The Buddha told the bhikshus, "The absorptions which the Buddha enters into and comes out of are such that Śāriputra and Maudgalyāyana have not even heard their names. How much the less would they be able to know what they are all about."

There are, for example, the Samādhi King Samādhi, the Lion's Sport Samādhi, and so forth. When the Buddha enters into them, he is able to cause the worlds of the ten directions to shake and move in six ways. He emits a great brilliant light that transforms into an incalculable number of buddhas who fill the ten directions. As a case in point, Ananda once thought to himself:

> "In the past, at the time of Burning Lamp Buddha, the world was a fine one, the lifespan of the people was long, and they were easy to teach and bring across to liberation. Now, in the time of Śākyamuni Buddha, the world is an evil one, the lifespan of the people is short, and they are difficult to teach. Will the Buddha nonetheless go ahead

and enter nirvāṇa even though the Buddha's work will not have been completed?"

Early in the morning, he expressed this concern to the Buddha. The sun had already risen. The Buddha then entered into the sunrise samādhi. Just as when the sun rises, its light illuminates all of Jambudvīpa, so too it was with the body of the Buddha. His hair pores all sent forth light which illuminated all of the worlds as numerous as the Ganges' sands throughout the ten directions.

Each and every one of the rays of light put forth a seven-jeweled thousand-petaled lotus blossom. Atop each and every one of the blossoms, there was a seated buddha. Each and every one of those buddhas sent forth an immeasurable number of rays of light. From within each and every one of those rays of light there was put forth a seven-jeweled, thousand-petaled lotus blossom. Atop each and every one of those blossoms, there was a seated buddha.

All of these buddhas filled up all of the worlds as numerous as Ganges' sands throughout the ten directions and carried on with the transformative teaching of beings. In some cases, they spoke Dharma. In some other instances, they remained silent. In yet other instances, they were engaged in meditative walking. Sometimes they displayed transformations wrought by the spiritual superknowledges in which their bodies poured forth water or fire. In ways such as these, they used all sorts of skilful means with which they led across to liberation the beings of the five destinies of rebirth throughout the ten directions.

By receiving assistance from the awesome spiritual power of the Buddha, Ānanda was able to completely observe these phenomena. The Buddha then withdrew his manifestation of spiritual powers, emerged from samādhi, and asked Ānanda, "Did you see these things, or not? Did you hear these things, or not?

Ānanda replied, "Having received the assistance of the Buddha's awesome spiritual powers, I have indeed seen these things and heard these things."

The Buddha asked, "Given that the Buddha possesses power such as this, is he or is he not thereby able to bring the Buddha's work to ultimate completion?"

Ānanda replied, "World Honored One, even if beings filled up worlds of the ten directions as numerous as the Ganges' sands, were the Buddha to employ powers such as these for just a single day of his life, he would certainly be able to completely implement the work of the Buddha." Ānanda exclaimed, "This is something that has never been before. World Honored One, the Dharma of the Buddhas is measureless, inconceivable, and ineffable."

We can know from this that the Buddha has completely perfected the *dhyāna* absorptions.

H. The Buddha's Accumulation of Wisdom

Furthermore, the Buddha's accumulation of wisdom has also been completely perfected. From the time he first brought forth the resolve [to attain bodhi], over the course of *asaṃkhyeya* kalpas, there is no dharma that he has not cultivated. In lifetime after lifetime, he has accumulated all manner of meritorious qualities. He has single-mindedly focused his energies in the pursuit of wisdom, not sparing even his own bodies and lives, doing so in just the same ways as did Sadāprarudita Bodhisattva.[6]

Additionally, it is on account of having well cultivated the great compassion together with wisdom that he has completely perfected the accumulation of wisdom. Others lack such great compassion. Although they may possess wisdom, they are unable to completely perfect it. [That the Buddha was able to accomplish this] is because, in seeking the many different types of wisdom, he relied on the great compassion as he strove to liberate beings. It is also because he cut off the affection for dharmas, extinguished the sixty-two types of erroneous views, and refrained from falling into the two extremes, whether through indulgence in the pleasures of the five types of desires, whether through cultivating the path of physical asceticism, or whether through [clinging to views positing the ultimacy of] annihilationism, eternalism, existence, or non-existence, or other such extreme views with respect to dharmas.

Moreover, the wisdom of the Buddha is unsurpassed. It is incomparable in its qualities of penetration and discernment. This is because it is born from within extremely deep *dhyāna* absorptions. It is also because it is unshaken by any gross or subtle afflictions. It is also because he has well cultivated all of the meritorious qualities inherent in the thirty-seven wings of enlightenment, in the four *dhyānas*, in the four immeasurable minds, in the four formless absorptions, in the eight liberations, in the nine sequential absorptions, and in other related practices.

It is also because he has achieved unobstructed, inconceivable and ineffable liberation by virtue of possessing the ten powers, the four fearlessnesses, the four unimpeded knowledges,[7] and the eighteen dharmas exclusive to the Buddhas. So it is that the Buddha's accumulation of wisdom has become entirely perfected.

Furthermore, he was able to defeat the great non-Buddhist dialectical masters, including Urubilvākāśyapa, Mahākāśyapa, Śāriputra,

Maudgalyāyana, Satyaka Nirgranthīputra, *Śreṇika Vatsagotra,[8] Dīrghanakha, and the others. Because the great dialectical masters were all defeated by him, one can therefore know that the wisdom of the Buddha is perfectly complete.

Additionally, as for the Buddha's three-fold treasury [of Dharma] with its twelve categories of scriptural text and its accumulation of eighty-four thousand dharmas, because one observes the sheer volume of discourse contained within it, one may deduce that the wisdom therein must also be vast. This is analogous to the account told of a layman who, in the early morning, observed the site of a great torrential rain and then exclaimed to others, "The strength of the rain dragon who manifest last night is extremely great."

The others said, "How can you know this?"

He replied, "I observed that the earth is wet, that there is much mud, that the mountains have broken apart, that trees have been broken off, and that every variety of bird and beast has been killed. It is on this basis that I have deduced that the power of that dragon is great."

The case of the Buddha is also just like this. Although one may not be able to observe his extremely profound wisdom with one's own eyes, still, when the Buddha let fall the great rain of Dharma, all of the great dialectical masters as well the heavenly kings, Śakra, and Brahmā, were defeated by it. One may realize on this basis that the wisdom of the Buddha is indeed abundant.

Moreover, because the Buddhas have gained unobstructed liberation, their wisdom is unobstructed in its fathoming of all dharmas.

Also, this wisdom of the Buddha is entirely pure and transcends all contemplations. It does not rely upon the contemplation of any dharma as marked by permanence, as marked by impermanence, as marked by limits, as marked by being limitless, as marked by disappearance, as marked by not disappearing, as marked by existence, as marked by nonexistence, as marked by the existence of contaminants, as marked by the nonexistence of contaminants, as marked by being composite, as marked by not being composite, as marked by being produced and destroyed, as marked by being neither produced nor destroyed, as marked by emptiness, or as marked by non-emptiness. It is eternally pure, immeasurable, and like empty space. Because of this, [one may conclude that] it is unobstructed.

[As for those contemplations which are transcended], one who is involved in the contemplation of "production and extinction" is not simultaneously able to contemplate "neither production nor extinction." One who is engaged in contemplation of "neither production nor extinction" is not simultaneously able to contemplate "production and extinction." If "neither production nor extinction" is held to be a reflection of reality, then "production and extinction" is not held to be a genuine reflection of reality. If "production and extinction" is held to be a reflection of reality, then "neither production nor extinction" is not held to be a genuine reflection of reality. All such contemplations as these are all of just such a sort. Because he has gained unimpeded wisdom [not subject to any such limitations], one may therefore realize that the Buddha's accumulation of wisdom is perfectly complete.

I. The Buddha's Accumulation of Liberations

Furthermore, [in one's recollection of the Buddha], one also bears in mind the fact that the Buddha's accumulation of liberations is perfectly complete. The Buddha has become liberated from all afflictions and habitual propensities. Because they have been extricated at the very root, his liberation is genuine and indestructible. Because he has perfectly realized all types of wisdom, his is referred to as "unobstructed liberation." Because the Buddha has realized the perfection of the eight liberations to the most extremely profound and universal degree, his liberation is referred to as perfectly complete liberation.

Moreover, because he has left behind "occasion-dependent liberation" (*samaya-vimukta*) as well as "liberation by resort to wisdom (*prajñā-vimukta*)," he has then completely perfected the "double liberation (*ubhayato-bhāga-vimukti*)." It is on account of perfecting liberations such as these that he is said to be perfectly complete in the collection of liberations (*saṃpanna-vimukti-skandha*).

Furthermore, it is on account of destroying Māra's armies that he has obtained liberation. It is because he has left behind the afflictions that he has gained liberation. It is on account of having left behind all dharmas that obstruct the acquisition of the *dhyānas* that he has gained liberation. It is also because he is possessed of unimpeded sovereign mastery in entering and emerging from all of the *dhyāna* absorptions.

Additionally, [when the Buddha was still] the Bodhisattva, he gained sixteen profound liberations on the path of seeing the truths (*satya-darśana-mārga*). The first was the conditioned liberation associated with the Dharma knowledge in regard to suffering (*duḥke-dharma-jñāna*). The second was the unconditioned liberation gained through the complete severance of the ten fetters (*saṃyojana*) related to the truth of suffering. And so it was on through to the comparative knowledge associated with the Path (*marge`nvayajñāna*).

On the path of meditation (*bhāvanā-mārga*), he gained eighteen liberations. The first was the conditioned liberation associated with either comparative knowledge (*anvaya-jñāna*) or with dharma knowledge (*dharma-jñāna*). The second was the attainment of the unconditioned liberation through the severance of the three fetters related to meditation (*bhavāna-saṃyojana*) within the formless realm. And so it was on through to the eighteenth, wherein he gained a conditioned liberation associated with knowledge of the cessation of the contaminants (*āsrava-kṣaya-jñāna*) and an unconditioned liberation associated with the destruction of all fetters. All of the liberations such as these are collectively referred to as constituting complete perfection of the collection of liberations.

J. The Buddha's Accumulation of the Knowledge and Vision of Liberation

Moreover, one also bears in mind the Buddha's complete perfection of the collection of the knowledge and vision associated with the liberations. There are two categories within the collection of knowledge and vision of liberation.

The first category refers to the fact that, in achieving liberation from all afflictions, the Buddha employed the knowledge of the cessation of the contaminants in his personally-attested awareness that he already knew the existence of suffering, had already cut off accumulation, had already realized cessation, and had already cultivated the path. This constitutes the collection of knowledge and vision of liberation achieved through the knowledge of the cessation of the contaminants.

"Having already known suffering, he had no need to pursue knowledge of it" and so forth until we come to "having already cultivated the Path, he had no need to engage in further cultivation of it" constitutes the collection of knowledge and vision associated with the liberations achieved through the knowledge of the non-arising of the contaminants (*āsrava-anutpāda-jñāna*).

The second category refers to [the knowledge and vision associated with liberation implicit in] the fact that the Buddha knows:

That this person will be able to gain liberation through entering the gateway of emptiness;

That this other person will be able to gain liberation through the gateway of signlessness;

That this other person will be able to gain liberation through the gateway of wishlessness;

That for this other person, there is no expedient means by which they may be influenced to gain liberation;

That this other person will be able to gain liberation after a long, long time;

That this other person will be able to gain liberation before long;

That this other person will be able to gain liberation immediately;

That this other person will be able to gain liberation through the use of gentle words, that this other person will be able to gain liberation through the use of instruction involving intense criticism;

That this other person will be able to gain liberation through the use of mixed forms of discourse;

That this other person will gain liberation through observing the spiritual superknowledges;

That this other person will gain liberation through the explanation of Dharma;

That this other person who is burdened by much lust will be able to gain liberation through the increase of his lust; and

That this other person who is burdened by much hatred will be able to gain liberation through the increase of his hatred. Instances of this sort are illustrated by the case of the dragons known as Nanda and Urubilva.

As illustrated here, there are many different kinds of causes and conditions conducing to the achievement of liberation. This is as discussed in [this work's discussion of] the Dharma eye.

It is the utterly complete knowledge and vision associated with all of these liberations that is referred to as the complete perfection of the collection of knowledge and vision of liberation.

K. Concluding Statement on Mindfulness of the Buddha Practice

Moreover, [in recollection of the Buddha], one is also mindful that the Buddha possesses omniscience, that he possesses all types of knowledge and vision, the great loving-kindness, the great compassion, the ten powers, the four fearlessnesses, the four unimpeded knowledges, the eighteen dharmas unique to the Buddhas, and so forth. One carries on one's recollection in a manner which corresponds to the actual realizations possessed by the Buddha, appreciating thereby his incalculable, inconceivable, and ineffable meritorious qualities. This is what is meant by "recollection of the Buddha."

This recollection may take place on seven grounds. It may be either "accompanied by contaminants" or "devoid of contaminants." In the case of those who are still subject to contaminants, there is a retributional reward. In the case of those who are beyond contaminants, there may be no retributional reward which occurs. It is associated with three faculties of bliss, joy, and equanimity.

It may be gained through practice or it may be gained as a resultant retributional reward. As for that which is gained through practice, it is such as occurs among those in this country who train in the mindfulness-of-the-Buddha samādhi. As for that which is gained as a resultant retributional reward, it is such as occurs with the inhabitants of the land of the Buddha of Limitless Life. People who are born there are naturally able to engage in recollection of the Buddha.

Considerations of this sort are extensively distinguished in the Abhidharma.

The End of "Nāgārjuna on Recollection of the Buddha."

Part Three Endnotes

1 As presented here, this discussion is found at T25.1509.218c28–219a02, 219b02–221b08.

2 KJ preserved the Sanskrit for "forest hermitage": *araṇya.*

3 This is a reference to the ten most standard names for the Buddha, which, when translated into English are: Thus Come One (*tathāgata*); Worthy of Offerings (*arhat*); the One of Right and Universal Awakening (*samyak-saṃbuddha*); the One Perfect in the Practice of the Clarities (*vidyā-caraṇa-saṃpanna*); the Well Gone One (*sugata*); the Knower of the Worlds (*lokavid*); the Unsurpassed Guide of Tamable Men (*anuttaraḥ-puruṣa-damya-sārathiḥ*); Teacher of Gods and Men (*śāstā-devamanuṣyāṇām*); Buddha (*buddha*); World Honored One (*bhagavat*).

4 This short introductory statement occurs somewhat earlier than the rest of the text which explores in greater detail the topic of "recollection of the Buddha" (T25.1509.218c27 - 219a02).

5 "*Vidyā-caraṇa-saṃpanna*" ("Perfect in Practice of Cognition") refers to the three types of cognition, namely: a) the heavenly eye; b) the cognition of past lives; and c) the extinguishing of all contaminants.

6 The story of the Bodhisattva Sadāprarudita ("Ever Weeping" Bodhisattva) is recounted in the *prajñāpāramitā* sutras. He is renowned for selfless pursuit of Dharma and for limitless compassion for beings.

7 The four unimpeded knowledges consist of unimpeded knowledge of meanings, dharmas, language, and eloquence.

8 The Sanskrit reconstruction for this name is slightly conjectural as it is a "one-off" rendering on the part of the Sanskrit-to-Chinese translation team. That said, the only other place this transliteration is mentioned in the entire *Taisho* canon is in a reference dedicated to reconstruction of the meanings of transliterations (翻梵語). This reconstruction is only ambiguously supported there (T54.2130.993c21).

Bibliography

Bodhi. (2000). *The Connected Discourses of the Buddha: A New Translation of the Saṃyutta Nikāya* ; translated from the Pāli ; original translation by Bhikkhu Bodhi. (Teachings of the Buddha). Somerville, MA: Wisdom Publications.

Bodhi. (2012). The Numerical Discourses of the Buddha: A Translation of the Aṅguttara Nikāya (Teachings of the Buddha). Boston: Wisdom Publications.

Burlingame, E., Buddhaghosa, & Lanman, Charles Rockwell. (1921). Buddhist legends (Harvard oriental series ; v. 28-30). Cambridge, Mass.: Harvard Univ. Press.

Conze, E., & Suzuki Gakujutsu Zaidan. (1967). Materials for a Dictionary of the Prajñāpāramitā Literature. Tokyo: Suzuki Research Foundation.

Dharmamitra. (2009) Nāgārjuna on the Six Perfections: An Ārya Bodhisattva Explains the Heart of the Bodhisattva Path. A translation of chapters 17-30 of Ārya Nāgārjuna's Exegesis on the Great Perfection of Wisdom Sutra. Seattle: Kalavinka Press.

Dharmamitra. (2009) Nāgārjuna's Guide to the Bodhisattva Path: Treatise on the Provisions for Enlightenment. A translation of the Bodhisaṃbhāra Śāstra by Ārya Nāgārjuna. Seattle: Kalavinka Press.

Edgerton, F. (1953). Buddhist Hybrid Sanskrit grammar and dictionary. (William Dwight Whitney linguistic series). New Haven: Yale University Press.

Hirakawa, A. (1997). Buddhist Chinese-Sanskrit Dictionary / Bukkyō Kan-Bon daijiten. Tokyo]; [Tokyo] :: Reiyūkai : Hatsubaimoto Innātorippusha; 霊友会 : 発売元いんなあとりっぷ社.

Kumārajīva (c. 405). Dazhidulun, *Mahāprājnāpāramitopedeśa (大智度論). T25, no. 1509).

Kumārajīva and Buddhayaśas (c. 408). Shizhu piposha lun, * Daśabhūmika-vibhāṣā (十住毘婆沙論). T26, no. 1521).

Malalasekera, G. (1937). Dictionary of Pāli proper names (Indian texts series). London: J. Murray.

Ñāṇamoli, & Bodhi. (1995). The Middle Length Discourses of the Buddha: A New Translation of the Majjhima Nikāya (Teachings of the Buddha). Boston: Wisdom Publications in association with the Barre Center for Buddhist Studies.

Nattier, J. (2003). A Few Good Men: The Bodhisattva Path According to the Inquiry of Ugra (Ugraparipṛcchā) (Studies in the Buddhist traditions). Honolulu: University of Hawai'i Press.

Powers, J. (2016). The Buddhist World (Routledge worlds). London ; New York: Routledge, Taylor & Francis Group.

Rahder, J. (1928). Glossary of the Sanskrit, Tibetan, Mongolian, and Chinese Versions of the Daśabhūmika-Sūtra. Compiled by J. Rahder. (Buddhica, Documents et Travaux pour l'Étude du Bouddhisme publiés sous la direction de J. Przyluski; Deuxième Série; Documents—Tome I). Paris: Librarie Orientaliste Paul Geuthner, 1928.

Rahder, J., & Vasubandhu. (1926). Daśabhumikasutra. Leuven: J.B. Istas.

Ruegg, D. (1981). The Literature of the Madhyamaka school of Philosophy in India (History of Indian literature ; v. 7, fasc. 1). Wiesbaden: Harrassowitz.

Stefania Travagnin (2013) Yinshun's Recovery of ShizhuPiposha Lun 十住毗婆沙論: a Madhyamaka-based Pure Land Practice In Twentieth-Century Taiwan, Contemporary Buddhism, 14:2, 320-343, DOI: 10.1080/14639947.2013.832497 To link to this article: https://doi.org/10.1080/14639947.2013.832497

Takakusu, J., & Watanabe, Kaigyoku. (1924). Taishō shinshū Daizōkyō. Tōkyō; 東京 :: Taishō Issaikyō Kankōkai; 大正一切經刊行會.

Vaidya, P. L., ed. Daśabhūmikasūtram. Darbhanga: The Mithila Institute of Post-Graduate Studies and Research in Sanskrit Learning, 1969.

Williams, M. Monier, Sir. (n.d.). A Sanskrit-English Dictionary. Delhi: Sri Satguru.

Zhonghua dian zi fo dian xie hui. (2004). CBETA dian zi fo dian ji cheng = CBETA Chinese electronic Tripitaka collection (Version 2004. ed.). Taibei; 台北 :: Zhonghua dian zi fo dian xie hui; 中華電子佛典協會.

Glossary

A

Abhidharma: A category of Buddhist texts devoted to detailed scholastic analyses of the teachings contained in the sutras.

afflictions: Otherwise known as "the three poisons" (*triviṣa*) these are: 1) greed (including lust and desire in general); 2) hatred (including all of the permutations of aversion such as irritation, anger, and rage); and 3) delusion or ignorance. There are many subcategories of afflictions (*kleśa*) listed in the various dharma schemas. For example, in the Sarvāstivāda school, there are six root afflictions and ten subsidiary afflictions.

aggregates: See "five aggregates."

anāgamin: The *anāgamin* or "nonreturner" is one who has gained the third of the four fruits of the individual-liberation path of the śrāvaka disciple.

anuttarasamyaksaṃbodhi: "Anuttarasamyaksaṃbodhi" refers to "the utmost, right, and perfect enlightenment" of a buddha.

arhat: An arhat is one who, having put an end to all of the afflictions, fetters, and contaminants and having put an end to rebirth, has gained the fourth and final fruit on the individual-liberation path of the śrāvaka disciple.

ārya: One who has realized one of the fruits of the path from which they can never fall away. This includes any one of the eight fruits of the arhat path, or any of the irreversible stations on the bodhisattva path to Buddhahood.

asaṃkhya, asaṃkhyeya: In Sanskrit, this is an incalculably and infinitely large number.

asura: As one of the paths of rebirth, this refers to a demi-god or titan. More loosely, this refers to beings much characterized by anger, hatred, jealousy, and contentiousness who may also appear as humans, animals, hungry ghosts (*pretas*), or hell-dwellers.

avadāna stories: Stories of the previous lives of a buddha.

avaivartika: one who has become irreversible on either the individual liberation path of the arhats or on the universal-liberation path of the bodhisattvas and buddhas. Throughout this text, "stage of certainty" (必定, 必定地) is most likely a translation of *avaivartika.*

B

bases of psychic powers: The four bases of psychic power (*catvāra ṛddhi-pāda*) are: zeal (*chanda*); vigor (*vīrya*); [concentration of] mind/

thought (*citta*); and reflective or investigative consideration, examination, or imagination (*mīmāṃsā*).

Bhagavat: "Bhagavat" is one of the titles of a Buddha. It may be translated as "Blessed One," "Lord," or, as rendered in Chinese Buddhist texts, "World Honored One," *shizun* (世尊).

bhikshu: A fully ordained celibate Buddhist monk within one of the traditional schools of Buddhism.

bhikshuni: A fully ordained celibate Buddhist nun within one of the traditional schools of Buddhism.

bhūta ghost: According to MW, one of the many meanings of *bhūta* is: "a spirit (good or evil), the ghost of a deceased person, a demon, imp, goblin." PDB: "A class of harm-inflicting and formless obstructing spirits (i.e. 'elemental spirits')..."; "...sometimes equivalent to *preta* (hungry ghosts)...."; "Because they obstruct rainfall, the *bhūta* are propitiated by rituals to cause precipitation."

bodhi: "Enlightenment" or "awakening." In its most exalted form this refers exclusively to the utmost, right, and perfect enlightenment (*anuttarasamyaksaṃbodhi*) of a buddha.

bodhimaṇḍa: A *bodhimaṇḍa* is the "site of enlightenment" wherein enlightenment is cultivated and fully realized. It may be used as a general reference to Buddhist temples, though it often refers specifically to the site beneath the bodhi tree where a buddha gains complete realization of the utmost, right, and perfect enlightenment.

bodhisattva: A bodhisattva is a being who, in his pursuit of the utmost, right, and perfect enlightenment of buddhahood, is equally dedicated to achieving buddhahood for himself while also facilitating all other beings' achievement of buddhahood. His primary practice is classically described as focusing on the six (or ten) "perfections" (*pāramitā*): giving, moral virtue, patience, vigor, meditative skill (*dhyāna*), and world-transcending wisdom (*prajñā*).

bodhi tree: The tree in Bodhgaya in the Indian state of Bihar under which the Buddha reached enlightenment approximately 2600 years ago.

Brahmā: Per PDB: "An Indian divinity who was adopted into the Buddhist pantheon as a protector of the teachings and king of the Brahmaloka ["Brahma world"] (in the narrow sense of that term)." "Brahmaloka" here refers to the first three heavens of the form realm.

brahmacārin: Per MW, "A young Brahman who is a student of the veda (under a preceptor) or who practises chastity, a young Brahman before marriage (in the first period of his life)."

brahmacarya: Celibacy.

brahmin: Someone who belongs to the highest caste in Hinduism; a member of the Hindu priestly caste.

buddha: Anyone who has achieved the utmost, right, and perfect enlightenment (*anuttarasamyaksaṃbodhi*), whether we speak of the Buddha of the present era in this world, Shakyamuni Buddha, any of the seven buddhas of antiquity, or, in Mahāyāna cosmology, any of the countless buddhas of the ten directions and three periods of time.

C

clear knowledges: "Clear knowledges" refers to the "three knowledges" (*trividyā*): 1) The remembrance of previous lives (*pūrvavanivāsānusmṛti*); 2) Knowledge of beings' rebirth destinies (*cyutyupapattijñāna*); and 3) Knowledge of the destruction of the defiling contaminants or "taints" (*āsravakṣaya*).

contaminants: "Contaminants" (āsrava) are usually defined as either threefold or fourfold: 1) sensual desire (*kāma*); 2) [craving for] becoming (*bhāva*), i.e. the craving for continued existence; 3) ignorance (*avidyā*), i.e. delusion; 4) views (*dṛṣṭi*) This fourth types is not included in some listings. Often-encountered alternate translations include "taints" and "outflows" and, less commonly "influxes" and "fluxes."

D

dāna pāramitā: The perfection of giving

deva: Devas are divinities residing in the heavens that collectively constitute the highest of the six rebirth destinies within the realm of *saṃsāra*. There are 27 categories of devas and their heavens in the desire realm, form realm, and formless realm. Although the lifespans of the devas in these various heavens may be immensely long, when their karmic merit runs out, they are all still destined to eventually fall back into the other five paths of rebirth wherein they are reborn in accordance with their residual karma from previous lifetimes.

dhāraṇī: *Dhāraṇīs* are of many types, but the two main types are mantra-like spells that serve the purpose of protection from negative spiritual forces such as ghosts and demons and formulae that aid the retention even for countless lifetimes of the Dharma teachings one has acquired in this and previous lives.

Dharma: The teachings of the Buddha

dharmas: 1) Fundamental constituent aspects, elements, or factors of mental and physical existence, as for instance, "the 100 dharmas" with which Vasubandhu analytically catalogued all that exists. In this sense, dharmas are somewhat analogous to the elements of the periodic table in chemistry; 2) Any individual teaching, as for instance in "the dharma of conditioned origination."

Dharma realm: As a Buddhist technical term, "Dharma realm" or "dharma realm," *dharma-dhātu*, has at least several levels of meaning:

1) At the most granular level, "dharma realm" refers to one of the eighteen sense realms, dharmas as "objects of mind" (*dharma-āyatana*);

2) In the most cosmically and metaphysically vast sense, "Dharma realm" refers in aggregate to all conventionally-existent phenomena and the universally pervasive noumenal "true suchness" (*tathatā*) that underlies and characterizes all of those phenomena. In this sense, it is identical with the "Dharma body" (*dharma-kāya*);

3) As a classifying term, "dharma realm" is used to distinguish realms of existence (as in the ten dharma realms consisting of the realms of buddhas, bodhisattvas, śrāvaka disciples, *pratyekabuddhas*, devas, *asuras*, humans, animals, hungry ghosts, hell-dwellers) or metaphysical modes of existence (as in the "four dharma realms" of the Huayan hermeneutic tradition that speaks of: a] the dharma realm of the "noumenal" [synonymous with emptiness or śūnyatā]; b] the dharma realm of the "phenomenal"; c] the dharma realm of the unimpeded interpenetration of the phenomenal and the noumenal; and d] the dharma realm of the unimpeded interpenetration of all phenomena with all other phenomena in a manner that resonates somewhat with quantum entanglement and non-locality).

Dharma wheel: The "wheel of Dharma" or "Dharma wheel" (*dharma-cakra*) refers to the eight-spoked wheel emblematic of the Buddha's teaching of the eight-fold path of the Āryas or "Noble Ones" consisting of right views, right volition or intentional thought, right speech, right physical action, right livelihood, right effort, right mindfulness, and right meditative concentration. This term is also synonymous with the three turnings of the four truths as initially taught by the Buddha to his original five disciples.

dhūta, *dhūtaṅga*, or *dhūtaguṇa* austerities: In contrast to the non-beneficial ascetic practices of non-Buddhists (lying on a bed of nails, etc.), these are austerities beneficial to progress on the path such as wearing only patchwork robes sewn from discarded cloth, eating only food obtained on the alms round, eating only a single meal each day, always sitting and never lying down, dwelling at the base of a tree, residing in a charnel field where one observes the stages of the body's decomposition.

dhyāna: "*Dhyāna*" is a general term broadly corresponding to all forms of Buddhist meditative skill. The Chinese "*ch'an*" or "*chan*" (禪) and the Japanese term "*zen*" are transliterations of the same Sanskrit word "*dhyāna*." All forms of Buddhist "calming" and "insight" meditation are subcategories of "*dhyāna*."

dhyāna pāramitā: The perfection of meditative skill.

E

eight difficulties: Birth in the hells, birth as a hungry ghost, birth as an animal, birth as a long-lived deva, birth in a border region (where there is no Buddha Dharma), birth as someone who is blind, deaf, mute, or otherwise possessed of impaired physical or mental faculties, birth as someone who is possessed of merely worldly knowledge and intelligence (and hence who uses his cleverness to deny the truth of the Dharma); and birth at a time before or long after a buddha appears in the world.

eight precepts: Eight vows involving abstaining from: 1) killing; 2) taking what is not given; 3) sexual misconduct; 4) false speech; 5) intoxicants; 6) use of perfumes, jewelry, other personal adornments, dancing, singing, or watching such performances; 7) sleeping on high or wide beds; and 8) eating after midday.

eighteen sense realms: These consist of the six sense faculties (eye, ear, nose, tongue, body, and mind), the six sense objects (visual forms, sounds, smells, tastes, touchables, and ideas, etc. as objects of mind), and the six sense consciousnesses (visual, auditory, olfactory, gustatory, tactile, and mental).

F

fetters: The fetters (*saṃyojana*) are ten mental characteristics of unenlightened existence that bind beings to uncontrolled rebirths in the six destinies of rebirth. They are: 1) "Truly existent self view," the wrong view that believes in the existence of an eternally existent self in association with the five aggregates; 2) "Skeptical doubt" about the truth of the Dharma and the path to enlightenment; 3) "Clinging to [the observance of] rules and rituals" in and of themselves as constituting the path to spiritual liberation; 4) Sensual desire; 5) Ill will; 6) Desire for rebirth in the form realm [heavens]; 7) Desire for rebirth in the formless realm [heavens]; 8) "Conceit," i.e. the belief that "I" exist; 9) "Agitation" or "restlessness" that prevents deep concentration; and 10) "Ignorance."

five aggregates: 1) form; 2) feelings (i.e. sensations as received through eye, ear, nose, tongue, body, or mind); 3) perceptions; 4) karmic formative factors (such as volitions); and 5) consciousness (visual, auditory, olfactory, gustatory, tactile, and mental).

five desires: Wealth, sex, fame, flavors, and leisure or, alternatively, the objects of the five basic sense faculties (visual forms, sounds, smells, tastes, and touchables).

five faculties: faith; vigor; mindfulness; concentration; wisdom.

five powers: faith; vigor; mindfulness; concentration; wisdom.

five precepts: Five vows involving abstaining from killing, stealing, sexual misconduct, false speech, and intoxicants.

four bases of meritorious qualities: truth, relinquishment, quiescence, and wisdom. (Per VB, the Sanskrit correlates of the Pali *saccādhitthāna, cāgādhitthāna, upasamādhitthāna* (= base of peace), and *paññādhitthāna* would be *satyādhiṣṭhāna, tyāgādhiṣṭhāna, upaśamādhiṣṭhāna*, and *prajñādhiṣṭhāna*.)

four bases of supernatural power: Zeal; vigor; mind; investigation.

four great elements: earth, water, fire, wind.

four right efforts: Causing already arisen evil to cease; causing not yet arisen evil to not arise; causing already arisen goodness to increase; causing not yet arisen goodness to arise.

four requisites: Food obtained on the alms round; robes; residences; medicines.

four stations of mindfulness: Mindfulness of the body; mindfulness of feelings or sensations (experienced via the eye, ear, nose, tongue, body, and mind consciousnesses); mindfulness of thoughts or mind states; mindfulness of dharmas.

four truths / four truths of the Āryas: Suffering; its origination; its cessation; the path to its cessation.

G

gandharva: *Gandharvas* are a type of celestial music spirit that is said to rely on fragrances as their means of survival.

garuḍa: *Garuḍas* are a type of spirit that manifests as an immense golden-winged bird that feeds on young dragons.

ground, grounds: These are levels or planes of spiritual development through which a practitioner proceeds on the way to complete enlightenment.

H

hindrances: "Hindrances" usually refers to "the five hindrances" which are desire, ill will, lethargy-and-sleepiness, excitedness-and-regretfulness, and afflicted doubtfulness. These five hindrances must be overcome in order to successfully enter deep states of meditation.

I

inverted views: The four inverted views (*viparyāsa-catuṣka*) consist of imputing permanence to the impermanent, pleasure to what cannot deliver it, self to what is devoid of any inherently existent self, and purity to what does not actually possess that quality. Standard objects of such upside-down perception are: thought, or mind states, the six categories of "feeling" manifesting in association with the six sense faculties, dharmas (as components of the falsely imputed "self"), and the body.

K

kalaviṅka bird: The Himalayan cuckoo bird that sings with an incomparably beautiful sound even before it breaks out of its shell.

kalpa: The Sanskrit "*kalpa*" roughly corresponds to the English term "eon" with the primary distinction being that, in Buddhist and Hindu cosmology, kalpas occur in various relatively precisely designated immensely long durations.

kāṣāya robe: The robes of an fully ordained bhikshu or bhikshuni.

kinnara: *Kinnaras* (skt. *kiṃnara*) are a type of celestial music spirit with the body of a human and the head of a horse.

kumbhāṇḍa: According to MW: "Having testicles shaped like a *kumbha* [a winter melon]," a class of demons (at whose head stands Rudra). PDB: "In Sanskrit, a type of evil spirit, and typically listed along with especially *rākṣasa,* but also *piśāca, yakṣa,* and *bhūta* spirits. Virūḍhaka, one of the four world-guardians, who protects the southern cardinal direction, is usually said to be their overlord, although some texts give Rudra this role instead. The *kumbhāṇḍa* are also sometimes listed among the minions of Māra, evil personified.

koṭī: A *koṭī* is a number that is defined in the Flower Adornment Sutra Chapter Thirty as the product of multiplying a *lakṣa* (100,000) by a *lakṣa*. Hence it equals 10,000,000, i.e. ten million.

kṣaṇa: A *kṣaṇa,* corresponds to a micro-moment. This is variously defined, one traditional definition being "a ninetieth of a finger-snap." Elsewhere in the text, this may be referred to as "a single thought," "a mind-moment," or "a thought-moment" as approximate translations of the term.

kṣānti pāramitā: The perfection of patience.

kṣatriya: The second of the four castes of traditional Indian culture consisting primarily of the warrior and royalty class.

kṣetra: The Sanskrit word *kṣetra* refers to a land or realm or field and in Buddhist texts it may refer specifically to a "buddha land."

M

mahāsattva: A *mahāsattva* is a great bodhisattva, one who has cultivated the bodhisattva path for countless kalpas.

mātṛkā: *Mātṛkās* are "matrices" consisting of lists of dharmas, technical terms, and concepts discussed in the sutras. They served as the basis for the Abhidharma.

Māra, *māras*: In Buddhism, Māra is generally regarded as the personification of evil and death who is also a particular deity dwelling in one of the desire realm heavens who delights in interfering with spiritual liberation from perpetual rebirths in *saṃsāra*. More specifically, there are said to be four kinds of *māras*: 1) the *māra* of the five mental and physical aggregates in association with which all beings wander endlessly in *saṃsāra*; 2) the *māra* of the afflictions consisting of the three poisons of greed, hatred, and delusion and all of their subcategories; 3) the *māra* of death; and, as mentioned above, 3) the deity known as Māra as well as all of his *devaputra* minions. Additionally, there are also "ghost and spirit" *māras* who may manifest in countless ways to interfere with a practitioner's cultivation of the path.

mind-moment: See *kṣaṇa*.

mahorāga: *Mahorāgas* are a type of serpent spirit often portrayed as having the upper body of a human and the lower body of a snake.

N

nayuta: A very large number, usually defined as a one hundred billion.

nirvāṇa: Nirvāṇa is the ultimate goal of the path of Buddhist spiritual cultivation that corresponds to the elimination of the three poisons (covetousness, aversion, delusion) and the ending of compulsory and random rebirth in *saṃsāra*, the cycle of existences in the deva realm, the demigod realm, the human realm, the animal realm, the hungry ghost realm, and the hell realms.

In the case of the individual liberation path practitioner exemplified by arhats and *pratyekabuddhas*, all future existence ends for them with the acquisition of nirvāṇa.

In the case of the universal liberation practitioners exemplified by bodhisattvas and buddhas, they achieve the direct cognition of the emptiness of all beings and phenomena and realize an ongoing realization of a nirvana-like state even as, by force of vow, they continue to take on intentional rebirths within *saṃsāra* in order to facilitate the spiritual liberation of all beings.

nirvāṇa without residue: The final nirvāṇa realized at death by fully awakened beings whether they be arhats, *pratyekabuddhas*, or buddhas.

nivāsana robe: The *nivāsana* is the monastic's skirt-like inner robe.

O

once-returner: See *sākṛdāgāmin*.

P

pāramitā: One of the six (or ten) "perfections" cultivated and perfected by the bodhisattva on the path to buddhahood.

Paranirmita Vaśavartin Heaven: The Paranirmita Vaśavartin Heaven is the sixth of the six desire realm heavens. PDB: "The heaven of the gods who have power over the creations of others, or the gods who partake of the pleasures created in other heavens."

piśāca: PDB: "In Sanskrit, "flesh-eater," a class of ogres or goblins, similar to rākṣasa and yakṣa, who eat human flesh." The female is called *piśācī*.

prajñā: *Prajnā* is the world-transcending wisdom that cognizes and understands all phenomena associated with "self," others, and the world as they truly are and in accordance with ultimate reality.

prajñā pāramitā: The perfection of wisdom.

pratyekabuddha: One who, in the absence of a buddha or his Dharma, achieves a level of enlightenment comparable to that of an arhat, doing so on his own through the contemplation of the cycle of dependent origination (*pratītyasamutpāda*). Mahāyāna literature attributes this ability to awaken in the absence of a buddha or his Dharma to direct exposure to the Dharma in previous lives, the seeds of which enable enlightenment in the present life.

pratyutpanna samādhi: The *pratyutpanna* samādhi is a samādhi wherein one becomes able to see the buddhas of the present and listen to them teach the Dharma.

provisions (for enlightenment): The provisions for enlightenment (*bodhisaṃbhāra*) are the spiritual prerequisites for enlightenment that must be accumulated in order to fully realize the path to buddhahood. These are usually considered to be merit (*puṇya*) and knowledge (*jñāna*).

pūtana: Per PDB: "Stinking hungry demons."

R

rākṣasa: A swift flying malignant flesh-eating demon which changes its form to seduce humans and eat them.

S

sakṛdāgāmin: The *sakṛdāgāmin* or "once-returner" is one who has gained the third of the four fruits of the individual-liberation path of the śrāvaka disciple.

samādhi: Samādhi refers both to any single instance of one-pointed concentration and also, more usually, to enduring states of persistently maintained one-pointed concentration.

saṃghāṭī robe: The *saṃghāṭī* is the monastic's outer robe.

saṃkakṣikā robe: The *saṃkakṣikā* is the monastic's robe that is worn over the left shoulder and under the right arm.

saṃsāra: *Saṃsāra,* for which the usual Sino-Buddhist rendering is "births-and-deaths," *shengsi* (生死), refers to the endless cycle of rebirths in the six realms of rebirth: devas (gods), *asuras* ("demi-gods" or "titans"), humans, animals, hungry ghosts (*preta*), and hell-dwellers.

Sangha: A community of at least ten fully ordained bhikshus in Buddhist countries or at least five fully ordained bhikshus in countries where Buddhism is only just being established for the first time. As the third object of refuge in "the Three Refuges" or "the Three Jewels," this refers exclusively to those persons who have already acquired one of the fruits of the path from which they can never fall away, whether on the individual-liberation paths of the arhats or *pratyekabuddhas*, or on the bodhisattva path.

śarīra: *Śarīra* are the remains or "relics" of eminent monks, bodhisattvas, or buddhas that are contained in their cremation ashes.

seven enlightenment factors: assessment or skillful selection of dharmas; vigor; joy; mental pliancy; concentration; equanimity with respect to the saṃskāra (karmic formative factors) aggregate.

śīla pāramitā: The perfection of moral virtue.

six rebirth destinies: gods (*deva*), demi-gods or titans (*asura*), humans, hungry ghosts (*pretas*), animals, and hell-dwellers.

skandha: See "aggregates."

skillful means: "Skillful means" (*upāya*) are individually tailored skillful techniques adopted by the bodhisattva in teaching the various kinds of beings. These various techniques are adopted precisely because all beings are possessed of different capacities, karmic obstacles and predilections due to which they respond best to individually tailored teachings.

spiritual superknowledges: The usual Sanskrit antecedent for "spiritual superknowledges" is *abhijñā* ("superknowledges") or *ṛddhi* ("supernatural powers"). This includes such abilities as "the six superknowledges" (the spiritual powers, the heavenly eye, the heavenly ear, the cognition of others' thoughts, past life recall for both self and others, and complete elimination of all "defiling contaminants" or "taints" [*āsrava*]).

śramaṇa: More generally, a *śramaṇa* is a mendicant, one who has left the home life and relies on alms for sustenance. In the Buddhist context, this refers specifically to a bhikshu, i.e. a Buddhist monk.

śrāvaka, *śrāvaka* disciple: A follower of the individual-liberation path to arhatship.

stream enterer: The stream enterer (*srota-āpanna*) is one who has gained the first of the four fruits of the path to arhatship.

śūdra: A member of the fourth and lowest caste of traditional Indian culture consisting primarily of servants and such.

sutra: A scripture attributed to the Buddha.

T

tathatā: "Suchness," i.e. the true nature of the ultimate reality of any and all things as it really is.

Tathāgata: "*Tathāgata*" ("Thus Come One") is one of the ten primary titles by which all buddhas are known.

Ten directions: North, south, east, west, the four midpoints, the zenith, and the nadir.

Thirty-seven wings of enlightenment / thirty-seven enlightenment factors: These consist of: the four stations of mindfulness; the four right efforts; the four bases of supernatural powers; the five faculties; the five powers; the seven enlightenment factors; and the eightfold path of the Āryas.

Three Jewels: The Buddha, the Dharma, and the Ārya Sangha.

Three periods of time: Past, present, and future.

Three Refuges: The Buddha, the Dharma, and the Ārya Sangha, the Three Jewels in which one "takes the refuges" to become a Buddhist disciple and upon which one must rely to advance on the Buddhist path.

Three Vehicles: The Śrāvaka-disciple Vehicle, the Pratyekabuddha Vehicle, and the Great Vehicle (Mahāyāna) the endpoints of which are arhatship, pratyekabuddhahood, and Buddhahood.

three wretched destinies: The three wretched destinies are rebirth as either an animal, a hungry ghost (*preta*), or a hell dweller.

trichiliocosm: A world system consisting of countless worlds.

tripiṭaka: The three divisions of the three-fold Buddhist canon, otherwise known as "the Tripiṭaka": the sutras (scriptures attributed to the Buddha or disciples authorized by the Buddha), the commentarial treatises (śāstra), and the moral codes (*vinaya*).

tripiṭaka master: A "*tripiṭaka* master" is someone who has completely mastered the three divisions of the three-fold Buddhist canon.

twelve sense bases: the six sense faculties (eye, ear, nose, tongue, body, and mind) and their respective sense objects (visual forms, sounds, smells, tastes, touchables, and ideas, etc. as objects of mind).

Two Vehicles: The two individual liberation vehicles taught by the Buddha, the Śrāvaka-disciple Vehicle leading to arhatship and the Pratyekabuddha Vehicle leading to pratyekabuddhahood.

V

vaiśya: A member of the third caste in traditional Indian culture comprised primarily of the merchant and agricultural classes.

vajra: An indestructible substance equated with the diamond. A symbol of indestructibility. Also, a pestle shaped sceptre or "thunderbolt" weapon held by Dharma protectors and deities.

vibhāṣā: A *vibhāṣā* is an extensively detailed explanatory treatise.

vinaya: The Buddhist moral codes.

vīrya pāramitā: The perfection of vigor.

W

wheel-turning king: In Buddhism, a "wheel-turning king" (*cakravartin*) is a universal monarch.

worthy: In Mahāyāna literature, a "worthy" (*bhadra*) is a bodhisattva practitioner who has brought forth the bodhisattva vow but who is still cultivating the preparatory stages and thus has not yet reached the ten bodhisattva grounds and has not yet become an ārya.

Y

yakṣa: *Yakṣas* are a kind of either good or evil spirit possessed of supernatural powers that may either serve as a guardian or a demon.

yojana: A measure of distance in ancient India usually defined as being the distance that an ox cart would travel in a day without unharnessing (somewhat less than ten miles).

About the Translator

Bhikshu Dharmamitra (ordination name "Heng Shou" – 釋恆授) is a Chinese-tradition translator-monk and one of the earliest American disciples (since 1968) of the late Guiyang Ch'an patriarch, Dharma teacher, and pioneer of Buddhism in the West, the Venerable Master Hsuan Hua (宣化上人). He has a total of 34 years in robes during two periods as a monastic (1969–1975 & 1991 to the present).

Dharmamitra's principal educational foundations as a translator of Sino-Buddhist Classical Chinese lie in four years of intensive monastic training and Chinese-language study of classic Mahāyāna texts in a small-group setting under Master Hsuan Hua (1968–1972), undergraduate Chinese language study at Portland State University, a year of intensive one-on-one Classical Chinese study at the Fu Jen University Language Center near Taipei, two years of course work at the University of Washington's Department of Asian Languages and Literature (1988–90), and an additional three years of auditing graduate courses and seminars in Classical Chinese readings, again at UW's Department of Asian Languages and Literature.

Since taking robes again under Master Hua in 1991, Dharmamitra has devoted his energies primarily to study and translation of classic Mahāyāna texts with a special interest in works by Ārya Nāgārjuna and related authors. To date, he has translated more than fifteen important texts comprising approximately 150 fascicles, including most recently the 80-fascicle *Avataṃsaka Sūtra* (the "Flower Adornment Sutra"), Nāgārjuna's 17-fascicle *Daśabhūmika Vibhāśa* ("Treatise on the Ten Grounds"), and the *Daśabhūmika Sūtra* (the "Ten Grounds Sutra"), all of which are current or upcoming Kalavinka Press publications.

Kalavinka Buddhist Classics

(http: www.kalavinka.org)

Fall, 2019 Title List

Meditation Instruction Texts

The Essentials of Buddhist Meditation

A marvelously complete classic *śamathā-vipaśyanā* (calming-and-insight) meditation manual. By Tiantai Śramaṇa Zhiyi (538–597).

Six Gates to the Sublime

The early Indian Buddhist meditation method involving six practices used in calming-and-insight meditation. By Śramaṇa Zhiyi

Bodhisattva Path Texts

On Generating the Resolve to Become a Buddha

On the Resolve to Become a Buddha by Ārya Nāgārjuna

Exhortation to Resolve on Buddhahood by Patriarch Sheng'an Shixian

Exhortation to Resolve on Buddhahood by the Tang Literatus, Peixiu

Letter from a Friend - The Three Earliest Editions

The earliest extant editions of Ārya Nāgārjuna's *Suhṛlekkha*:

Translated by Tripiṭaka Master Guṇavarman (*ca* 425 CE)

Translated by Tripiṭaka Master Saṇghavarman (*ca* 450 CE)

Translated by Tripiṭaka Master Yijing (*ca* 675 CE).

Marvelous Stories from the Perfection of Wisdom

130 Stories from Ārya Nāgārjuna's *Mahāprājñāpāramitā Upadeśa.*

Nāgārjuna's Guide to the Bodhisattva Path

The *Bodhisaṃbhāra Treatise* with abridged Vaśitva commentary.

The Bodhisaṃbhāra Treatise Commentary

The complete exegesis by the Indian Bhikshu Vaśitva (*ca* 300–500).

Nāgārjuna on Mindfulness of the Buddha

Ch. 9 and Chs. 20–25 of Nāgārjuna's *Daśabhūmika Vibhāṣā*

Ch. 1, Subchapter 36a of Nāgārjuna's *Mahāprājñāpāramitā Upadeśa.*

Nāgārjuna on the Six Perfections

Chapters 17–30 of Ārya Nāgārjuna's *Mahāprājñāpāramitā Upadeśa.*

A Strand of Dharma Jewels (Ārya Nāgārjuna's *Ratnāvalī*)

The earliest extant edition, translated by Paramārtha: *ca* 550 CE

The Ten Bodhisattva Grounds

Śikṣānanda's translation of The Flower Adornment Sutra, Ch. 26

The Ten Grounds Treatise
Nāgārjuna's 35-chapter *Daśabhūmika Vibhāṣā*

The Ten Grounds Sutra
Kumārajīva's translation of the *Daśabhūmika Sūtra*

Vasubandhu's Treatise on the Bodhisattva Vow
By Vasubandhu Bodhisattva (*ca* 300 CE)

Printed in the USA
CPSIA information can be obtained
at www.ICGtesting.com
LVHW091443231023
761891LV00045B/536

9 781935 413141